D1171793

THE BOOK OF HOURS

THE BOOK OF HOURS

WITH A HISTORICAL SURVEY
AND COMMENTARY BY
JOHN HARTHAN

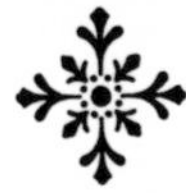

PARK LANE
NEW YORK

First published in Great Britain by Thames and Hudson Ltd.
This 1982 edition published by Park Lane Books,
Distributed by Crown Publishers, Inc.

h g f e d c b a

Filmset by Keyspools Ltd, Golborne, Lancashire
Printed and bound in Italy by Amilcare Pizzi spa, Milan

Library of Congress Cataloging in Publication Data

Harthan, John P.
The book of hours

Reprint. Originally published: London: Thames & Hudson, c1977.
Bibliography: p.
Includes index.
1. Hours, The book of. 2. Illumination of books and manuscripts, Medieval. I. Title.
ND3363.A1H37 1982 745.6'7'094 81-18718
ISBN 0-517-36944-3 AACR2

CONTENTS

In memory of
MONICA BALDWIN
(†1975)
and
MIRANDA GREEN
(†1976)

PREFACE

BOOKS OF HOURS were described by Dr L. M. J. Delaissé (d. 1972) as 'the late medieval best-seller'. Their contents were derived from the official service-books of the Church, but they were produced as the personal prayerbooks of the laity. They were thus not subject to clerical control and could be decorated with greater or lesser elaboration according to the wealth and position of the owner. No two are alike, each example, whether magnificent or modest, has something individual to tell us. Combining sacred and secular elements in a manner found in no other type of illuminated manuscript, Books of Hours have an especial significance in the history of religious sentiment and in the development of painting.

Since this, like most anthologies, is addressed to a general rather than to a specialist audience, English translations have been supplied for quotations or extracts from texts usually in Latin. Thirty-four individual Books of Hours are discussed and illustrated, each represented by one or more pages with an introductory description of the miniatures reproduced followed by a more general commentary on the owner. The selection has ultimately to be a personal one; an attempt has been made to diversify the representation not only by choosing Books of Hours of different dates, styles and countries but by including little-known as well as famous examples.

Throughout the anthology the emphasis is on the devotional aspects of Books of Hours and on the lives and characters of their owners. Since these were often personages well known in their time, the commentaries provide a highly selective review of fourteenth- and fifteenth-century history, seen from an unusual and intimate viewpoint. Certain related groups of Books of Hours considered here are, indeed, connected so closely with specific families that brief historical excursions have been inserted on the Houses of Berry, Anjou, Burgundy and Brittany; there are pedigrees for Books of Hours as well as for their owners.

Anybody familiar with the specialist literature will realize how much I have drawn on recognized authorities for what I have to say about the artistic aspects of Books of Hours. But here also, my aim has been to examine the miniatures in their devotional context and not as isolated examples, however resplendent, of the illuminator's art. There is therefore little attempt at stylistic analysis.

My acknowledgments are brief but none the less grateful. Through the courtesy of the Lady Abbess of Stanbrook Abbey, Worcester, I have been able to discuss Part One with several members of her community; in particular I am indebted to Dame Felicitas Corrigan, Dame Hildelith Cumming and Dame Gertrude Brown for several important additions and corrections. Among friends and colleagues at the Victoria and Albert Museum I have received much help from Dr Michael Kauffmann, Mr Ronald Lightbown, Mr John Fuller, Miss Irene Whalley and Mrs Jeanne-Marie Piat. My brother, the late Mr Antony J. Harthan, and Mr Peter James (British Museum, Natural History) generously supplied ornithological information. I am grateful also to Professor Julian Browne; Mr Brian Collie; the late Lady Cox (M. D. Anderson), whose suggestions about possible links between the illustrations in Books of Hours and Mystery Plays I wish I could have followed up; Dr Albinia De La Mare (Bodleian Library, Oxford), who kindly arranged for me to have access to the papers of the late Dr L. M. J. Delaissé; Miss Phyllis Giles (sometime Librarian at the Fitzwilliam Museum, Cambridge); Dr Ruth Harvey (Oxford); Dr Elfriede Knauer (formerly of Berlin, Staatliche Museen, Antikenabteilung), who not only examined the Hours of Mary of Guelders on my behalf but also most kindly read much of the text of the commentaries and made useful comments; the late Miss Dorothy Miner (The Walters Art Gallery, Baltimore), with whom I discussed my project at a very early stage; Miss Marguerite de Revel for invaluable insights into French history; Miss Dorothy Stroud (Sir John Soane's Museum, London); and Dr Frank Taylor (Principal Keeper, The John Rylands University Library of Manchester). My greatest debt is to my editor, Mr David Britt, of Thames and Hudson, who reduced an over-long and enthusiastic typescript to manageable proportions.

January, 1977 JOHN HARTHAN

PUBLISHER'S NOTE

Measurements are included in the captions to the colour reproductions, and from these it will be seen that an attempt has been made to reproduce pages in their actual size. In a few instances some enlargement has been necessary for reasons of visual balance; and in one case, that of the Duke of Berry's *Grandes Heures* (p. 59), the reproduction is smaller than the original.

THE BOOK OF HOURS

AN HOUR now means a division of time lasting sixty minutes. In the Middle Ages, before time-keeping became mechanized, the Hours indicated less exact portions of the day which were set aside for religious or business duties. The Christian Church, following both Roman secular practice and Jewish religious tradition, established rules or canons for the recital of certain prayers and devotions at specific times. These formed the Canonical Hours in which the daily liturgy or Divine Office of the Church was celebrated. The Psalmist's cry 'Seven times a day do I praise thee because of thy righteous judgments' (Psalm 119:164) anticipated, centuries before Christ, what was to become the Church's practice.

In medieval times devout layfolk followed the example of the professed religious. They wished to have their personal prayerbook and to follow, in their own manner, the Church's programme of daily devotion. Books of Hours, though originating in the Church's liturgy, were used by men and women who lived secular lives. They also served a secondary, worldly purpose as status symbols, as gems in the collections of rich bibliophiles. Religion, art and secular life come together in them in a remarkable synthesis which now constitutes, perhaps, their greatest appeal. Their popularity was such that they form the largest single category of illuminated manuscripts which now exists. After centuries of loss and destruction thousands survive today, not only in public and private collections but also in the commercial market. It is still just possible for the determined, wealthy amateur to collect Books of Hours, or at least leaves from them, in number and quality impossible in other types of illuminated manuscripts. So many were made, so many still exist, that nobody can hope to see or record them all.

Individual Books of Hours have been studied in learned monographs, and a considerable literature is available about the schools of illumination which specialized in their production. But no general study appears to exist. In 1927 the Abbé Leroquais published a masterly catalogue (with a supplement issued in 1943) of 335 Books of Hours in the Bibliothèque Nationale, Paris. This monument of scholarship remains the starting-point for any study of Books of Hours. More recently the researches of Dr L.M.J. Delaissé have greatly extended our knowledge of them, provided new insights into how they were made, and emphasized their importance not only for the history of book production but in the development of religious sentiment.

Much of the charm of Books of Hours comes from the realization that each example was personally commissioned or bought, and decorated with greater or lesser elaboration according to the taste, status and wealth of the owner. Across the centuries they still preserve this connection, intimate and often revealing, with a specific individual. It is in this spirit that they are examined here.[1]

Historical Evolution

'The World can be likened to books written by the hand of the Lord,' wrote the Saxon-born monk Hugh, who became Prior of the Augustinian monastery of Saint-Victor in Paris in 1133. His statement is an arresting reminder of the gulf which divides our scientific, technological age from the religiously orientated world of the Middle Ages. Books then possessed a mystique which had little to do with personal expression. They revealed the purposes of God and enabled man to know and worship his Creator. The most important books were those in which Christ's saving work, his redemption of mankind, was remembered and honoured in the liturgy of the Church. In both the Orthodox Church of the Byzantine Empire and the Catholic Church of Latin Christendom this liturgy was ceaselessly celebrated, in accordance with the texts in the Missal and the Breviary. The Missal contains the texts necessary for the celebration of Mass; the Breviary the Divine Office (*Divinum Officium* or 'godly work'), the prayers, hymns and other texts sung by monks and nuns in choir at the Canonical Hours (and read over daily, under the breath, by all ordained deacons and priests). There are seven services, comprising the night Hours of Matins and Lauds (usually taken together), recited between midnight and dawn, followed at approximately three-hourly intervals by the day Hours of Prime, Tierce, Sext and None, and the evening Hours of Vespers and Compline. Changes in methods of time-keeping and the varying practice of different religious foundations, as well as variations in the summer and winter timetables of monasteries, mean that the timing of the hours is less rigid than it might seem.

The Divine Office for each day takes an hour or two to read through privately. For a monastic community who sing the Office every day of the year, it takes much longer. They are kept busy most of the time – as was the intention when the Breviary was last expanded, at the instance of the Cistercians and other reformed Orders, in the eleventh century. The composition of the Breviary has changed little since then. First comes a Calendar, essential for making sure that the right devotions are performed on each day in the year; for the content of each service varies according to the season, the day of the week, the saints' days and other feasts, both fixed and moveable. The Ordinary (*Ordinarium*), with which the Breviary proper begins, sets out the constant elements of each Hour, with certain seasonal variations. It is mainly a list of instructions and has, indeed, been called 'a prompter's script'. Next follows the Psalter containing the psalms, canticles and hymns to be used for each Hour on every day of the week. The Proper of Time (*Proprium temporale*) which follows contains the Office (i.e. text) of the various prayers to be recited on each day of the liturgical year; the Proper of Saints (*Sanctorale*) contains the texts for the major saints' days; and the Common of the Saints (*Communale*) the texts for categories of saints (apostles, martyrs, confessors) and such as do not have an individual Office.

The Breviary, despite the suggestion of brevity in its title, contains the whole text of the Divine Office, with the Psalter forming an essential constituent. But it contains also a number of additional prayers and devotions to be recited in choir at regular times. They were introduced by St Benedict of Aniane (*c.* 750–821), reformer of the French monasteries and counsellor to Louis the Pious, son of Charlemagne. Among these devotional accretions is a short service or *cursus* in honour of the Virgin Mary, which first appeared in the tenth century. Its recitation was made obligatory in the Benedictine monastery of Monte Cassino in central Italy at an early date, but the widespread popularity in clerical circles of this extra devotion to the Virgin has been attributed to the piety of St Ulric (d. 973), Bishop of Augsburg, and of Berengar (d. 962), Bishop of Verdun. Urban II (1088–99) gave Papal approval by ordering the service to be recited by clerics for the success of the first Crusade.

With these historical testimonies we reach the heart of our subject. For it was this 'Little Office of Our Lady' (*Officium parvum beate Marie Virginis*) which was to become the basic text of Books of Hours. The devotional practice of reciting it spread from the religious orders to the clergy and from the clergy to the laity. What had started as an accretion to the Breviary became the favourite prayerbook of layfolk everywhere. Until the thirteenth century the Little Office was usually attached, as a kind of appendix, to the Psalter, the only prayerbook normally used by the laity. During the thirteenth century it became detached, like fruit falling off a tree, to borrow the charming simile used by the Abbé Leroquais, and became a separate prayerbook: the Book of Hours. The earliest known English example of a separate Book of Hours appears to be the mid-thirteenth-century Hours of the Sarum Use executed by William de Brailes (British Library, Add. ms. 49999). William is thought to have been a clerk and illuminator who worked in Oxford between *c.* 1230–60. His name appears on f.43 of the British Library manuscript beside a picture of a tonsured clerk with the words *qui me depeint*.

The fact that the Little Office was from the first concentrated on the Virgin Mary is of great significance. With no martyrdom or miracles associated with her during her lifetime, she became, though the mystery of the Incarnation, the central figure in an unprecedented devotion in which many of the deepest emotions of men and women were involved. The multiplicity of traces left in cathedral, chapel and shrine bear witness to this. Through their Books of Hours, with their personal prayers and private images, layfolk were to identify themselves with *Dei genitrix*, the Mother of God.

In the full Divine Office the Canonical Hours are interpreted as a commentary on Christ's Passion; in the context of the Little Hours they are principally seen as episodes in the life of the Virgin and in the operations of the Holy Spirit. At Lauds she visits St Elizabeth; at Vespers she begins the Flight into Egypt. The three Little day Hours of Tierce, Sext and None represent the Descent of the Holy Spirit at Pentecost, the Ascension, and the Death of Christ upon the Cross (None, the ninth hour: Luke 23:44). Alternatively, the Holy Trinity may be contemplated at Tierce, the Son at Sext and the Father at None. These plural, non-contradictory interpretations suggest how owners might use their Books of Hours for private devotional purposes.

But it was to the Virgin Mary, Mother of God, that they turned most often. Through the intensity and multiplicity of her cult she became the most popular expression of faith and devotion in the Middle Ages. She was the mother-substitute of all, the new Eve, the intercessor with God. 'Mary was more powerful than the saints and less awful than God,' wrote Eileen Power; 'as His mother she had a quite peculiar influence with Christ; and her position between man and his maker, as the middle ages pictured it, is exactly expressed by St Bernard, when he says that Christ desires us to have everything through Mary.'[2] For the devout laity her image was always before them in their Books of Hours.

Contents

The Abbé Leroquais established a basic classification of the contents of Books of Hours. Three elements are distinguished: essential, secondary and accessory texts. The essential texts are those extracted from the Breviary: the Calendar, the Little Office or Hours of the Virgin, the Penitential Psalms, the Litany, the Office of the Dead and the Suffrages of the Saints. Like the Breviary, the Book of Hours in its turn attracted further texts which extended its devotional scope as well as increasing the variety of its contents.

These secondary texts comprise the Sequences, which are the passages from the four Gospels in which the Evangelists Matthew, Mark, Luke and John describe the coming of Christ; the account of the Passion given in the Gospel of St John; two special prayers to the Virgin which enjoyed great popularity, the *Obsecro te* ('I implore thee') and *O intemerata* ('O matchless one'); a number of shorter alternative Offices, the Hours of the Cross, of the Holy Spirit and (less often) of the Holy Trinity; the Fifteen Joys of the Virgin; and the Seven Requests to the Saviour.

Even this substantial addition was not enough to satisfy the yearning for devotion among the laity. It was increased by Leroquais' third element, the accessory texts. These comprise more extracts from the Psalter, and miscellaneous prayers. The Fifteen Gradual Psalms (also present in the Breviary in this form) and the Psalter of St Jerome represent a further appropriation of the inexhaustible riches of psalmody. The Gradual Psalms comprise numbers 119–33, the short and beautiful psalms sometimes considered to be those recited by Jewish pilgrims 'going up' (*gradus*, a step) to Jerusalem. The Psalter of St Jerome is an anthology of 183 verses from the Psalms compiled for the use of the sick by an unknown writer but traditionally associated with St Jerome, the translator of the Bible into Latin and author of three versions of the Psalms. The miscellaneous prayers were of widely diverse character. Many were of venerable antiquity, going back to the prayerbooks (*libelli precum*) of Carolingian times. Most were anonymous, but some were attributed to major saints or Fathers of the Church to give them status and perhaps greater efficacy.

The arrangement of a 'typical' Book of Hours is given below. Only the essential and secondary texts are included. It must always be remembered that no two manuscript Books of Hours are exactly alike. Except for the Calendar at the beginning, the order of the separate parts was never fixed, and the number of texts included could vary as much as their position in the book.

1 Calendar
2 Sequences of the Gospels
3 The prayer *Obsecro te*
4 The prayer *O intemerata*
5 Hours of the Virgin
6 Hours of the Cross
7 Hours of the Holy Spirit
8 Penitential Psalms
9 Litany
10 Office of the Dead
11 Suffrages of the Saints

Books of Hours invariably begin with a Calendar, except when this introductory section has been lost through wear and tear. Its purpose was to indicate the days for celebrating the feasts of the Church and of the saints. Calendars in Books of Hours follow the pattern established in Missals, Psalters, Breviaries and other liturgical texts; but they were often carelessly compiled and invoked the wrath of clerics: it was nobody's job to check the accuracy of the lay scribes who copied them out.

Entries in the Calendar are written in different coloured inks – gold, red, blue – which besides giving sparkle to the pages have a functional purpose. Important Church festivals such as Christmas, Easter and many more, as well as the feast days of apostles and other major or universal saints, are commonly written in gold or red (hence 'red-letter days'), the lesser festivals and saints' days in black. But local saints with a restricted cult, especially those who evangelized a district in early Christian times, may also appear in gold, red or blue. The same applies to anniversaries of the consecration of churches, the translation of relics and the obits or commemorations of notable deceased persons connected with the diocese. A Calendar thus conveys to the trained eye a synopsis of the history of a region and suggests where the book in which it appears originated or was intended to be used.

The days of the month are not numbered consecutively in the modern manner. Instead, the Roman notation of Kalends, Ides and Nones is used, in which the days are reckoned from three fixed points in each month. The abbreviation KL for Kalends is written in emblazoned initials at the head of each month. Columns in the left margin show the Golden Numbers (I–XIX) used for calculating the date of the Paschal moon (essential for fixing Easter), the days of the week marked by lower-case letters of the alphabet *a–g*, and the abbreviations of Kalends, Ides and Nones.[3]

After the Calendar come the Gospel Sequences, already described, and the universally popular prayers to the Virgin, *Obsecro te* and *O intemerata*. Following these we reach the most important text of all, the indispensable Hours of the Virgin. They are usually introduced by title in the phrase *Incipiunt hore beate Marie virginis*, or *Officium parvum beate Marie virginis*, or *Hore beate Marie secundum usum romanum* or some other variant. From these descriptions derives the shortened name 'Hours' (*Horae*, *Heures*) as a term for the whole book, and always used in the plural.

In each Hour the basic texts comprise an opening verse and response (or *invitatorium*), followed by the *Gloria*, antiphon, psalms, *capitula* (short extracts from the Psalms) and hymns, divided by verses, responses and prayers or collects (*orationes*). These subdivisions are usually indicated by abbreviated rubrics written in red or blue, e.g. *Ant* for Antiphon, *Ps* for Psalm and so on. Each Hour has its initial verse, to be spoken after a silent *Ave Maria*. At Matins this is *Domine labia mea aperies* . . . ('O Lord, open thou my lips . . .'); at Lauds and all subsequent Hours up to and including Vespers, *Deus in adjutorium meum intende* ('Haste thee, O God, to deliver me'); at Compline *Converte nos Deus salutaris noster* ('Convert us, O God our Saviour'). These opening exhortations, especially *Deus in adjutorium meum intende* which occurs so often, provide a quick means of recognizing pages from the Hours of the Virgin.

The length of text varies. Matins, Lauds and Vespers are the longest Hours. In the Breviary, Matins and Lauds constitute the 'Night Office', with Matins including three Nocturns or night prayers, each with three psalms, which correspond with the three night-watches between midnight and dawn. In Books of Hours these are usually replaced by three Lessons followed by the *Te Deum*. It is appropriate that the theme of Lauds, the Hour which marks the end of the night and beginning of day, should be one of praise and thanksgiving. Prime and the Little day Hours of Tierce, Sext and None are quite short, with a simplified text composed of verse, response, hymn, three psalms, antiphons, *capitulum* and collect (*oratio*). Vespers, the evening Hour and a favourite devotion, includes five psalms, the hymn *Ave maris stella* ('Hail, Star of the Sea') and the *Magnificat* ('My soul doth magnify the Lord'). Compline, the last Hour, contains three psalms and the *Nunc dimittis* ('Lord, now lettest thou thy servant depart in peace, according to thy word').

The Hours of the Cross and the Hours of the Holy Spirit are both quite short, each Hour consisting of a hymn, antiphon and prayer but with no psalms, lessons or responses. They usually come after the Hours of the Virgin, but sometimes appear in the midst of them, after Matins and Lauds, or they may alternate with them in what are known as 'mixed Hours'.

The Seven Penitential Psalms constitute one of the basic texts of Books of Hours. It is rare to find an example without these passionate outpourings of grief, consciousness of sin and hope of pardon. They owe their name to the sixth-century monk Cassiodorus, a former Roman prefect, who described them in this manner in his *Commentary* on the Psalms. They may be easily recognized by the opening words of the first Penitential Psalm (no. 6 in the Psalter), *Domine, ne in furore tuo arguas me* ('O Lord, rebuke me not in thine anger').

The Litany, which customarily follows the Penitential Psalms, is one of the oldest forms of liturgical prayer, dating back to the earliest days of Christian worship. It is a cry for help. After the threefold call for mercy, *Kyrie eleison, Christe eleison, Kyrie eleison*, the text continues with invocations of the Holy Trinity, the Virgin Mary, the Archangels Michael, Gabriel and Raphael, and then a long roll-call of universal saints (the Apostles and others) in which are sometimes included the 'local' saints venerated in the diocese where the book was intended to be used.

The Office of the Dead (*Officium defunctorum*) is another essential component of Books of Hours. The text is not that of the Requiem Mass (which belongs to the Missal) but of the prayers said over the coffin as it lies on a bier in the church choir during the wake-night or vigils before burial. The Office itself is an old one dating back at least to the early ninth century, but its widespread adoption as an impressive and no doubt expensive public ritual with mourners and candles did not become common until the early fifteenth century. The solemn celebration of death in late medieval times, so different from modern attitudes which trivialize the subject, was in part a reaction to the traumatic experience and memory of the Black Death and recurrent plagues; it was important to know how to die well.

The presence of the Office of the Dead in Books of Hours shows that it was the habit of layfolk to read it regularly in private. This was not out of morbid preoccupation with death, although few today would be prepared to face such a nightly task: it arose, rather, from the traditional Christian belief in the need for constant penitence and preparation before the inevitable Divine judgment. Thomas à Kempis, in chapter 23, 'Of Meditation on Death', in the first book of *The Imitation of Christ* (a key work for understanding late medieval religious sentiment), instructs his reader as follows: 'Always, therefore, be thou ready, and so live that death may never take thee unprepared ... Tomorrow is a day uncertain, and how knowest thou if thou shalt have a tomorrow? ... Few by sickness grow better, now are the days of salvation.'

The choir service in the Office of the Dead is in two parts: Vespers said in the evening, and Matins and Lauds in the morning. Though the dead are in eternity and outside time, the living mourners continue to pray for them according to the Hours. The two parts of the service are often known as the *Placebo* and the *Dirige* (or dirge), from the opening words of their respective antiphons, *Placebo Domino in regione vivorum* ('I will praise the Lord in the land of the living'), said in the evening, and *Dirige, Domine Deus meus, in conspectu tuo viam meam* ('Direct, O Lord my God, my way in thy sight'), in the morning. Together with the Litany and the Penitential Psalms, the Office of the Dead represents the consciousness of sin in Books of Hours, which is a matter quite different from modern psychological 'guilt'. A sense of sin is an intolerable state of mind about which one can and must do something; guilt is a nagging disquiet, characteristic of neurotic psyches, which many people live with for years without resolving.

After the Penitential Psalms, Litany and Office of the Dead, the Fifteen Joys of the Virgin and the Fifteen O's or Orisons of St Bridget of Sweden restore the element of gladness. They do not belong to the Breviary, and usually appear in a vernacular language, most often French. They recall the joys of the Virgin both on earth and in Heaven. St Bridget's prayers were considered especially efficacious in rescuing souls from Purgatory.

The final and one of the most interesting sections in Books of Hours consists of the Suffrages, *Memoriae*, or invocations of the saints. These are short devotions consisting of an antiphon, verse, response and prayer. The series usually opens with the Trinity, followed by prayers to the Virgin Mary, St Michael, St John the Baptist, the Apostles and then a succession of universal and local saints, named in the order in which they appear in the Litany and chosen to some extent according to the wishes of the owner. The Suffrages usually appear at the end of a Book of Hours, very occasionally at the beginning after the Calendar which lists each saint's day. Their number ranges from a mere half dozen or so to twenty or thirty in large Books of Hours and a hundred or more in a few special examples (surely a case of safety in numbers).

Devotion to the saints, especially to one's patronal or some other personal saint, was an essential part of medieval religious life. It united all classes of society. The saints had preceded the living into the after-life and could there intercede for them. 'Make now friends to thyself by honouring the saints, and imitating their actions,' wrote Thomas à Kempis. The varying cast of saints found in Books of Hours contributes greatly to the individuality of these books. The name of an obscure or unfamiliar saint in the Calendar, Litany or Suffrages may well help to establish the locality to which the book belongs.

After this brief résumé of the contents of Books of Hours a final word must be devoted to the subject of Uses. In liturgiology, a Use is a distinctive form of prayer and ritual followed in a particular church or diocese. A celebrated example is the Sarum Use followed in England in pre-Reformation times. Some of the mendicant orders such as the Franciscans (or Friars Minor) and Dominicans, religious whose way of life in the world made it impossible to sing the Divine Office, took to using Books of Hours in which special forms of prayer or Uses appear. Uses are indicated by variations in the text of certain prayers. These are found mainly in alternative versions of the hymns, antiphons and *capitula* at Matins, Lauds and Vespers in the Hours of the Virgin, and in the Office of the Dead. The differences between the Rome and Paris Uses, the two most commonly found in Books of Hours, and between these and more local Uses are matters of detail rather than of substance. The various Uses can nonetheless be most helpful in determining the history of a Book of Hours.[4]

Decoration

In a memorable phrase Ruskin affirmed that 'illumination is only writing made beautiful'. Today this definition no longer seems adequate, especially when (as seldom happens) the words following are quoted – 'the moment illumination passes into picture making it has lost its dignity and function' (*Lectures on Art*, v). It is not the writing alone which is made beautiful, but rather the whole page, in which writing is but one component in an ensemble.

Illumination is the art of decorating books with colours and metals (usually gold, occasionally silver), a form of ornamentation chiefly practised during medieval times when all books were written by hand. The vellum pages of these books were regarded as spaces to be filled by the joint labours of the scribe who wrote the text and the artist who painted the borders and pictures. A simultaneous presentation of text, decoration and illustration resulted, in which one or other element might predominate. The decorative borders and the pictures (or miniatures, see below) were sometimes supplied by different artists, for embellishment of the more elaborate manuscripts was often a joint enterprise in which several craftsmen might collaborate.

The varying stress laid at different times on decoration and illustration, the problems of reconciling the inventive fantasy of the artist with the demands of the text, and the several solutions adopted for combining the separate units of text, initial, miniature and border into a decorative ensemble, represent book illumination considered as an art form. The historical development is concerned with the emergence and decline of various national and local schools (between which there existed complex relationships and mutual influence), the connection in the fifteenth century, if not earlier, between book illumination and panel painting, and the important question of patronage.

The basic elements in illumination are the initial, the miniature and the border. To describe the pictures in manuscripts as 'miniatures' does not necessarily imply small size. The term derives from the Latin word *minium*, the red pigment (lead oxide) used by scribes to rubricate or emphasize initial letters at important places in the text. Illumination had its origin in this practice. *Miniare* meant to write or paint in vermilion; and the artist who did so was the miniator. The word 'miniature' was later extended to include pictorial illustrations of whatever size and however displayed (in frames, medallions or initials). Medieval miniatures are a different art form altogether from the diminutive portraits, painted in later centuries on ivory or playing-cards and framed in lockets, which we associate with Nicholas Hilliard and his successors.

Initials, when painted, may be either decorative or historiated. If the former, the letter shapes are filled with interlacing foliage or other ornament according to the illuminator's fancy. Scribes sometimes added penwork flourishes and patterned 'in-filling' to initial letters, using coloured inks to increase the decorative effect. In such cases the term 'calligraphic' or 'penwork' initials is appropriate. Historiated initials are those in which small pictures (*ystoires*) instead of ornament appear inside the loops of the letter shapes. Initials and miniatures are thus closely connected, and in historiated initials come together as a unit. But when the *ystoire* escapes from the initial we have the miniature as the term is commonly understood, a separate illustration complete with its frame or border. It may be small or large, occupying a part only or the whole of the page.

The third element in illumination is the border which surrounds the miniature and frequently the whole page of text. Originally introduced to enclose the miniature and separate it from the text, the rectangular frame-border in Anglo-Saxon and Romanesque manuscripts (for example, in the English Winchester School of illumination) was often enlarged to form wide panels round the miniature, which were filled with a variety of closely packed acanthus ornament or an interlace of foliage with climbing beasts and human figures. Towards the end of the Middle Ages, in the Gothic period of the late thirteenth and early fourteenth centuries, a second type of border appeared, with irregular edges. Beginning as a tail-like extension of the initial into the margin, it developed into the prolific ivy- or vine-leaf border composed of curling tendrils from which sprouted tiny leaves picked out in gold. The ivy-leaf border was to become one of the most characteristic decorative features of northern Books of Hours in the fourteenth and early fifteenth centuries.

Books of Hours, as volumes detached from Psalters, were a late arrival among the religious texts of the Middle Ages. By the time they appeared, the production of illuminated manuscripts was no longer the monopoly of monastic *scriptoria* but had been taken over by lay scribes and artists whose workshops were located in the larger cities where there was a wealthy clientele. The decoration applied to Books of Hours in these lay workshops displays the successive phases of the Gothic style of illumination during a period of over two hundred years, from around 1300 to the early sixteenth century. Most of the books were small in size, as befitted their personal nature, compared with the massive Bibles and Psalters of the Romanesque age, but reduction of scale in no way inhibited luxury of presentation.

In earlier examples historiated initials remain the commonest type of picture (p. 43). When the miniatures escape outside the letter shapes, in the early fourteenth century, they are still often painted against diapered or chequered backgrounds. But already the figures are characterized by plasticity of form and modelling of draperies, a movement towards realism which is reinforced when the figures are placed in landscape settings of trees and rocks (p. 55). The increasing prominence of the miniature is reflected in the introduction around 1420 of the arched frame at the top which intrudes into the upper margin (p. 30). A further development is the depiction of successive episodes in a story within a single miniature. These 'travel landscapes', as they are sometimes called, are a favourite pictorial theme (p. 122). The simultaneous depiction, with no regard for perspective, of events which in real life occur in a time sequence, gives such incidents as the Adoration of the Magi or the Flight into Egypt a peculiarly vivid intensity. The laws of perspective, even when known and mastered, are not necessarily an asset in book illumination.

Parallel with the miniature, the borders are undergoing a similar evolution. At first the blank margins of the text are filled only sparsely by the tail-like extensions of initials from which sprout the first shoots of vine- or ivy-leaf ornament. But when these 'tails' extend to the corners they throw out cusped bars at right angles which provide platforms to support drolleries, grotesque figures, monsters, birds and animals (pp. 43, 50–51). Playful secular imagery of this kind is sometimes said, on not very clear grounds, to indicate the artists' emancipation from clerical control. It derives more immediately from the natural inventiveness of artists and from the willingness of their clients to be diverted from their religious texts during long services in church or periods of private devotion; Books of Hours were taken to church as well as read at home. In the late fourteenth century the emphatic 'bar borders' supporting drolleries and little human figures gradually give way to lighter and more graceful ivy-leaf designs which now completely frame the miniature and text with a dense but delicate mass of foliated scrolls or *rinceaux* (pp. 30, 87).

By this time, too, the proportions of the border, narrow at the inner margin and successively wider at the head, outer and foot margins, have become established. In the early fifteenth century sprays of acanthus, a leaf form much used in Romanesque illumination, reappear in the tightly packed ivy-leaf borders; together with flowers, fruits (especially strawberries) and assorted fauna, the mixed ivy- and acanthus-border acquired a diverse and colourful repertoire (p. 114). Nor does the appearance of the text itself remain unaltered. Elegant, angular Gothic scripts replace the more rounded hands of the preceding period and contribute to the general 'spikiness' of effect. The text is moreover continually broken up by emblazoned or coloured initials and decorative line-endings (*versets*), filling blank spaces left empty when the words stop short of the margins.

When assimilation of the various elements in the decorated page – script, miniatures, initials, marginal decoration – had reached a stage which allowed no further development, illuminators were faced with the problem of finding a new synthesis. They met this challenge in two ways. The first was to increase the size of the miniatures until they became full-page illustrations from which all marginal decoration was banished (p. 127). The miniature now resembled a panel or easel painting which happened to be incorporated in a book. The second solution was to turn the border into a frame through which one looks at the miniature as if from a window. This optical illusion is achieved by increasing the size of the flowers, insects or other objects in the border so that they appear to be close to the spectator while the miniature recedes into the distance, and the text, if present, occupies a neutral zone (p. 151). A variant of this method was to reverse the respective parts and bring forward the text. It now appears as if written on a panel superimposed upon the miniature, much of which is concealed; the miniature assumes the place of the border and consequently appears to be painted on another plane. This new relationship between border and miniature ignores the flat surface of the vellum page, hitherto respected by artists, by introducing a spatial effect. It is often said to have broken the unity of script, miniature and border so characteristic of Gothic illumination and to mark the disintegration of book painting as an independent art. Nevertheless, some three centuries later, William Blake adopted precisely these late medieval expedients when designing his series of illuminated books.

In the fifteenth century Books of Hours were near mass-produced in lay workshops situated in Paris (always the chief centre for book illumination, as Dante recorded) and in other prosperous cities in France and the Low Countries where there was a buyers' market. The grander examples were joint enterprises to which a number of craftsmen contributed under the supervision of a *chef d'atelier*. The planning and execution of a Book of Hours was a complex operation. The gatherings of vellum sheets (paper was seldom used before the coming of printed Books of Hours late in the fifteenth century) had first to be assembled and ruled with vertical and horizontal lines before the scribe could begin his work. Spaces were left for initials and miniatures. The book was then passed to the miniator, who added coloured decoration to the borders and initials. Finally, came the artist who painted the *ystoires* or miniatures. The design was first drawn in outline and a covering of sized clay applied to the vellum within the design; gold leaf was then laid on direct with an adhesive and burnished. An alternative method was to apply the gold in powdered form mixed with an adhesive producing a matt, less glittering effect. The final stage was the application of colour, usually red and blue, but also yellow, green and pink.

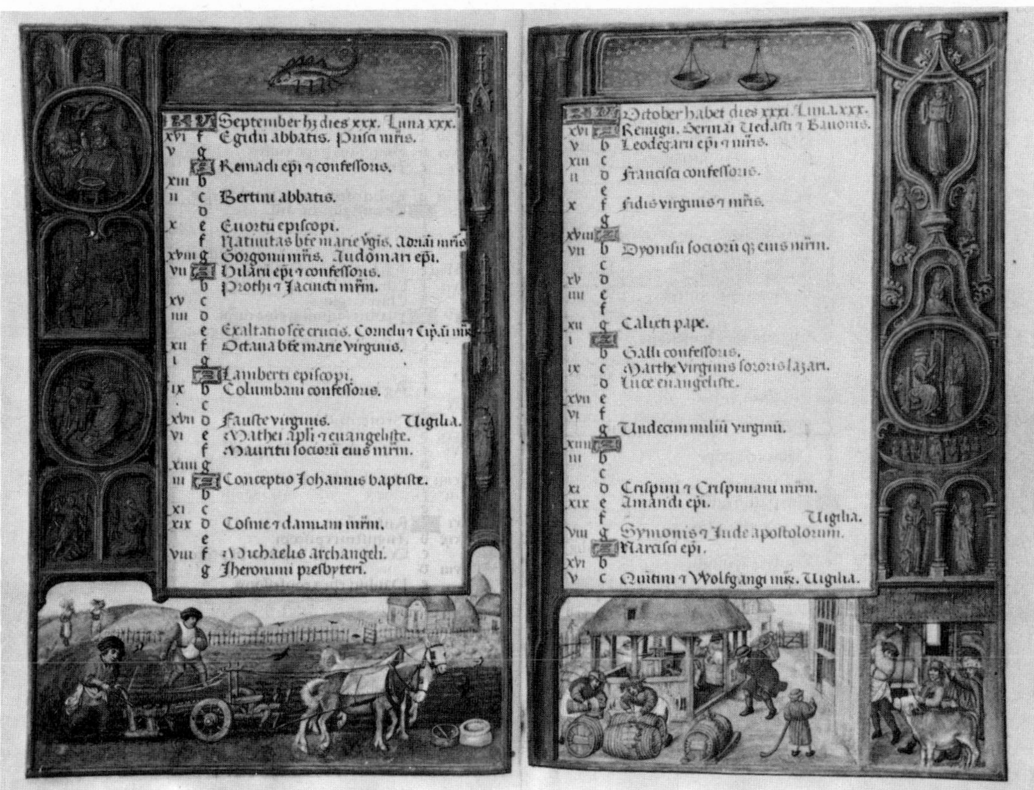

The Soane Hours (*see* p. 152). September–October Calendar (with Libra and Scorpio in the wrong order).

Books were compiled in sections, not written page by page, and there must have been many delays in the progression from the plain vellum leaves to the final decorative ensemble. The occasional appearance of incomplete or uncoloured drawings is evidence of this. The Calendar was often a fill-up or supplement. One may suppose that a large workshop owned a stock or at least reference copies of Calendars of different Uses.

Artists had often to work in a hurry; and it is known that pattern books were used, though few have survived. One important specimen is the Göttingen Model Book, an incomplete manual of the fifteenth century containing both written instructions and painted specimens for the use of illuminators.[5] Decorative motifs from playing cards are also found in manuscript illumination, and it is easy to imagine how useful and labour-saving a pack of cards lying about a workshop might have been. But the precise way in which motifs were transferred into manuscripts, and the principles governing the choice of subject, are obscure.[6]

Although many details of workshop organization are unknown, it must always be remembered that the miniatures in a Book of Hours were part of an ensemble, not individual pictures. The standard and degree of ornamentation depended to a large extent on what the owner was prepared to pay; religious texts were always thought worthy of as much *de luxe* presentation as the owner could afford.

To understand the traditional scheme followed in the illustration of Books of Hours, and to fix in our minds the types of pictures customarily found in them we shall imagine that we hold in our hands a 'typical' example and go through it section by section to see how each is decorated. The Calendar comes first. In most Books of Hours each month occupies two leaves, beginning on the recto and finishing overleaf on the verso. Occasionally Calendars are found with each month filling one leaf only, as in the Soane Book of Hours (p. 23). The two-page format meant that there was more space for displaying the most important pictorial features of Calendars – the labours or occupations of the months with their corresponding sign of the zodiac. In Calendars occupying two pages for each month the occupation usually occurs on the first leaf and the zodiacal sign on the second; in the Soane Hours they occur respectively at the bottom and top of the page.

The occupations are taken from the seasonal labours of the peasants and the pastimes of their feudal lords. A standardized sequence became established for Books of Hours:

JANUARY	*Feasting*
FEBRUARY	*Sitting by the fire*
MARCH	*Pruning*
APRIL	*Garden scene*
MAY	*Hawking or boating*
JUNE	*The hay harvest*
JULY	*Reaping the corn*
AUGUST	*Threshing*
SEPTEMBER	*Treading the grape*
OCTOBER	*Ploughing and sowing*
NOVEMBER	*Gathering acorns for pigs*
DECEMBER	*Killing the pig or baking bread*

It is pleasant to find all classes occupied during the winter months of January and February in feasting or sitting by a warm fire; the weather – colder in late medieval times than now – made outdoor activity impossible in northern climates.

Artists apparently had complete freedom in how they depicted the occupations and the signs of the zodiac. In routine Books of Hours the treatment of these subjects is conventional or perfunctory; but in the more costly examples artists had scope for landscape painting and naturalistic observation. The zodiacal signs provided them with an opportunity for figure painting and for varied animal and fish designs; also, in the Gemini sign for June, an excuse, sometimes, for depicting a naked man and woman embracing –

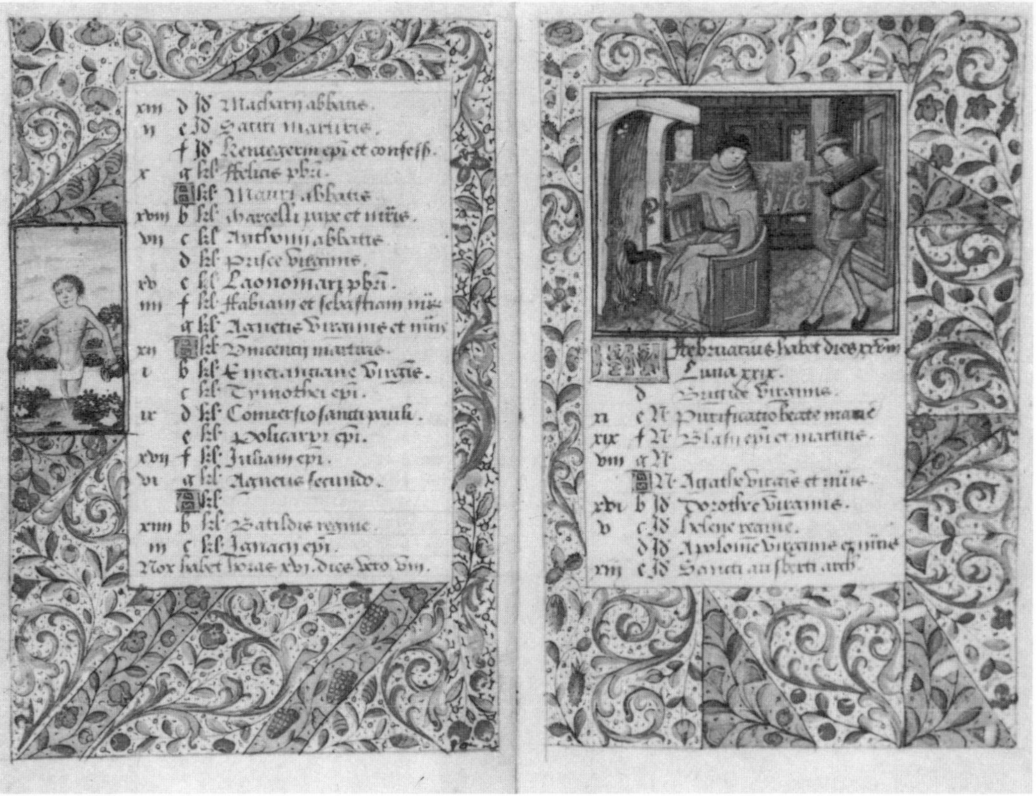

The Playfair Hours. Northern France, late 15th c. Victoria and Albert Museum, London, L.475–1918. January–February Calendar: Sitting by the fire.

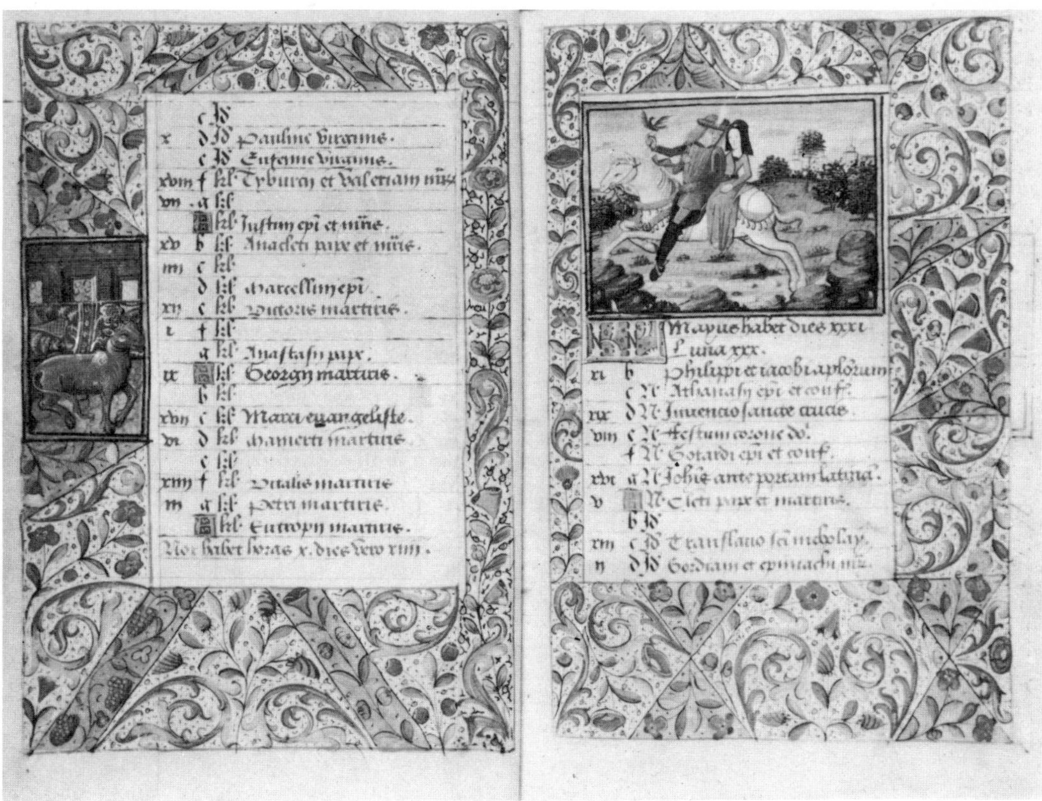

The Playfair Hours. April–May Calendar: Hawking.

one of the few places in Books of Hours, apart from pictures of St Sebastian and Bathsheba in her bath, where artists could safely give their patrons a mild erotic *frisson* by portraying nudity.

The pictures of the occupations of the months contain material of the greatest interest for students of social history, costume and agriculture. In them can be found illustrations of domestic interiors, agricultural implements, methods of pruning, ploughing, reaping, shearing sheep, wine-making and baking, while the courtly scenes show how the leisured class disported themselves in hawking, hunting, boating and dalliance in gardens dressed in their finest clothes. Nor do the seasonal changes pass unrecorded: wintry scenes in January and February with snow on the ground, trees broken by the frost being pruned in March, the springtime flowers in their green verdure, and brown leaves on the trees in autumn (in the *Très Riches Heures*). Already in this opening Calendar section the unique character of each Book of Hours is revealed in the artist's personal interpretation of traditional themes.[7]

Following the Calendar are the Sequences or Gospel passages from the four Evangelists describing the coming of Christ. Each is announced by a miniature of the Evangelist writing his Gospel and accompanied by his attribute. St John is often shown on the isle of Patmos; in superior Books of Hours this can be a beautiful seascape, with his eagle holding in its beak an inkwell which a mischievous devil tries to steal. The other Evangelists are shown in their studies, usually writing, but sometimes sharpening their quill pens or occupied in some other useful manner. In certain Books of Hours, particularly those of the Rouen School, all four Evangelists are shown together in one miniature divided into four compartments (p. 27); a notable example of this practice, though not of the Rouen School, is the black prayerbook at Vienna (p. 106). The Passion according to St John, which follows the Sequences, may be illustrated by a Passion scene, most commonly the Crucifixion, or sometimes by St John in his cauldron of boiling oil.

We next find the two universally popular prayers to the Virgin, the *Obsecro te* and *O intemerata*. Both may be introduced by a picture of the Virgin and Child or by a *Pietà*, though the second prayer is often unillustrated. At the *Obsecro te* we may also find a portrait of the owner, especially if a woman, kneeling in prayer. But the most common place for owners to appear, like donors on an altarpiece, is at Matins, the first of the Hours of the Virgin.

To this section, which we now reach, the most important and indispensable text in a Book of Hours, the richest embellishment is applied. Each Hour is introduced by a full or half-page miniature. The subject matter of these miniatures usually concerns the life of the Virgin, but another cycle, that of the Passion, is found in many English Books of Hours of the Sarum Use, and also in Dutch examples (it derives from Psalter illustrations, where a Passion sequence is frequently found following the Calendar). In some Books of Hours (such as that of Jeanne d'Evreux) both cycles occur together (p. 42).

The Playfair Hours. August–September Calendar: Treading the grape.

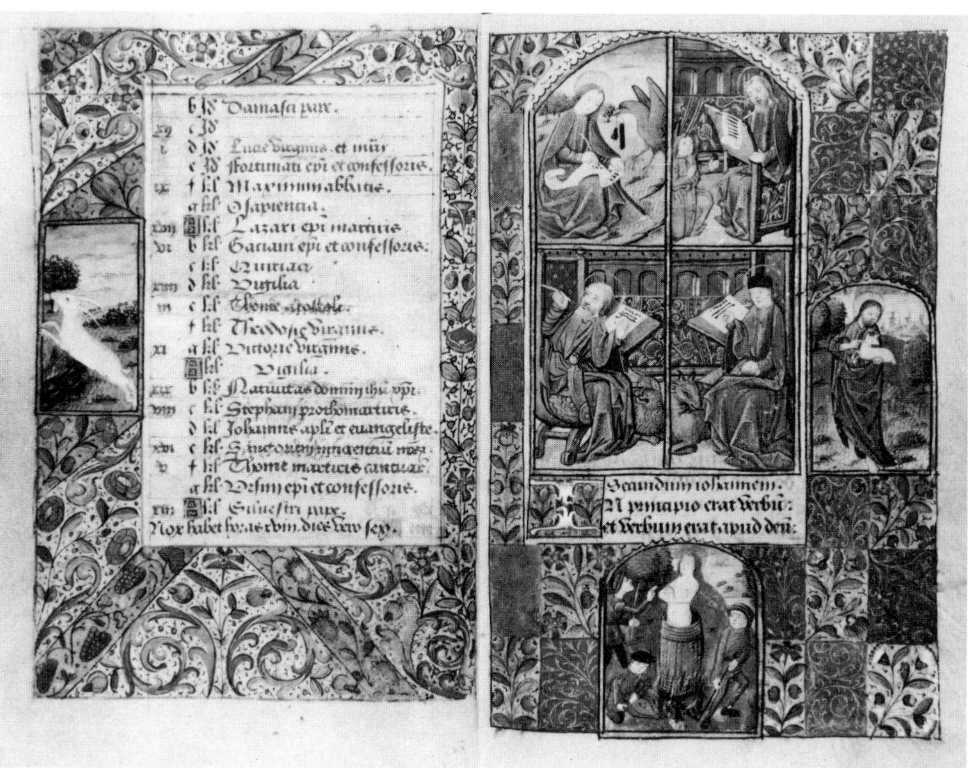

The Playfair Hours. December Calendar: Four Evangelists.

The Hours of the Virgin are usually illustrated with the following scenes:

MATINS	*The Annunciation*
LAUDS	*The Visitation*
PRIME	*The Nativity*
TIERCE	*The Angel's Announcement of Christ's Nativity to the Shepherds*
SEXT	*The Adoration of the Magi*
NONE	*The Presentation in the Temple*
VESPERS	*The Flight into Egypt, and/or the Massacre of the Innocents*
COMPLINE	*The Coronation of the Virgin*

Mary is present, it may be noted, in every one of these scenes except for the Angel's Announcement to the Shepherds. The Annunciation miniature in which she first appears is, in many Books of Hours, of a higher quality than the others. It is the most important image in the whole book from a devotional point of view, and for this reason was often undertaken by the master of the workshop, the other miniatures being distributed among his assistants. In the case of manuscripts made for stock and not personally commissioned there was a more mundane reason for concentrating on the Annunciation; it came early in the book and would be one of the first pictures to catch the eye of a prospective purchaser.

The Angel's Announcement to the Shepherds is a miniature always worth close scrutiny in Books of Hours. The scene gave artists an opportunity for depicting a landscape inhabited by peasants in their working clothes. The essential tool of the shepherd, his *houlette*, a hooked staff with a little shovel at the end, is an attribute as distinctive as the bishop's crozier. It was used to recapture straying animals, and the shovel for throwing earth and stones at marauding beasts or at sheep from another flock. The *houlette* does not appear in miniatures before the fourteenth century, when sheep-raising on a commercial scale became organized. In the late fifteenth century, and especially in printed Books of Hours, the Angel's Announcement turns into a pastorale, with the shepherds, accompanied by their wives, dancing to the music of bagpipes as they receive or ignore the celestial message. The gathering of the shepherds around the Christmas crib provided another setting for a rustic scene.[8]

The remaining pictures in the Hours of the Virgin are best studied in the examples reproduced in the plates. When the Hours are illustrated by the Passion the sequence is usually:

MATINS	*The betrayal of Judas*
LAUDS	*Christ before Pilate*
PRIME	*The Scourging*

TIERCE	*Christ carrying the Cross*
SEXT	*The Crucifixion*
NONE	*The Deposition*
VESPERS	*The Entombment*
COMPLINE	*The Resurrection*

The Hours of the Cross and of the Holy Spirit have much shorter texts than the Hours of the Virgin; the pictorial element is correspondingly reduced. It is usual to find a miniature at the first Hour only; at Matins of the Cross, the Crucifixion (occasionally the finding of the True Cross by the Empress St Helena); and at Matins of the Holy Spirit, the Descent of the Holy Ghost at Pentecost. Only in a few very elaborate examples (such as the Hours of Louis de Laval in the Bibliothèque Nationale) is each Hour of these two Offices illustrated.

Next come the Penitential Psalms. In the earlier sections the themes and subjects available to artists have been largely standardized, but at the Penitential Psalms there is considerable choice. The most obvious subject is an incident from the life of their supposed author, King David. He is often shown as an old man kneeling in penitence with his crown beside him before God or an avenging angel (p. 139). In the latter half of the fifteenth century a new theme appears, David watching Bathsheba in her bath,though this scene is noticeably absent from the *Grandes Heures* of the prudish Anne of Brittany.

It is unlikely that we shall find any miniatures at the Litany of the Saints which follows the Penitential Psalms, though occasionally individual saints are portrayed in the margin. In the Saint-Omer Hours (*see* p. 52), for example, St Lawrence on his gridiron and St Stephen nonchalantly juggling with blue and white stones, the emblems of his martyrdom, appear beside the text where their names appear. An illustration of a very special kind at the Litany is found in a few isolated manuscripts – the procession of St Gregory through the streets of Rome imploring Heaven for release from the plague (pp. 66–67, 151).

For the Office of the Dead, one of the most important sections in Books of Hours, there was an even wider choice of subjects for illustration than at the Penitential Psalms. The Last Judgment, with angels lifting the souls of the risen dead in a sheet to Christ, is found in early manuscripts. This tends to be replaced in later examples by the Vigil of the Dead, the service of prayers said in church over the coffin of the deceased the night before burial. The procession to the graveyard or the interment appear as alternatives in many French Books of Hours. Other subjects comprise a dying man, attended by friends and mourners, with a devil and angel competing for his soul above the bed; the Poor Man at the Rich Man's Feast (Dives and Lazarus), the Raising of Lazarus, and Job on his dunghill visited by the Comforters. The latter subject is explained by the passages from the Book of Job which appear in the lessons of the Office of the Dead.

Differing from these subjects in having no Biblical or liturgical source is the

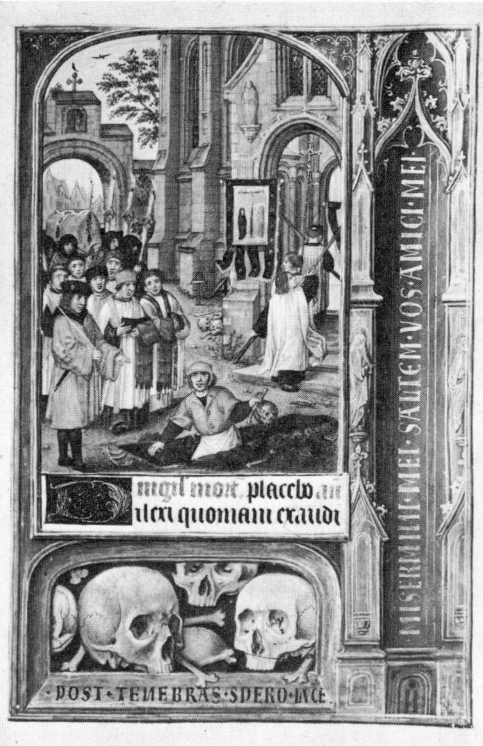

Book of Hours. Flanders, late 15th c. British Library, London, Add. MS. 35313.
Three Living and Three Dead; funeral procession. A very similar scene, with one female rider, is in a Book of Hours (Staatliche Museen, West Berlin) which once belonged to Mary of Burgundy, and commemorates (or did it prefigure?) her death in a riding accident.

Book of Hours (Use of Le Mans). France, *c.* 1420–30 and later. Victoria and Albert Museum, London, A.M. 181–1894. Vigils of the Dead.

popular theme of the Three Living and Three Dead. In this allegory on the vanity of earthly rank and riches, three men in the prime of youth and vigour are shown on horseback or walking, with falcons on their wrists. They encounter three skeletons, or corpses in varying stages of decomposition. This abrupt reminder of mortality in the midst of life anticipates the Dance of Death which frequently appears in the borders of printed Books of Hours.[9]

After these vivid scenes of death and judgment we turn a number of pages of text (the Office of the Dead is one of the longer sections in a Book of Hours) until we reach the Fifteen Joys of the Virgin. Here Our Lady, who has not been seen since her Coronation at Compline in her own Little Office, reappears with the infant Jesus in her arms. The change of mood is heightened by finding the prayers written in French or another vernacular language instead of Latin.

We now come to the last section, the *Memorie* or Suffrages of the Saints. After the Hours of the Virgin this is the most profusely illustrated section in the book. The saints appear in the same order as in the Litany, and are identified by conventional 'portraits' with their appropriate attributes or emblems. In modest Books of Hours, where no portraits are included, the saint's name is given in a red rubric.

As we reach the end of our imaginary Book of Hours it is important to realize that another specimen might contain more of the secondary and accessory texts, most of which had their appropriate miniatures, or have the contents arranged in a different order. On the other hand, it must not be supposed that every Book of Hours would be as richly decorated.

Social Aspects

Two questions must already have occurred to anybody who has read so far. What did these books mean to their owners, and how were they used? Some answers can be supplied by two types of evidence: written records and the arts.

Joan Evans described Books of Hours as 'a form of prayer that was both cause and consequence of the development of castle chapels'.[10] This definition perhaps over-emphasizes the aristocratic connection: the main purpose of Books of Hours was to provide every class of the laity from kings and royal dukes down to prosperous burghers and their wives with personal prayerbooks. All literate people, and even some who could not read, aspired to own one. In contemplating the superior specimens with their overwhelming richness of decoration it is easy to forget the thousands of humble examples, made for everyday use, which have been preserved only by accident. Yet the latter were the more influential in the democratization of religion which took place in the later Middle Ages. Books of Hours were the vehicle both of intellectual Christianity at its loftiest and of popular devotion on the most primitive level. One does not get far in understanding them by looking at the miniatures alone, or by concentrating exclusively on the best examples.[11]

It is sometimes said that Books of Hours reflect the vanity and affluence rather than the piety of their owners. There is some truth in this, but we should be cautious, at a distance of five hundred years or more, in thinking that we can enter into the minds of the men and women whose Books of Hours we now hold in our hands; the relationship between a soul and God is one of the most private mysteries. In the Middle Ages piety was an important means of self-expression, obligatory for the professed religious, unquestioningly accepted by the vast majority of layfolk. With piety often went display; luxury cannot be kept out of religion. Processions and pilgrimages were collective expressions of piety, complementing the private recitation of the Hours. It was only later that Puritanism questioned the sincerity and doubted the value of ostentatious prayer; there are no Quaker Books of Hours.

Those of the Duke of Berry are a special case. A prototype Rothschild, he was a compulsive collector of the finest examples of jewellery, goldsmiths' work and illuminated manuscripts that his money could buy. His resplendent Books of Hours have influenced the study of the subject too exclusively; their fame has resulted in the popular but inaccurate image of Books of Hours as belonging only to the rich and great.

Circumstances and temperament obviously determined how much or little use the lay owner made of his Book of Hours. But references by chroniclers and other writers to the devotional habits of their patrons are too precise to be ignored. It is easy to dismiss as courtiers' conventional flattery the reiterated statements that a great man daily said his Hours, recited the Vigils of the Dead at bedtime and found time to hear two or three Masses a day. Individual anecdotes make one think again. We are told that tough old Arthur III, Duke of Brittany, the hammer of the English, recited his Hours on his knees the day he died (like Elizabeth I of England, he refused to take to his bed). The flighty Queen Isabeau, wife of Charles VI, owned several Books of Hours which she read at night-time, a fact established by entries in the royal accounts recording payments for candles, sconces and ivory lamps specifically supplied for this purpose.[12] Philip the Good of Burgundy was reading from his Hours in the palace chapel in Brussels after Mass when he began a colossal row with his son Charles, described in Monstrelet's Chronicle. Henry VI of England recited the Little Office every day, as might be expected of a candidate for sanctity who could perhaps have been canonized but for Henry VII's meanness. Margaret Beaufort, Countess of Richmond, the latter's mother, began her devotions at five in the morning by reading Matins with one of her gentlewomen. In reporting this habit to his government, the Venetian Ambassador observed of the English that 'if any can read they take the Office of Our Lady to church and recite it in a low voice in alternate verses, after the manner of the religious orders'. Catherine of Aragon, first consort of Henry VIII, recited this Office daily on her knees. Sir Thomas More said Matins, the seven Penitential Psalms, the Litany and 'manie times the Graduall Psalms'. A visitor to Esher Place, one of the homes of Cardinal Wolsey, in 1529 found Thomas Cromwell, a few years later to become the destroyer of the monasteries, leaning in a window of the great chamber reading his Hours.[13]

There is often evidence in Books of Hours of much use. Bindings are rubbed, the introductory Calendar section lost, edges of the pages thumb-marked, stained with wax spots from lamp or candle, torn, and blank pages and even margins used for additional prayers copied out by later hands. Leaves from the Hours of Philip the Bold of Burgundy are black from fingering and much kissing; a repulsive habit, we may think, but evidence of prolonged use even if not necessarily by him. The fact that many choice Books of Hours survive in near immaculate condition does not necessarily imply indifference but more probably that their owner possessed more than one. The everyday copy would be discarded when worn out, the best carefully preserved and brought out on special occasions.

From wills and inventories it is clear that Books of Hours were regarded as important, precious objects. Owners left careful instructions for their disposal. Three entries for Books of Hours mentioned in the will of Blanche of Navarre, wife of Philip VI of France, are worth citing in full. Queen Blanche died at an advanced age in 1398. She owned a considerable library which was carefully divided among her relatives, friends and servants. Her mother's finest Book of Hours went to her 'very dear son' the Duke of Berry: *Item, nous laissons à nostre très chier filz le duc de Berry, noz plus belles heures que nostre très chiere dame et mère, que Dieux pardoint, nous laissa à son trepassement.* (The Duke of Berry was in fact her step-grandson, but in her will she refers to him and his brothers in the royal manner as her *filz*.) To her sister Jeanne de Navarre, Queen Blanche left her mother's second-best Hours, those which she herself used every day: *Item, noz heures de Nostre Dame, ou nous disons touz les journs noz heures, que furent madame nostre mère, que Dieux absoille, qui sont les meilleures que nous ayons après celles que nous laissons à nostre dit filz de Berry.* The third Book of Hours, identified by the *Gloria* which followed the Calendar, was one formerly owned by Queen Jeanne d'Evreux (but not the little volume illustrated on p. 42): *Item, un livre d'oreisons et devocions qui fu à la ditte madame la royne Jeanne d'Evreux; et le nous donna la duchesse d'Orlions, sa fille derrenière trepassée: et se commence après le Kalendrier Gloria in excelsis.* These entries tell us that a great lady might own several Books of Hours, often inherited, and could identify them from the text. Queen Blanche also specifically mentions which was the one she used every day.[14]

The inventory of Marguerite of Brittany, first wife of Duke Francis II (pp. 124–25), lists fifteen books belonging to her at her death in 1469, of which five were Books of Hours. Among the latter were two *Grandes Heures* of the Use of Paris, *armoyées aux armes de la duchesse ysabeau*, her mother, either of which could have been the Hours of Isabella Stuart, now in the Fitzwilliam Museum, Cambridge (pp. 114–17). A third Book of Hours, in a binding with golden clasps, *armoyées aux armes de feu madame d'Estampes*, may have been the exquisite volume now in the Bibliothèque Nationale (ms. lat. 1156B), made in the 1420s for Marguerite of Orleans, wife of Richard d'Etampes, the father of Duke Francis II.[15] These entries show how ladies might accumulate several Books of Hours formerly belonging to different members of their family; they demonstrate also how difficult it is to identify the books today from the descriptions of the vanished original bindings.

It was not only the rich and great who owned more than one Book of Hours and made provision for them to pass to suitable persons after their death. On a more humble level the evidence from English archives is equally explicit. Specific Books of Hours (or Primers) are described in terms such as 'my prymer with gilt clasps, whereupon I am wont to say my service' (in the will of a fifteenth-century grocer), 'my best prymer', 'my mydell prymmer', 'my grete prymmer'. In 1429 Ralph Avirley left his 'red Primer' to Thomas Stone, and in 1443 Henry Market of York his 'second best prymer' to his second son Henry. A lady in 1498 left her god-daughter a prayerbook 'clasped with silver and gilte for a Remembrance to pray for me'.[16]

For the living, the most obvious occasion for acquiring a Book of Hours was on marriage. Prayerbooks were frequently commissioned or bought as a wedding present from a husband to his bride. The Hours of Jeanne d'Evreux were illuminated by Jean Pucelle on the order of Charles IV of France as a gift to his third wife in 1324–25. The Grey-FitzPayn Hours are another example (pp. 43, 45). These 'wedding' Books of Hours started a fashion which survived for centuries. On the occasion of the marriage of her second son Alfred, Duke of Edinburgh, to the Czar's daughter in 1874, Queen Victoria sent a plain and an illuminated prayerbook to St Petersburg, the first for the groom, the second for the bride. It is interesting to note that at this late date illumination was considered to have a feminine appropriateness, an idea quite foreign to the Middle Ages.

An often-quoted ballade by the poet Eustache Deschamps (1346–1406), employed by Charles VI and Louis of Orleans, satirizes the vogue for Books of Hours among the wives of the prosperous bourgeois. It seems they could not appear in church without one:

Heures me fault de Nostre Dame
Qui soient de soutil ouvraige,
D'or et d'azur, riches et ceintes,
Bien ordonnées et bien peintes,
De fin drap d'or bien couvertes,
Et quant elles seront ouvertes,
Deux fermaulx d'or qui fermeront.

A Book of Hours, too, must be mine,
Where subtle workmanship will shine,
Of gold and azure, rich and smart,
Arranged and painted with great art,
Covered with fine brocade of gold;
And there must be, so as to hold
The pages closed, two golden clasps.[17]

Much written evidence survives in Books of Hours to tell us about the varied purposes they served. Like the family Bibles of later times, they often served as *livres de raison* in which details of births and deaths were recorded. A more specialized use was as albums for the safe keeping of pilgrims' badges, *ex-votos* and other *objets de piété*. A few examples survive with actual specimens sewn into the pages, but more common are painted *bondieuseries* or religious knick-knacks, such as those found in the Soane Hours (p. 150).

The presence of rosaries among the objects of piety depicted in the Soane Hours is a reminder that this form of popular devotion developed more or less simultaneously with Books of Hours in the later Middle Ages. The rosary cult was, indeed, even more widespread than that of Books of Hours, for even the totally illiterate could learn how to pray by 'saying their beads'. As an aid to devotion the rosary is sometimes described as the poor relation of Books of Hours, though specimens could range from a simple knot of beads to elaborate confections of enamelled gold, coral, crystal and jewels. Even more than the Book of Hours the rosary was an object which could be carried about or worn on the person. The conjunction of the rosary with the Book of Hours is seen in the Hours of Mary of Burgundy and in a striking page from the Hours of Catherine of Cleves, where the border of an Adoration of the Magi miniature is filled by a painted rosary of red beads, tasselled with gold and pearls to which is attached a cross, a seven-pointed star and a blue purse.[18]

Books of Hours served medicinal as well as spiritual purposes. In a general sense every example might be therapeutic; for a particular saint would be invoked against a specific malady or ailment in a particular part of the body. One cannot help thinking that the frequent appearance in Books of Hours of the obscure third-century saint Apollonia of Alexandria, a reputed sister of St Lawrence, who suffered martyrdom by having her teeth extracted one by one, must have some connection with the prevalence of toothache in the Middle Ages. An anguished prayer *contra dolorem dentium*, addressed to St Apollonia, was inserted in a later hand at the Suffrage of St Margaret in a French Book of Hours now at Lille, perhaps by someone named Margaret who was suffering grievously from toothache. St Apollonia appears in a memorable miniature from the dismembered Hours of Etienne Chevalier at Chantilly. The brutality of the scene is mitigated only by the realization that it here represents part of a Mystery Play.[19]

An invocation against bed-bugs, found in a Spanish Book of Hours, is a reminder of another common hazard of daily life. Such a quasi-superstitious prayer would never have been allowed in an official service book; and its inclusion illustrates the freedom Books of Hours enjoyed from clerical control. Prayers against the plague are also frequent and include the 'Grand Supplication', derived from the procession of St Gregory illustrated in the *Très Riches Heures* (pp. 66–67). The plague prayer *Stella celi extirpavit* is also occasionally found, an English version appearing in the Salisbury Hours (Victoria and Albert Museum, London). This prayer alludes to the then common belief that illness, like most accidents of mortal life, is controlled by the stars.

One of the most curious medieval methods of preventive medicine was calculation based on the *Dies mali*, *Dies egri* or *Dies aegyptiaci*. These were the 'unlucky' days, unpropitious for beginning any enterprise and especially for purging or blood-letting, then the commonest form of medical treatment. A Shakespearian echo is heard in the first scene of *Richard II* when the King, in postponing the trial of arms between Bolingbroke and Mowbray, observes: 'Our doctors say, this is no month to bleed.' In the Calendars of Books of Hours these dangerous days were marked with a small *d*.

The Egyptians were credited with this useful aid in medical treatment, hence the expression *Dies aegyptiaci*.[20] The Romans also had their *Dies atri*, or black days, on which disasters had occurred in the past and might happen again if any affair of importance was begun on a similar day. The *Dies egri* prayer appears in verse form as early as the Hymns attributed to Bede (before AD 731), but had previously been denounced by SS. Augustine and Ambrose as a pagan survival. This bizarre example of medieval superstition and pseudo-science has considerable antiquarian interest in England, where the *Dies mali* appear to have been specially popular, or rather feared; they are found marked in the Calendars of both Books of Hours and Psalters, including the Queen Mary and Gorleston Psalters (British Library).

Generally speaking, Books of Hours were expensive. One got what one was prepared to pay for, as so often in life. For their cost it is necessary to consult inventories where much information is found which cannot, however, often be related directly to existing manuscripts. An entry in the book of accounts of Guy VI de La Trémoille, covering the years 1395–1406, records that Robin Jaquin, *escrivain et enlumineur*, refurbished a Book of Hours for Guy's wife, Marie de Sully. He supplied new quires or sections (*quayers neufs*) for her *grans heures* which he also rebound, regilded, cleaned and generally put in order (*mettre à point*). For this work he received five francs.[21] This interesting entry establishes that at this date the skills of writing and illuminating might be combined in one craftsman and that owners took the trouble to keep their Books of Hours in good condition. No work by Robin Jaquin is now known.

The *Belles Heures* of the Duke of Berry were acquired after his death by

Yolanda of Aragon, Duchess of Anjou, for what is said to have been the bargain price of 300 *livres tournois*. His most valuable book, the *Très Riches Heures*, though not completed at his death, was valued at 4,000 *livres*. Nearly a century later Anne of Brittany issued an order from Blois, dated 14 March 1508, that Jean Bourdichon should be paid 1,500 *livres tournois* in the form of 600 *écus d'or* for painting her *Grandes Heures*. Owing to the different currencies used it is difficult to give modern equivalents.

Few Books of Hours survive in their original covers. These were not normally of leather before the period of near mass-production in the second half of the fifteenth century. The more usual practice for the grander specimens at least was to bind the leaves in silk or velvet, to which were attached gilt and jewelled clasps and corner-pieces made by professional goldsmiths. Inside the spine of the book a pearl-studded metal rod known as a *pippe* was inserted to which the *signaux* or book-marks were attached. When completed the book was either provided with a box for safe keeping or sewn into a covering known as a *chemisette* (or chemise), usually made of a fine kid-leather called *chevrotin* or of *cendal*, a silk fabric. When picked up by the corners the *chemisette* formed a bag in which the book could be conveniently carried. When laid open on a *prie-dieu* or held in the hands for reading the *chemisette* was unwrapped to serve like a napkin to keep the pages clean.[22]

Books of Hours in these *chemisette* bindings may often be encountered in paintings in the hand of saint or donor. Van Eyck frequently introduced Books of Hours with pearl-studded *pippes* and *chemisette* covers into his pictures. In the Ghent altarpiece of the *Adoration of the Holy Lamb*, the richly attired Virgin reads from a prayerbook in a green *chemisette* binding edged with gold from which hang four brown tassels at the corners.[23] No less than three Books of Hours, shown closed and open, appear in the triptych of *Mary in the Burning Bush* by Nicolas Froment in the Cathedral of Saint-Sauveur at Aix-en-Provence. The donors, René of Anjou and his second wife Jeanne de Laval, kneel with their books in front of them. René's is closed, his wife's open at a page where the text can be read: *In his omnibus requiem quaesivi et in hereditate Domini morabor*, a quotation from Ecclesiasticus which appears in the first lesson of Matins in the Hours of the Virgin. On the outer shutter of the triptych the Virgin Mary, painted in grisaille, stands with her thumb marking the place she had reached in her Book of Hours before receiving the Archangel's message.[24]

The bindings found today on Books of Hours usually date from a later period than the text inside. After a century or more of use the *chemisette* and original cover became worn out and were discarded. The volume was then rebound as an act of piety by descendants or successors of the first owner and put away in a drawer or cupboard to be forgotten for many years. (The chance finding in the late 1950s of the Llangattock Hours, now in the H.P. Kraus Collection, New York, in a chest of silver, is one of the most spectacular discoveries of forgotten Books of Hours. The manuscript, illuminated in Ghent around 1450, contains miniatures in the manner of Jan van Eyck and Petrus Christus. More recently, an hitherto unrecorded Flemish Book of Hours, executed *c.* 1510, from an anonymous German collection, fetched the record sum of £407,000 in a London saleroom in July 1976.)[25]

A sense of mild incongruity or anachronism is aroused when we find an illuminated Gothic Book of Hours encased in a sixteenth-century binding *à la fanfare*, a seventeenth-century *pointillé* or eighteenth-century *dentelle* binding. In the early nineteenth century connoisseurs, influenced by the current romantic interest in medieval history and art, attempted to give their Books of Hours a more appropriate external presentation by having them rebound *à la cathédrale* with decorative motifs on the covers taken from Gothic architecture. While recognizing this laudable attempt to achieve a period fitness, one may deplore the liturgical ignorance so often shown in labelling the spines as 'Missals'. This was, indeed, the 'Missal Age', when English bibliophiles described almost any 'monkish' manuscript by this term.

Indicative of this enthusiastic if uninformed interest was the account of the Bedford Hours (British Library, Add. ms. 18850) published in 1794 by Richard Gough, the antiquary, under the title of *An Account of a Rich Illuminated Missal executed for John Duke of Bedford, Regent of France under Henry VI, and afterwards in the Possession of the late Duchess of Portland.* The Bedford Hours has the distinction of being the first individual Book of Hours to be the subject of a special study. Richard Gough's detailed description established the fame of this peerless example dating from the 1420s and a masterpiece of the anonymous Bedford Master (so called after his patron).[26]

Ruskin was one of the last representatives of the 'Missal Age'. His observations about book illumination are perceptive, but his treatment of manuscripts as recorded in his diaries makes horrific reading: 'Spent the day cutting up a missal, hard work', 'Cut leaves from large missal', 'Put two pages of missals in frame', 'Missals for use not curiosities'.[27] Ruskinian scholars excuse his barbarous habit of cutting up illuminated manuscripts as being prompted by the wish to share his treasures and to make them more accessible to students. This may be so, but there is surely, a psychological explanation. After the first disturbing realization 'that all beautiful prayers were Catholic' he resisted any attempt to relate the miniatures in the manuscripts he was fortunate enough to acquire with their textual and devotional context. How much happier he might have been in later life, if he could have accepted the implications of his profound sympathy with medieval art!

Ruskin could recognize a Book of Hours when he saw one. The first illuminated manuscript he acquired was an early French Book of Hours (Use of Rheims) illuminated around 1280–1300 and now in the Victoria and Albert Museum (Reid ms. 83). He describes it in *Praeterita* (III, i) as

> a little Hours of the Virgin, not refined work, but extremely rich, grotesque, and full of colour. The new world which every leaf of the book opened to me, and the joy I

had, counting their letters and unravelling their arabesques as if they had been of beaten gold – as many of them indeed were – cannot be told ... Not that the worlds thus opening themselves were new, but only the possession of any part of them; for long and long ago I had gazed at the illuminated missals in noblemen's houses with a wonder and sympathy deeper than I can now give ... for truly a well-illuminated missal is a fair cathedral full of painted windows.

Before turning to the minute sample of Books of Hours represented in the plates, their later development must be briefly outlined.[28] The invention of printing, which is often claimed to have killed the art of illumination, increased rather than diminished the vogue for Books of Hours. But it was in the form of printed editions that they achieved their widest diffusion during the sixteenth century. An enormous number were produced, of which only the best examples have been preserved. A brief essay on printed Books of Hours is included on pp. 169f. Here it is only necessary to stress that this abundance of editions was marked by radical changes in their contents, as new texts were added and arranged in quasi-liturgical manner for use at church services, especially the Mass and Vespers, the latter being one of the most popular devotions.

All subsequent prayerbooks derive from Books of Hours, and it is significant that the old title was retained for manuals of devotion which bore only a general resemblance to the medieval Book of Hours. From the seventeenth century onwards compilations were issued with a variety of titles which sometimes included the name of the author or compiler. Typical examples are the *Heures à l'usage de ceux qui assistent au service de l'Eglise avec les Vespres* (1691), *L'Office de la Sainte Vierge pour les trois tems de l'Année avec l'Office des Morts, les prières du Soir & du Matin* (1700), and the *Heures nouvelles paroissien complet, latin-français à l'usage de Paris et Rome par l'abbé Dassance* (1841). This proliferation of prayerbooks using the old title, and in which only the Hours of the Virgin might be retained intact, witnesses to the popularity and success of Books of Hours in earlier centuries – as does the official title of the new post-Vatican II Breviary: *The Divine Office: The Liturgy of the Hours According to the Roman Rite.*

Jan van Eyck. The Virgin Mary, detail of the *Altar of the Holy Lamb*, 1432. Church of St Bavon, Ghent.

The Hours of Jeanne d'Evreux, Queen of France

Dominican Use. France, *c.* 1325. 9 × 6 cm ($3\frac{5}{8} \times 2\frac{3}{8}$ in), 209ff.
25 miniatures with marginal vignettes, initials and drolleries painted in grisaille.
The Metropolitan Museum of Art, New York, The Cloisters Collection, ms. 54.1.2

page 42 **Betrayal of Christ; Annunciation** ff.15v–16
Christ carrying the Cross; Angel and Shepherds ff.61v–62

THE FIRST EXAMPLE in this anthology is one of the choicest of early Books of Hours, with miniatures as delicate as contemporary ivory carvings and displaying a freshness of spirit which looks to the future. There are strong grounds for believing the owner to have been Jeanne d'Evreux, wife of Charles IV of France (reigned 1322–28). Her tiny prayerbook is written in a beautifully regular script, on vellum so thin that it is transparent; the scribe's name is unfortunately not recorded. The miniatures are all in grisaille, a technique of painting in grey tones, with touches of colour for the faces and hands of the figures, which is peculiarly suited to book illumination, where it blends harmoniously with the black script of the text and gives decorative unity to the page. These delicate pictures are from the workshop of Jean Pucelle, one of the few fourteenth-century book illuminators known both by name and documented works. He excelled particularly in the *de blanc et de noir* style, as grisaille was then called.

The miniatures in the first section follow two traditional cycles. At the beginning of each Hour of the Office of the Virgin Mary, scenes from the Passion of Christ face, on the opposite page, events in the life of his mother. The Passion cycle came from the traditional illustrations in the Psalter, from which Books of Hours detached themselves around 1300 as independent prayer-books of layfolk. Scenes from the life of the Virgin, beginning with the Annunciation at Matins, were to become the accepted pictorial sequence for illustrating Books of Hours during the following two centuries. In this early example we find both cycles together.

At each Hour the confronting miniatures, marginal illustrations and animated little scenes at the bottom of the page are designed as a unit. On the right of the first double-page reproduced here (p. 42) is the Annunciation. The Archangel Gabriel and the Virgin Mary are inside a Gothic hall, the front of which has been swung back like a door by a crouching angel. In the open gable at the top are praying angels, with two more at the sides holding musical instruments. In the historiated initial *D* of *Domine labia mea aperies* ('O Lord open thou my lips'), Jeanne d'Evreux herself appears, as a diminutive, crowned figure kneeling at a *prie-dieu*. In the border below the two lines of text a group of ladies play a game of tag known as 'hot cockles'. The scene on the left page shows the Betrayal of Christ, beneath which a rubric written in red announces the Hours of the Virgin with another incongruous *bas-de-page* group of two men riding a goat and a ram and tilting at a barrel.

The second opening shows Christ carrying the Cross, with the Angel's announcement of his Nativity to the shepherds on the facing page. The lively angels and other figures in the margins are extensions of the scene. Gothic cresting along the top of both miniatures gives a sense of balance, almost of symmetry, to the double-spread. The two crouching 'caryatid' figures supporting the frame of the miniature recall the angel who holds the Annunciation picture on the earlier page.

QUEEN JEANNE'S PRAYERBOOK, enchanting in its own right, introduces us to questions of ownership, artistic origin and subsequent history which will confront us often in this survey of Books of Hours. To begin with the artist: Jean Pucelle's name is mentioned in two early fourteenth-century manuscripts, the Billyng Bible and the Belleville Breviary (both in the Bibliothèque Nationale, Paris), which, together with the present one, convey a clear impression of his style.[1] It is fully Gothic, characterized by the double or S-bend pose of the standing figures as found in ivories of the period, and an overall refinement of manner. Less immediately obvious is an Italian influence, indicated in the Evreux Hours by the use of box-like architectural interiors open on one side to display the figures within, already inhabiting a spatial area even if the laws of perspective may not be perfectly understood. The crowd scenes at the Betrayal of Christ and the Crucifixion also show the influence of Italian painting. Pucelle is thought to have been in Italy at some time in the early 1320s, visiting Florence, Siena and possibly Rome. A memory of Duccio's *Maestà*, then to be seen intact with its predella in Siena cathedral, has been discerned in the miniatures of Jeanne d'Evreux's Book of Hours.

Pucelle's workshop transformed the art of book illumination in Paris during the second quarter of the fourteenth century. Its influence remained dominant, despite his seemingly early death, for many years; to such an extent, indeed, that Pucelle has become as much the name of a style as of an artist. Yet almost nothing is known about him except for five documents in which his name is mentioned, his death in 1334 (recorded in the accounts of the Confraternity of Saint-Jacques-aux-Pèlerins in Paris, for whom he designed the great seal sometime between 1319–24),[2] and what may be deduced from his manuscripts.

In the so-called International Gothic style of the early fifteenth century, the Pucelle tradition was revivified by the impact of northern influences which produced a Franco-Flemish synthesis, itself in turn to develop into the separate Flemish-Burgundian and the more specifically French School of Tours associated with Fouquet and his followers.

Ownership of a Book of Hours, in the absence of an inscription or coat of arms, often cannot be established with absolute certainty. But the presence in the Cloisters example of a young crowned queen in the historiated initial of the Annunciation page, and the inclusion of the Hours of St Louis, the royal saint, which follow the Hours of the Virgin, point unmistakably to a royal provenance; and the most likely candidate for ownership is Jeanne d'Evreux.[3]

She was the eldest daughter of Louis de France, Count of Evreux in Normandy, and married her

Continued on page 44

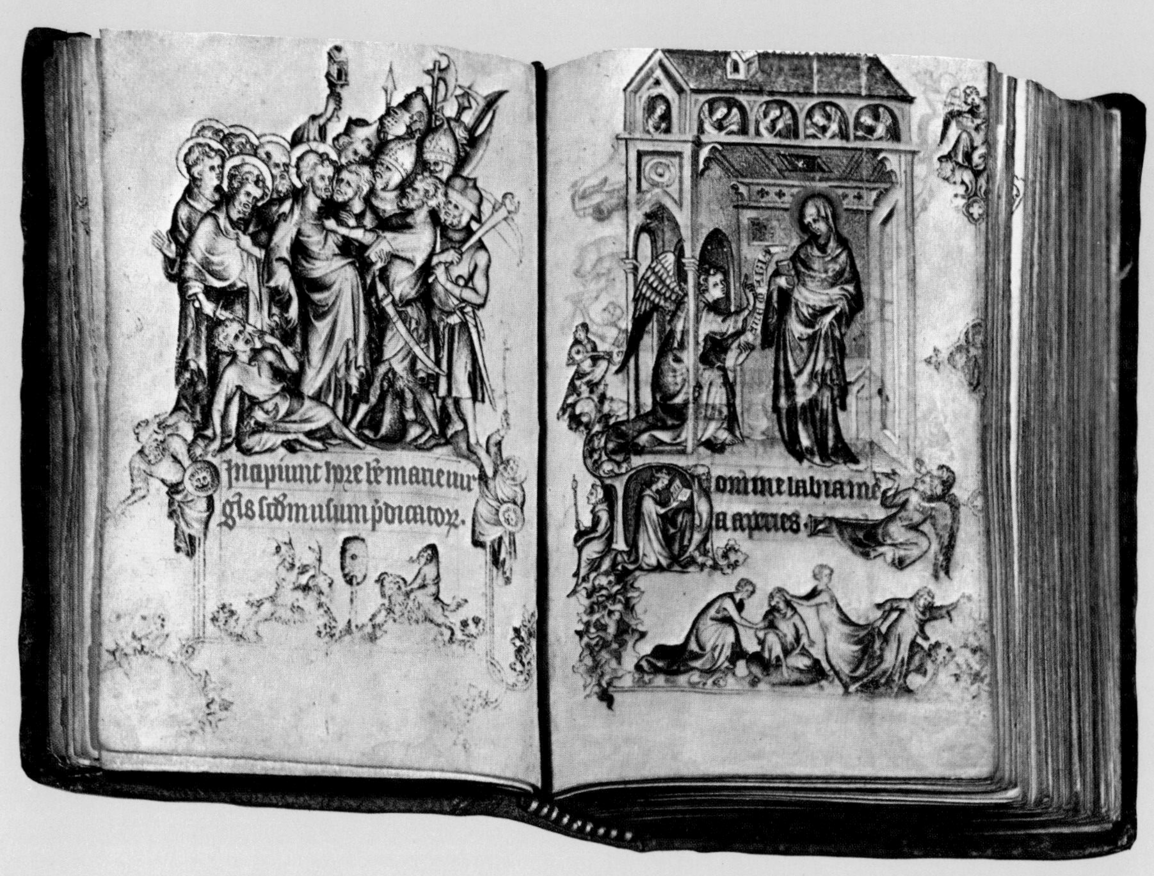

Domine labia mea a
peries et os me
um annunci
abit laudem
tuam Deus
in adiutoriu̅
meum intende Domine ad adiuua̅
me festina Gloria patri et filio et spu
sco Sicut erat in principio et nu̅c et
semp et in secula seculorum amen.
Deum uerum unum in trinitate et trinitate̅
in unitate. uenite adoremus.
Venite exultemus domino iubile
mus deo salutari nro preocupem
faciem eius in confessione et in psalmis
iubilemus ei Deum uerum unum in trini
tate et trinitatem in unitate. uenite adoremus.
Quoniam deus magnus dominus et

first cousin King Charles IV (a Papal dispensation was necessary) in 1325 as his third wife. It has been suggested that the King commissioned this book from Jean Pucelle either as a wedding present for his new Queen, or for her coronation in Rheims cathedral.

Charles IV was the last of the Capetian kings, a somewhat shadowy figure of whom few personal details are known except that he was nicknamed 'the Handsome' (*le Bel*) like his father Philip IV. All three sons of Philip were slim, personable young men who in turn briefly inherited the throne after the death of their father in 1314: Louis X, the Impetuous (*le Hutin*); Philip V, the Tall (*le Long*); and Charles IV. Petrarch observed that the last three Capets 'passed like a dream'. By 1328 all were dead, leaving no male heirs. This unexpected event brought the Crown to the Valois family, a collateral branch of the royal house, and plunged France into the disasters of the Hundred Years War, fought with the King of England over a disputed succession. From 1328 to 1498 the Valois family ruled in direct father-to-son succession through seven generations. This was also the High Gothic age, when, as rarely happens, an artistic style evolved chronologically within a parallel dynastic period. Jean Pucelle was an early, forward-looking exponent of this style.

Jeanne d'Evreux survived a long widowhood spent in retirement at the royal abbey of Maubuisson, near Vincennes. She died in 1371 after enriching the Church with works of art and providing for perpetual Masses. She also concerned herself with the religious orders to whom she made many benefactions; and this Book of Hours follows the Dominican rather than the more usual Paris Use.

It is of great importance for our subject that on her death Queen Jeanne bequeathed her Book of Hours to the reigning Valois King Charles V: *Premièrement, au roy nostre sire . . . un bien petit livret d'oroisons que le roy Charles, dont Diex ait l'âme, avoict faict faire por Madame, que pucelle enlumina* ('Firstly, to the king our lord a very small prayerbook which king Charles, may God have his soul, had made for Madame, which Pucelle illuminated'). The mention of the artist's name suggests that he was remembered in the royal family long after his death, though there is no evidence that he received a court appointment as a *varlet de chambre*.

Queen Jeanne's mention of Pucelle establishes that a prayerbook illuminated for her by the artist was once in the library of the royal bibliophile Charles V. Thence it seems to have migrated (as a gift?) to his brother John, Duke of Berry, another dedicated if more flamboyant book-lover. In inventories of the Duke of Berry's possessions made in 1401, 1413 and 1416 there appears a manuscript described as: *Item unes petites heures de Nostre Dame, nommées Heures de Pucelle, enluminées de blanc et de noir, à l'usaige des Prescheurs* ('Item a little Hours of Our Lady, called Pucelle Hours, illuminated in white and black, following the Use of the Preachers [the Dominican Order]').[4]

This description fits very closely the manuscript now in the Cloisters Collection, New York. Whether it can be identified beyond doubt with the book described in Queen Jeanne's will as *un bien petit livret d'oroisons* – not, it may be noted, as a *livre d'heures*, and with no mention of *de blanc et de noir* illuminations – has been questioned; but the combination of stylistic, iconographical and documentary evidence carries conviction. Jeanne d'Evreux certainly confirmed the new fashion for owning finely illuminated, personal Books of Hours and established a tradition long followed in the French royal family.

At some time in the nineteenth century this pearl among Books of Hours was acquired by the Rothschild family, always zealous collectors of rare and beautiful objects. In 1953 it was purchased by the Metropolitan Museum from Baron Maurice de Rothschild.

The Grey-FitzPayn Hours

Use of Sarum. England, Midlands, *c.* 1300–08. 24.5 × 17 cm ($9\frac{5}{8} \times 6\frac{5}{8}$ in), 93ff. 2 full-page miniatures, 3 large historiated initials, decorative initials and bar borders.
Fitzwilliam Museum, Cambridge, ms. 242

43 **Christ blessing, inside initial D** f.29

THIS IS A LARGE VOLUME, unlike the tiny Hours of Jeanne d'Evreux, which it predates by at least twenty years. Its size reminds us that in the early fourteenth century Books of Hours had only recently become detached from Psalters to follow an independent role as personal prayerbooks of the laity. This early English example was probably written and illuminated for Sir Richard de Grey, of Codnor Castle, Derbyshire, as a wedding present to his bride, Joan FitzPayn. In the page reproduced, blue predominates, lit up by the heraldic tinctures of the shields which display the coats of arms of the families of Clifford differenced by FitzPayn, Grey and Creye. The text is that of the Hours of the Trinity, with the opening words marked by a large initial *D* (*Domine labia mea aperies*), in which appears Christ in Majesty blessing Joan FitzPayn, who kneels before him on the left wearing an heraldic mantle.[1]

The bar border springing from the historiated initial incorporates the smaller initial with its portrait bust, lower down the page, and extends into both top and bottom margins to provide a platform for lively hunting scenes. At the top, dogs in pursuit of a rabbit are unnoticed by a boar and a sleeping lion. A stag hunt appears at the bottom of the page. Here a rabbit crouches immobile with flattened ears beneath the stricken beast, which has been shot through the neck by an arrow from the archer on the right, as it springs towards a lion and a fox-tailed animal which appear to be watching some quarry. The goat in the outer margin climbing a tree in search of succulent foliage is a motif as old as Mesopotamian art, but an incident the artist could have seen any day by looking into his back garden. The birds, a favourite subject in English manuscripts of this period, are finely depicted as they attentively regard the heraldic shields and the more distant figure of Christ blessing.

The heraldic shields introduce an emphatic note. They are used functionally, to announce family alliances, as well as to provide a decorative motif in the borders; already at this early date we see the important role heraldry was to play in the embellishment of Books of Hours.

THE GREY-FITZPAYN wedding took place in 1300/1, and since Joan is thought to have died in 1308 the date of the manuscript can be fixed to within a few years (her husband did not die until 1334/5). Their portraits, in the guises of a kneeling armoured knight and his lady, appear in the borders and historiated initials of the two frontispieces.

Stylistically, the miniatures and borders of the Grey-FitzPayn Hours show French Gothic influence combined with an English sharpness of observation, especially in the representation of birds and animals. The drolleries, grotesques and hunting scenes which give such animation to the pages of this book are found in other manuscripts of the period. These form a distinct group, of which the Tickhill Psalter (New York Public Library, Spencer Collection, ms. 26) is the finest example. They are thought to have been illuminated in the Nottingham area, only twelve miles from Codnor Castle.

Though this prayerbook is not related artistically to the Taymouth Hours, the next item in this anthology, there is a tenuous historical link. Edward II visited Sir Richard de Grey, his greatest supporter, at Codnor in 1322 after repulsing one of the Scottish forays into Yorkshire; but his failure to achieve his father Edward I's ambitions in Scotland led to a patched-up peace and the marriage of the King's daughter Joan, the probable owner of the Taymouth Hours, to the child King David II of Scotland.[2]

The text of the Grey-FitzPayn Hours is somewhat incomplete, the Calendar having vanished entirely and several of the Hours lacking their opening pages. The surviving contents comprise the normal elements – Hours of the Virgin, Hours of the Trinity, Hours of the Holy Ghost, Penitential Psalms, Litany, Gradual Psalms and Office of the Dead. There are no rubrics announcing the different Hours and prayers, though each verse is marked by a small decorative initial. This was a practice taken from the Psalter, and one with which we may assume Richard de Grey and Joan FitzPayn to have been well familiar, since they needed no guidance other than these initials in finding their way about their Book of Hours.

December.

Nonas
Nicholai epī et conf.
Oct. sci andree apli
Conceptio Marie
O Sapiencia
Vigil.
Sci Thome apostoli
Vigil.
Nativitas domini
Stephani prothom.
Iohis euangeliste
Scorum innocencium
Thome archiepiscopi
Silvestri epī et conf.

Oreison avaunt la messe.
Douz sire al comencement
De ceste messe en present
De celui prestre vous bien a dire

S. Jeronimus

miserere nostri. Deo grās. R̄
Felix namq; es sacra virgo maria et
omni laude dignissima. quia ex te ortus
est sol iusticie xp̄c deus noster. V̄ Ora pro
populo interveni pro clero intercede pro de
voto femineo sexu senciant omnes tuū
levamen quicumq; celebrant tuam cō
memoracionem. Quia ex te ortus est
sol iusticie xp̄c deus noster. Gloria patri
et filio et spiritui sancto. Xp̄c deus noster.
Te deum laudamus: te
dominum confitemur.
Te eternum patrem: omnis
terra veneratur.

Tibi omnes angeli: tibi celi
et universe potestates.
Tibi cherubim et seraphin: in
cessabili voce proclamant.
Sanctus Sanctus Scs.
Dominus deus sabaoth.
Pleni sunt celi et terra maiesta
tis glorie tue.
Te gloriosus: aplōr chorus
Te prophetarum: laudabilis
numerus.
Te martirum candidatus: lau
dat exercitus.
Te per orbem terrarum: sancta

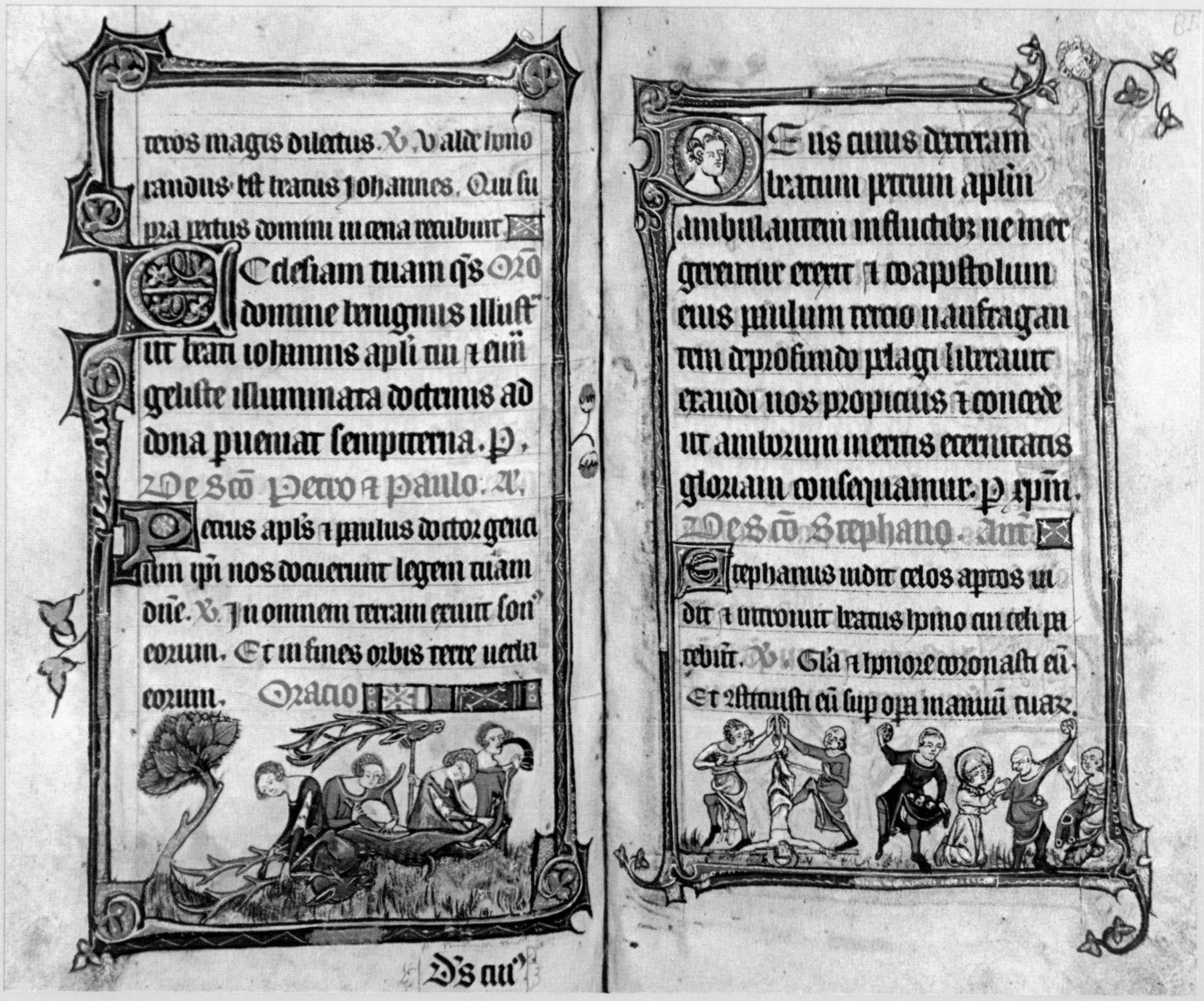

teros magis dilectus. V. Valde hono-
randus est beatus Johannes. Qui su-
pra pectus domini in cena recubuit.
Ecclesiam tuam qs Oro
domine benignus illustra
ut beati iohannis apli tui et euangeliste illuminata doctrinis ad
dona perueniat sempiterna. P.
De sco Petro et paulo. A.
Petrus apls et paulus doctor genci-
um ipsi nos docuerunt legem tuam
dne. V. In omnem terram exiuit son'
eorum. Et in fines orbis terre uerba
eorum. Oracio

Ds cui'

Deus cuius dextera
beatum petrum aplm
ambulantem in fluctibus ne mer-
geretur erexit et coapostolum
eius paulum tercio naufragan-
tem de profundo pelagi liberauit
exaudi nos propicius et concede
ut amborum meritis eternitatis
gloriam consequamur. P. xpm.
De sco Stephano. Ant.
Stephanus uidit celos apertos uidit et introiuit beatus homo cui celi pa-
tebant. V. Gla et honore coronasti eu.
Et constituisti eu sup opa manuu tuar.

nomen tuum domine uiuifica-
bis me in equitate tua.
Educes de tribulacione animam meam: et in mia tua dis-
perdes inimicos meos.
Et perdes omnes qui tribulat
animam meam: quoniam e-
go seruus tuus sum.
Gloria patri. Antiphona.
Ne reminiscaris domine delicta
nostra uel parentum nostrorum ne-
que uindictam sumas de peccatis nostris.

Ci uont les ames vers paradys

Hic incipiunt quindeci psalmi

Ad dominum cum tribularer cla-
maui: et exaudiuit me. psalm.
Leuaui oculos meos i. ps.
Letatus sum in his que. ps.

ames ames ames dolenz ames ames

The Taymouth Hours

Use of Sarum. England, *c.* 1325–40. 16.3 × 11.5 cm ($6\frac{3}{8} \times 4\frac{1}{2}$in), 195ff. Calendar illustrations, 397 marginal and other miniatures.
British Library, London, Yates Thompson ms. 13

46 **End of Calendar; lady at Mass; St Jerome in border** f.6v–7
Rabbit hunt in border ff.68v–69

47 **End of hunt; SS. Peter and Stephen** f.84–85
Owner before throne of Christ; Heaven and Hell ff.138v–139

THE FIRST OWNER of the Taymouth Hours was a fourteenth-century royal lady (very probably Joan, daughter of Edward II of England and consort of David II of Scotland) who is seen at an *oreison avaunt la messe* ('prayer before Mass') which follows the Calendar, kneeling before an altar where a priest is officiating. She wears a crown and is dressed in a pink robe lined with vair, the heraldic fur with a distinctive shield shape. At the bottom of the page the author of the prayer, St Jerome, is writing its opening words, *Douz Sire al comencement de ceste messe* ('Sweet Lord, at the beginning of this Mass'). The prayer, like several others in this prayerbook, is in French, a more appropriate language than English for a fourteenth-century princess – particularly one who, like Joan, had a French mother. The last page of the Calendar shows the month of December, here occupying one page only and embellished both with the occupation of the month (killing a pig) and the zodiacal sign of Capricorn.

The prayerbook is remarkable for lively drawings of religious and secular subjects which occur at the bottom of almost every page. Lauds in the Hours of the Virgin is accompanied by thirty hunting scenes in which all the participants are ladies. They are shown hunting rabbits, ducks, boars and stags in such an engaging manner that even the most dedicated opponent of blood sports must here temporarily suspend disapproval. First comes the rabbit hunt, in which a lady is seen shooting a bolt-headed arrow at a rabbit which sits remarkably composed outside its circular burrow. On the facing page the lady sends her dog after it, while two of her companions watch from a castle on the left. One must turn the pages of the manuscript to follow the ladies as they pursue their varied quarry.

On the third opening illustrated (p. 47 *above*), the ladies have reached the final stage in the hunt of the royal stag. The hunting rituals are here meticulously depicted, the *curée* or removal of the beast's entrails, the *présent* in which its head is set on a pole, and the *mort* announcing the kill, which a huntress sounds on her horn. On the facing page we see the Crucifixion, head downwards, of St Peter, and the stoning of St Stephen; their Suffrages (*Memorie*), with those of other saints, are here, unusually, inserted in the text of Lauds.

The last opening reproduced from the Taymouth Hours comes at the beginning of the Fifteen Gradual Psalms (Psalms 120–34). The royal owner again appears, kneeling like a child before an enthroned Christ to whom she is presented by the Virgin; the difference in scale may be intended to distinguish the divine personages. The words in the banderole linking the figures appear to have been erased, or perhaps were never inserted. While the lady kneels before Christ, a group of naked souls at the bottom of the page is led away to Hell by devils at the direction of a stern angel with an upraised sword. Beneath the damned is the despairing inscription *alas alas tristes dolenz alas alas* ('Alas alas sad sufferers alas alas'). On the following pages their torments are shown in a lively sequence which must have evoked shivers of alarm in the owner of the book.

Facing the damned is the happier spectacle of saved souls, all dressed in identical cloaks and hoods, being received at the Gate of Paradise by St Peter. Two angels sound a fanfare from the battlements; other angels line the castellated walls of the Heavenly City to watch the new arrivals, who have miraculously been provided with clothes after the Resurrection of the Dead so that they may not arrive naked in Heaven. At the bottom of the page appears the inscription *Cy vount les almes vers paradys* ('Here souls approach Paradise').

THE TAYMOUTH HOURS owes its name not to the first owner but to the accident that in the late eighteenth century it belonged to the Earl of Breadalbane, of Taymouth Castle, Perthshire. Inside the cover his bookplate may be seen facing that of the next owner but one, Henry Yates Thompson, who acquired the manuscript at the Ashburnham sale in 1897. The earlier history of the manuscript is unknown, but it appears to have been in Scotland long before it entered the library at Taymouth Castle. Several pages contain notes in Scottish dialect dating from the sixteenth century, when the book was already two hundred or more years old. Its preservation in Scotland, where Presbyterian zeal systematically destroyed survivals of 'Popery', is a miracle. The fact that the Calendar entry for St Thomas à Becket of Canterbury is undefaced implies that the book was not in England at the time of the Reformation. One can only suppose that it was for many years hidden or forgotten.[1]

The first owner was a royal lady who appears several times in the manuscript. Wearing a crown, she is first seen on f.7 (p. 46). At Matins of the Holy Spirit she appears again, this time in the company of a man robed in blue but without a crown, her husband or, less probably, her chaplain. On f.118v, somewhat obscurely tucked away at the end of Compline, both figures are shown crowned and kneeling; her companion here must be her husband. Finally, on f.139, at the beginning of the Fifteen Gradual Psalms, she is seen for the last time (p. 47), a tiny figure kneeling before Christ.

The identity of this lady has never been established. A strong candidate is Joan of the Tower, fifth and youngest child of Edward II of England. She was born in the Tower of London in 1321 and was married as a child in 1328 to David II of Scotland, the son of Robert Bruce, and her junior by three years. This child-marriage developed into an eventful partnership in later years. Joan shared her husband's exile in France in 1334–41, after Edward Balliol seized the Scottish throne. When David returned home and was captured by the English at the Battle of Neville's Cross in 1346, Joan visited him during his imprisonment in her birthplace, the Tower of London. On his release in 1357 he returned to Scotland with a mistress, Catherine Mortimer, whom he had met in London. Joan replied to this betrayal by requesting a safe conduct from her brother Edward III to return to England, where she settled for the last years of her life at Hertford Castle, dying there in 1362 at the age of forty-one. David II died without children in 1371 and was succeeded by his nephew Robert Stuart, son of his sister Marjorie, and the first Scottish royal Stuart.

The miniatures are by an accomplished artist, possibly more than one, with the Annunciation at Matins of a finer quality than the others, as is often the case in Books of Hours. A brilliant effect is achieved by the punched gold or chequered grounds which set off the figures. According to Dr Otto Pächt, these are the only miniatures in an English manuscript of this date which could have been modelled on the Pucelle style, then current in France, which we have seen in the Hours of Jeanne d'Evreux (p. 42).[2]

It is not the miniatures, charming as they are, which give the Taymouth Book of Hours its special character, but the coloured drawings in the margins. Similar drawings are found in other English fourteenth-century illuminated manuscripts, of which the closest in style to the Taymouth Hours are the Smithfield Decretals (London, British Library, ms. Royal 10. E. IV) and the Carew-Poyntz Hours in the Fitzwilliam Museum at Cambridge (ms. 48). In all three books the marginal illustrations mingle religious and secular themes in a hectic, inconsequential manner which anticipates the modern strip-cartoon. In the Taymouth Hours there are, besides the curious *jeu de dames* or ladies' sport, not only drolleries, birds of all kinds, combats between monsters and scenes from daily life, but also subjects taken from the Bible, the lives of the saints, the bestiary, folklore and the *fabliaux* or romances which recorded the deeds of popular heroes such as Bevis of Hampton, Sir Eneas and Guy of Warwick.

Most of the margins show religious subjects. In addition to those already mentioned are Adam and Eve and other Bible stories, Prophets and Apostles, the Genealogy of Christ, the Pains of Hell, the Miracles of the Virgin and four episodes from the life of St Francis. The latter have considerable iconographical interest; for, in addition to the Call to Preaching, the Sermon to the Birds and the Stigmatization, a much rarer subject is also depicted: St Francis cutting out his habit with a pair of scissors beside him (f.180v).[3]

The decorative element, in contrast, receives perfunctory treatment. The bar borders surrounding text and miniatures are like a frame from which sprout only the most tentative leaf-tendrils. These were later to branch into the luxuriant ivy-leaf borders which characterize fifteenth-century Books of Hours.

It is sad that neither Joan's English nor her Scottish coat of arms appears anywhere in the book to establish her ownership. What heraldry there is relates to the Neville family of Castle Raby, Co. Durham, with whom Joan had close personal links: a Neville lady was buried at her side in the Church of Grey Friars, London. At some period in the later fourteenth century, Dr James cautiously suggests, the Neville family acquired the Taymouth Hours, possibly by gift or bequest from Queen Joan, and subsequently added their heraldry unobtrusively on a few pages (*see* note 1, p. 177).

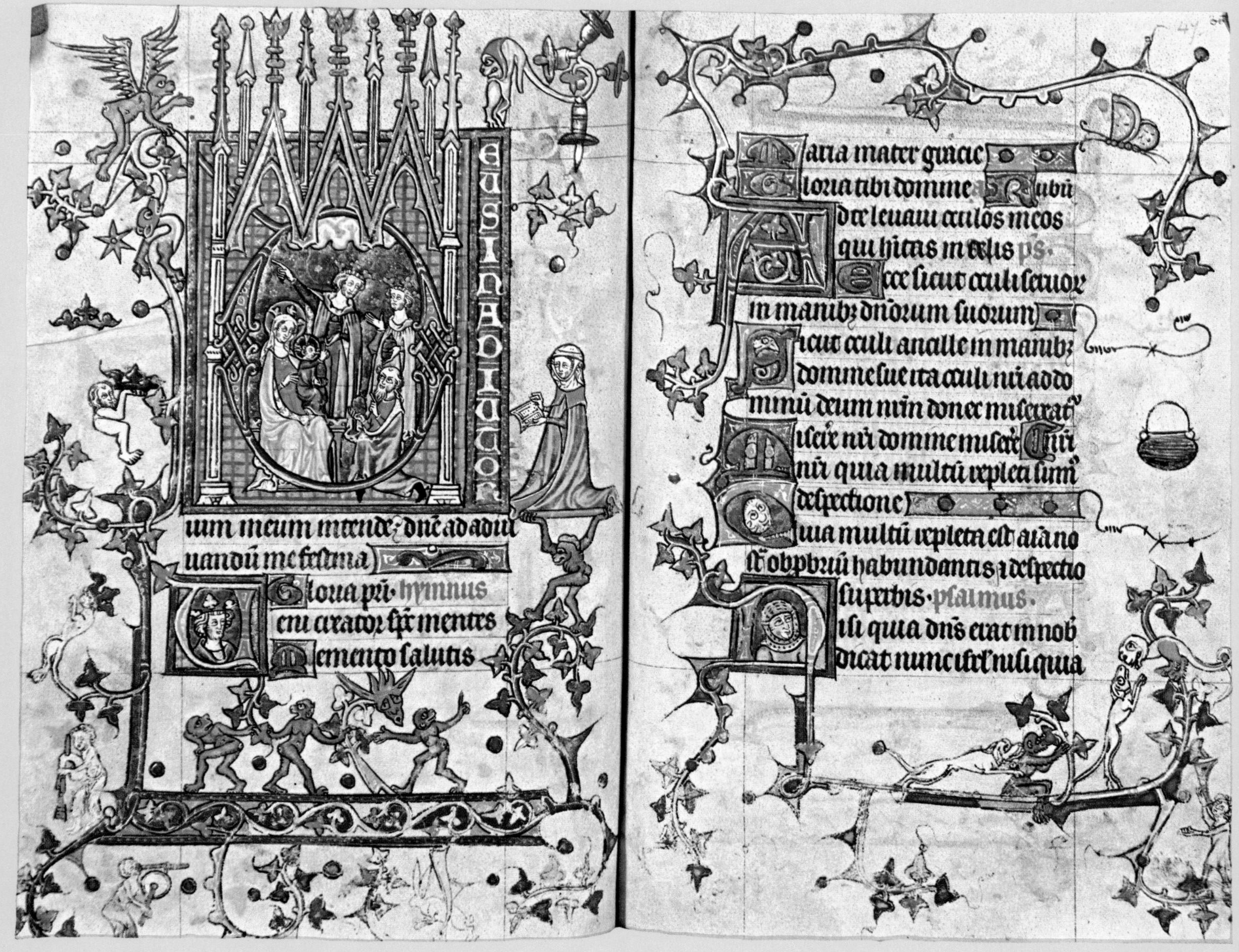

uod parasti ante faciem om
nium populorum.
umen ad revelationem gē
tium et gloriam plebis tu
e israhel.
loria patri ant.
ortus conclusus est dei genitrix ort
conclusus fons signatus surge
propera amica mea
omine exaudi Et clamor. Orem
ratiam tuam qs dne oro
mentibz nostris infunde
ut qui angelo nūtiante
xpi filii tui incarnationē cogno
uimus per passionē eius et crucē
ad resurrectionis gliā pducamur. p.d.
enedicamus dno. deo grās. vii ps.
OMINE NE IN FURO
re tuo arguas me neq; in ira tua
orripias me
iserere mei domine quoni
am infirmus sum sana me

The Saint-Omer Hours

Use of Arras. Northern France, *c.* 1350.
15.3 × 10.5 cm (6 × 4⅛ in), 155ff. Historiated initials on stippled gold and diapered grounds, bar and ivy-leaf borders with marginal drolleries and other figures.
British Library, London, Add. ms. 36684

50 **Adoration of the Magi** ff.46v–47
51 **Harrowing of Hell** ff.59v–60

THE SAINT-OMER HOURS is an enchanting book, which Chaucer might have had in mind when he wrote in *The Hous of Fame* (iii, 99–100) of

> Babewynnes and pynacles,
> Imageries and tabernacles.[1]

The pinnacles are immediately apparent, though the baboons need a moment's search. They are soon found supporting the platforms on which the lady owner of the Book of Hours kneels in prayer. Although the expression 'babewynnes' is used of other drollery figures, it refers especially to the apes and monkeys which invaded the borders of illuminated manuscripts in the fourteenth century. In the Saint-Omer Hours they make a relatively restrained appearance, useful as caryatids or supporters, decorative when they frolic in the margins.

The manuscript was written and illuminated for a lady whose name was probably Marguerite. She may have been Marguerite de Beaujeu, wife of Charles de Montmorency, *Grand Panetier* (Pantler or Butler) of France. Whoever she was, the lady appears frequently in the margins of pages where the principal divisions of text are indicated by miniatures. At Sext in the Hours of the Virgin she kneels on a platform supported by an ape and contemplates the Adoration of the Magi (p. 50). At the Penitential Psalms she appears again, this time at the Harrowing of Hell, a spectacle which seems to dismay her, for she has dropped or laid her prayerbook on the ground; her dog perhaps gives her some moral support.

The Harrowing of Hell, a dramatic and popular subject, is often found accompanying the Last Judgment in Books of Hours. The legend of Christ's descent into Limbo after the Crucifixion to rescue the souls of the Just came from the Apocryphal Gospel of Nicodemus, not from the Canonical Gospels. The *gueule d'enfer* or Hell-Mouth was usually depicted as the jaws of the monster Leviathan. In this form it appears in sculpture, alabaster panels and paintings, and as primitive stage scenery in Mystery Plays. In the page from the Saint-Omer Hours (p. 51) the frame of the *D* starts from the hind legs of a winged creature in the top left-hand corner, whose head and front legs subsequently get lost in interlacings. (The Adoration of the Magi initial depends in similar manner from a winged ape.)

THE SAINT-OMER HOURS in the British Library, an incomplete manuscript, is so called from having been written in the region of Saint-Omer in northern France. St Audomarus, Audemer or Omer, a Benedictine monk who evangelized the district in the seventh century and became Bishop of Thérouanne, appears in the Calendar at 17 and 21 October. These entries for the dedication of his church and the finding (*inventio*) of his relics are in blue. The book dates from the middle years of the fourteenth century, and is thus a near-contemporary of the Taymouth Hours. Though reminiscent of the latter, the Saint-Omer Hours has a more elaborate decorative ensemble characterized by emphatic bar borders and ivy-leaf sprays sprouting from initials. Several of the large initial-miniatures have architectural canopies which give the page a typical Gothic spikiness. But it is the cast of grotesque creatures, drolleries, rabbits, monkeys and other animals, including fish, disporting themselves in the margins with great liveliness of gesture, which give animation to this book. These margins convey a mood of bantering good humour and high spirits.

The cheerful tone of these early Books of Hours made in France and England has often been remarked on. The miniatures have a brisk quality, whatever their subject matter. Were the artists celebrating their escape from close clerical supervision, or trying to please and divert their patrons?

In the Calendar illustrations the occupations of the months and the zodiacal signs are shown in diminutive houses with crocketed spires. The same arrangement is found in another Saint-Omer book, a Psalter of the late thirteenth or early fourteenth century in the Pierpont Morgan Library (M. 79). In the same library is the second portion of the Saint-Omer Hours, consisting of 136 leaves (M. 754).[2] The British Library manuscript was once owned by John Ruskin, and carries his bookplate inside the upper cover.

THE DUKE OF BERRY

Under the feudal system it was customary for lands and territorial dignities – duchies or counties – to be granted by a king to his sons, in order to provide them with an income and to secure their loyalty to the Crown. These grants were known as *apanages*, and reverted to the Crown in default of male heirs. The obvious dangers, the loss of revenue and the virtual independence of these royal dukes and counts, were never adequately foreseen.

The Duke of Berry (1340–1416) was one of four brothers, the sons of John II, the Good, King of France (reigned 1350–64), and all of them patronized the arts with a gusto and extravagance never before or since encountered in a single generation of one family. For the three younger brothers this was made possible by the stupendous financial endowments which came to them from their *apanages*. The eldest brother was Charles V, the Wise, who reigned from 1364 to 1380. He was the wisest and most learned of the brothers, and his early death was a disaster for France. Next came Louis, Duke of Anjou, then John, Duke of Berry, and finally Philip the Bold, Duke of Burgundy. Berry was the most pacifically minded of the younger brothers, the most 'French' in outlook. More interested in his art collections than in politics, he tried to hold the balance between the Orleans-Armagnac and Burgundian rival factions, at first with some success.[1] He outlived all his brothers, dying on 15 June 1416 at the age of seventy-five after surviving one wife, three sons and several nephews. He might have been surprised to know that his reputation as a medieval Maecenas, an early connoisseur and aesthete in an age before such terms were known, is largely due to the *Très Riches* and other Books of Hours. He clearly valued his books but could not have regarded them as his most precious possessions. However, they are the only objects from his collections to survive in any number. About one third of an estimated 300 manuscripts still exists, ninety-three of them illuminated. Of his seventeen castles in Berry, Poitiers and the Auvergne only a few ruins remain at Bourges, Melun, Poitiers and Riom. His jewels and other *joyaux* have almost all vanished, the precious objects in gold and silver melted down by his heirs to help pay for the wars against the English. An enamelled gold cup and a Reliquary of the Holy Thorn may be seen in the British Museum, a few cameos and medals elsewhere. Apart from these, little remains.

The Berry Books of Hours have a special *éclat* as the most famous specimens of the genre. Their sonorous titles come from inventories of the Duke's treasures made during his lifetime or shortly after his death, and have no liturgical significance. Their mere recitation, despite their confusing similarity of title, invokes a sense of artistic opulence and resplendent piety. Identifying them in the inventories is, however, a difficult matter since sometimes only the vanished covers are described in detail and the names of artists often omitted. During his lifetime the Duke may have owned as many as eighteen Books of Hours. Some he inherited, but most were made by the group of *ouvriers* whom he personally employed. The six extant examples are discussed on pp. 54–69.

The manuscripts crackle with problems of chronology, changes in style, additions and interrupted campaigns of embellishment. These are specialist matters, the details of which may be pursued in the authorities mentioned in the Notes.[2] The artistic aspects of the Berry Books of Hours have been minutely studied, but it is not always appreciated how varied also are the texts of the surviving examples. So far from being stereotyped or restricted to the basic components, as might be expected of a bibliophile who collected examples as *joyaux* rather than as prayerbooks, the number of secondary and accessory texts included in the Duke's Books of Hours is impressive. Professional advice from his chaplains and from theologians must have been required, one cannot help thinking, in determining the texts to be included. The Duke was in no way peculiar in adopting special devotions but their inclusion in his Books of Hours presents him under a somewhat different guise from that of the acquisitive bibliophile, the role in which he is most often portrayed.

eus in adiutorium meum in
tende.
Domine ad adiuuandum
me festina.

letur. Per dominum. Ad terciam

Deus in adiutorium meum intende. Domine ad adiuuandum me festina. Gloria patri et filio et spiritui sancto. Sicut erat in principio et nunc et semper

The Très Belles Heures de Notre Dame of John, Duke of Berry

Use of Paris. France, begun *c.* 1382. 27.9 × 19.9 cm (11 × 7⅞in), 240 pp. 25 miniatures, historiated initials, *bas de page* pictures, borders.
Bibliothèque Nationale, Paris, ms. nouv. acq. lat. 3093

54 **Nativity; Angel and Shepherds** p. 42
For a note on the Duke of Berry see page 53

THIS WAS ONE OF THE FIRST Books of Hours to be begun to the order of the Duke. It was from the outset a work of collaboration, in which a number of artists took part over a considerable period. Like all but one of the Duke's prayerbooks, it remained unfinished at his death.

The first section dates from the early 1380s. It was planned by the Parement Master (so called after his major work, an altar frontal, the *Parement de Narbonne*, in the Louvre), who shared the embellishment between himself and his assistants. The ivy-leaf borders with their busts of angels holding scrolls, initials and *bas-de-page* pictures were done first, the miniatures completed later. Most of those in the Hours of the Virgin were painted or at least designed by the Parement Master himself. In the Nativity scene at Prime (illustrated), Mary, solicitously watched by Joseph, lies on a red mattress with her new-born son beside her. This traditional iconography, dating back to Byzantine sources, was soon to be replaced by the Virgin kneeling in adoration, a change of posture which owed much to the visions of St Bridget and the writings of St Bernard. Here the two traditions are seen at a transitional moment. Mary worships her son but still lies on a mattress. An Angel in the initial *D* announces the glad tidings of the Nativity to a group of shepherds down in the *bas-de-page*. The owl in the lower margin, traditionally a bird of ill omen, is an odd choice for this page. The gold border moulded like a picture frame which surrounds the miniature of the Holy Family is a reminder that the Parement Master was a panel painter as well as a miniaturist.

THE TRÈS BELLES HEURES DE NOTRE DAME is the most complicated of the Berry Books of Hours, both historically and artistically. Its title comes from the 1413 inventory. In that year the Duke presented the uncompleted manuscript to Robinet d'Estampes, his keeper of jewels. Even at this date the manuscript had a long history, having been worked on by a succession of artists. The Parement Master, André Beauneveu and the Limbourg brothers appear to have directed successive campaigns but failed to finish the decoration of the book.

Robinet d'Estampes divided the manuscript into two parts, keeping for himself the section which had already been supplied with illuminations. This is the manuscript now in the Bibliothèque Nationale, sometimes known as the 'Paris' or (after a former owner) 'Rothschild' fragment. The second, largely undecorated, part somehow passed at an early stage into the possession of a Wittelsbach prince, William IV of Hainault and Holland, cousin of the German-born Queen Isabeau, wife of Charles VI.

The undecorated pages were now embellished with miniatures, initials and *bas-de-page* pictures in a style so remarkable and different from the 'Paris' section that they have been attributed to the school if not to the hand of Jan van Eyck. A new Calendar was added, filled with Hainault saints.

This second section is next found in the possession of the Dukes of Savoy, descendants of John of Berry's daughter Bonne who married Amadeus VII. Before the early eighteenth century it was itself divided into two parts. One was given in 1720 by Victor Amadeus II of Savoy to the library of the new University he had founded in Turin. There the *Heures de Turin*, as they were subsequently called, remained until destroyed by fire in 1905. The second part of the manuscript, which comprised a series of special Masses (an unusual feature in a Book of Hours), was acquired in the early nineteenth century by the Trivulzio family of Milan; hence the later name of *Heures de Milan* by which it is known. Shortly before World War II it was purchased from the Trivulzio family by the Museo Civico of Turin.[1]

The Petites Heures of John, Duke of Berry

Use of Paris. France, Paris, *c.* 1388. 21.5 × 14.5 cm ($8\frac{1}{2} \times 5\frac{5}{8}$ in), 292ff. Calendar illustrations, over 100 miniatures, historiated initials, *bas-de-page* pictures, borders.
Bibliothèque Nationale, Paris, ms. lat. 18014

55 **St John the Baptist in the Wilderness** f.208

The Petites Heures is a small manuscript by comparison with the Duke of Berry's other prayerbooks; its title appears to be modern and not to come from the 1402 inventory, where the book is described as *unes très belles Heures, contenant pluseurs heures et commémoracions de Dieu et de ses sains* ('a very fine Hours containing several Hours and commemorations of God and of his Saints'). Among the latter are the Hours of St John the Baptist, a special Office in honour of the Duke's patron saint. This section is finely illuminated by the so-called Passion Master. At Tierce the youthful Baptist sits in his desert cave like a Christianized Orpheus or a Gothic Tamino from Mozart's opera, summoning beasts and birds around him, not by the music of his lyre or magic flute but by his sacred message. Rabbits peep nervously from their burrows. Other animals include apes, traditionally evil creatures, which here sit quietly watching. A snail extends its slimy length along the rock above the Baptist's shoulder. The birds, a hoopoe, woodpecker or jay, and finches, perch expectantly on tree and rock. In the curling ivy-leaf sprays in the ample margins are more birds which might at any moment flit off to join their companions around St John inside the miniature.

The illuminated initial *D* of the text encloses an heraldic semé of gold fleurs-de-lys on a blue field within a red engrailed border (*une bordure engreslée de gueules*). Through his coat of arms Berry associates himself directly with the picture of the Baptist, his patron saint. The bear in the foreground of the rocks may be a further personal allusion. A bear and a wounded swan were among the Duke's emblems and appear constantly in his Book of Hours.[1]

The manuscript was completed about 1388, according to some scholars; others date it to 1402, when it was inventoried. It contains a substantial complement of essential texts of Books of Hours. To this are added, as noted in the inventory, several extra Offices in which there seems to be a special emphasis on the Passion of Jesus Christ. Besides special prayers, there are the Hours of the Passion, a long exposition in French, *selonc les docteurs* ('according to the Doctors'), the lamentations of the Virgin at the foot of the Cross, called by the Abbé Leroquais the Hours of the Compassion of the Virgin, and a narration of the event described as the Virgin's own account, supported by prayers of St Bernard and followed by the Six Degrees of Charity by which one comes to perfect love of God. It is pertinent here to remember that in the Middle Ages people acutely identified themselves with the Passion in a manner scarcely possible today. The richness of contents in the *Petites Heures* transforms this Book of Hours into a devotional library. Also included are special prayers suitable for princely families in which the importance of early religious training, and in particular the recitation of the Hours, is stressed. The many portraits of the Duke in prayer before God, the Virgin and the Crucifixion, or receiving the sacrament at Mass, may be intended to exemplify the practice of piety.

Artistically, the *Petites Heures* was a joint enterprise in which five miniaturists took part. Among them were two of the Duke's *ouvriers*, Jacquemart de Hesdin and his *alter ego*, the 'Pseudo-Jacquemart', so-called because his scarcely less accomplished miniatures are often found together with Jacquemart's in the same manuscripts. The most individual of the several artists employed was the Passion Master, whose style depended from the Pucelle Master; the John the Baptist miniature is a beautiful example of his work.

There are indications that the *Petites Heures* may have been one of the Duke's favourite, much used Books of Hours, which he took with him on his frequent journeys. The 1413 inventory refers to a new binding in purple damask (*drap de damas violet*), and at the end of the book prayers for travellers were added together with a miniature by the Limbourg brothers (*see* pp. 62–67) of the Duke himself setting out on foot, accompanied by his chamberlain and a white greyhound, from a turreted gateway (f.228v).

Deus in adiuto
rium meum in
tende.
Domine ad adiuvandū
me festina.
Gloria patri et filio et spi
ritui sancto.
Sicut erat in principio et
nunc et semper et in secula se
culorum amen allā.
Veni creator spū. ant.
Veni sancte spū. psalmus
Deus in adiutoriū
meum intende: do
mine ad adiuvandum me
festina.
Confundantur et revere
antur: qui querunt animam
meam.
Avertantur retrorsum et
erubescant: qui volunt michi
mala.
Avertantur statim erube
scentes qui dicunt michi euge
euge.
Exultent et letentur in te
omnes qui querunt te et dicant
semper magnificetur dominus
qui diligunt salutare tuum.
Ego vero egenus et pauper
sum: deus adiuva me.
Adiutor meus et liberator
meus es tu: domine ne moreris.
Gloria patri. ant.
Veni sancte spiritus reple tuor
corda fidelium et tui amoris in eis ignē
accende qui per diversitatem linguarum
cunctarum gentes in unitate fidei cō

The Brussels Hours of John, Duke of Berry

Use of Paris. France, Paris, *c.* 1402–09.
27.5 × 18.5 cm ($10\frac{3}{4} \times 7\frac{1}{4}$ in), 276 pp. 18 full-page miniatures, 17 historiated initials, borders.
Bibliothèque Royale, Brussels, ms. 11060–61

58 **The Duke of Berry with SS. Andrew and John the Baptist before the Virgin** p. 14

The Duke of Berry's second *Très Belles Heures* is now conveniently known as the 'Brussels Hours' from the present location of the manuscript.[1] It is remarkable for containing two large miniatures, the first in diptych form, of the Duke being presented by his patron saints to the Virgin Mary. In the second, here reproduced, we see for the first time in this anthology a portrait of this compulsive collector of Books of Hours. The meeting of the celestial and earthly realms is skilfully suggested in the placing of the realistically posed group of the Duke and his companions SS. Andrew and John the Baptist against massed haloed heads in the background, and in the direct looks and gestures exchanged between the human and divine participants in the encounter; the Duke is the only figure without a halo. His cloak and John the Baptist's foot obtrude on to the platform of Mary's throne. The angels in attendance about her, and the little musical trio in the foreground, make enchanting groups.

The miniature is framed like a picture and placed inside a border where the Duke's coat of arms, bear and swan badges and mysterious EV cypher (perhaps for *En Vous*, 'In You') appear in regularly disposed quatrefoil medallions. This border serves as a second frame or mount for the miniature; in the absence of text the sprays have no initials from which to sprout and are independent of the rectangular frame. The hair-thin, pen-drawn tendrils terminate in leaves and flowers, among which we recognize the columbine or aquilegia, a flower whose shape resembles hanging doves (*columbae*), symbolizing in medieval art the gifts of the Holy Spirit ('and the Holy Spirit descended in a bodily shape like a dove upon him': Luke 3:22). The naturalistic birds and solitary butterfly should be noted; we shall meet them again in the *Grandes Heures* (p. 59).

The Brussels Hours is a challenging manuscript about which there is much dispute concerning its date and the number of artists involved in its embellishment. These difficulties arise largely from disagreement among scholars whether a Book of Hours described in the 1402 inventory of the Duke of Berry as *unes très belles heures, richement enluminées et ystoriées de la main Jacquemart de Odin* ('a very fine Hours, richly illuminated and historiated by the hand of Jacquemart de Hesdin') can be conclusively identified with the manuscript now in Brussels.

Lacking a Calendar, the Brussels Hours is generally considered to be an unfinished product of the Duke of Berry's personal studio of *ouvriers*. French, Flemish and Italian elements appear in the decoration. A north Italian artist painted the seventeen historiated initials; and in the eighteen large miniatures Italian influence may also be discerned, though there are indications of changes in the original designs.

The miniatures fill the pages on which they appear to the exclusion of all text, an innovation in French Books of Hours. They are painted with a new awareness of nature (e.g. in the Flight into Egypt miniature, set in a wintry landscape) and have been hailed as examples of the Avant-Renaissance. They can, indeed, be studied as individual panel paintings, an exercise which diminishes their significance in a devotional sequence. Professor Calkins considers the manuscript to be one 'in which the text, miniatures, historiated initials, and secondary decoration have an intrinsic relation to the volume as an *objet d'art*. By examining the manuscript as an artistic ensemble, we may find clues which can provide for a better understanding of the circumstances surrounding the execution of the book and for a more satisfactory appreciation of the style of the miniatures.'

The Brussels Hours was owned after the death of the Duke of Berry by Margaret of Bavaria, wife of his nephew John the Fearless, Duke of Burgundy; it appears in an inventory of her possessions made in 1424. The book may well be the manuscript which the Duke of Berry is known to have given his brother Philip the Bold of Burgundy in 1402 and which was subsequently acquired by Philip's daughter-in-law Margaret. But there is a long and tantalizing gap in its later history; the *Très Belles Heures* did not pass into the Belgian royal library until 1840.

The Grandes Heures of John, Duke of Berry

Use of Paris. France, Paris, 1409. 40 × 30 cm (15$\frac{3}{4}$ × 11$\frac{3}{4}$ in), 126ff. Calendar illustrations, 28 text miniatures, initials, borders.
Bibliothèque Nationale, Paris, ms. lat. 919

59 **The Duke of Berry received by St Peter** f.96

The status-symbol aspect of Books of Hours could not be developed further than in the *Grandes Heures* of the Duke of Berry.[1] It is, in the first place, the biggest example ever made; each leaf is nearly as big as two pages of this book. Obtaining animal skins large enough to provide vellum for 126 folios of this size must have been a major preliminary task for somebody. The text page reproduced comes from the Hour of Sext in the Office of the Holy Spirit. With matchless self-confidence the Duke presents himself at the Gate of Heaven, here represented by an attenuated Gothic chapel, with no welcoming angels as in the Taymouth Hours. On the threshold stands a stern-faced St Peter with a far from friendly expression who grasps the Duke firmly by the left hand almost as if taking him into custody rather than into Paradise. In his right hand St Peter holds up the key to Paradise in a somewhat minatory manner. To this gesture the Duke responds by indicating a jewel which hangs from a clasp around his neck. This is a large blue stone, probably a sapphire, surrounded, according to Professor Meiss, by six large pearls. In medieval symbolism pearls were associated with Christ, sapphires with the blue vault of Heaven; in presenting one of his choicest jewels like a holy relic the Duke is perhaps establishing his credentials for entry into Paradise.[2]

He is attended by an elderly, crusty-faced retinue. In the initial *D* below this group, a kneeling and younger Duke of Berry (his hair has not yet turned grey) raises his hands in fervent prayer. He is petitioning for future acceptance into Paradise, a prospect which the gestures of the supporting angel seem to encourage. In the borders of this magnificent, exhibitionistic page the arms, mottoes and emblems of the Duke appear in quatrefoil medallions. It would be interesting to know who painted this extraordinary miniature: the attribution to the Bedford Master, though long established, is not accepted by all specialists.

Finally, the birds and butterflies should be noted. They might have come straight out of manuscripts of the Pucelle School dating from nearly two centuries earlier. The birds perch on ivy-leaf sprays but are not an integral part of the border. They could have been painted separately by somebody specializing in this work and using a pattern book or even a Pucelle manuscript for his model. The varied species are depicted with considerable accuracy and most can be identified. Beginning at the top left corner they appear to be: 1) wren; 2) hair-streak butterfly(?) with closed wings; 3) wheatear or flycatcher; 4) pheasant; 5) clouded yellow butterfly; 6) pigeon; 7) goldfinch; 8) tortoiseshell butterfly; 9) flycatcher; 10) golden oriole(?); 11) red underwing moth(?); 12) great tit.

The Grandes Heures seems from the start to have been planned as a very special volume in which the Duke announced his patronage by assembling examples of the best illuminators of the time. In its original condition the manuscript contained not only miniatures at the principal divisions but also a set of full-page pictures as large as panel paintings and without any text. These were almost certainly the *grans histoires de la main Jacquemart de Hodin*, mentioned in the inventories. It is sad to record that all were later removed. Only one has been identified in modern times out of an estimated seventeen, the picture of Christ carrying the Cross now in the Louvre. These large pictures are mentioned not only in the Duke of Berry's inventories of 1413 and 1416 but also in an inventory made for King Charles VIII in 1488. The volume was then or at some later date rebound, the large miniatures removed and replaced by the present blank leaves.

The disappearance of the large miniatures curiously makes the outsize *Grandes Heures* more approachable as a Book of Hours than it may have been when intact. The twenty-eight 'small' miniatures are closely integrated with the double-columned text and elaborate ivy-leaf borders, though they are as large as many full-page miniatures in smaller Books of Hours. Jacquemart de Hesdin, the artist probably responsible for the large miniatures, disappears from the Duke's service around 1409, though it is not known whether he died in this year. He left the stage clear for the Limbourg brothers, the last and most scintillating of the Duke's *ouvriers*.

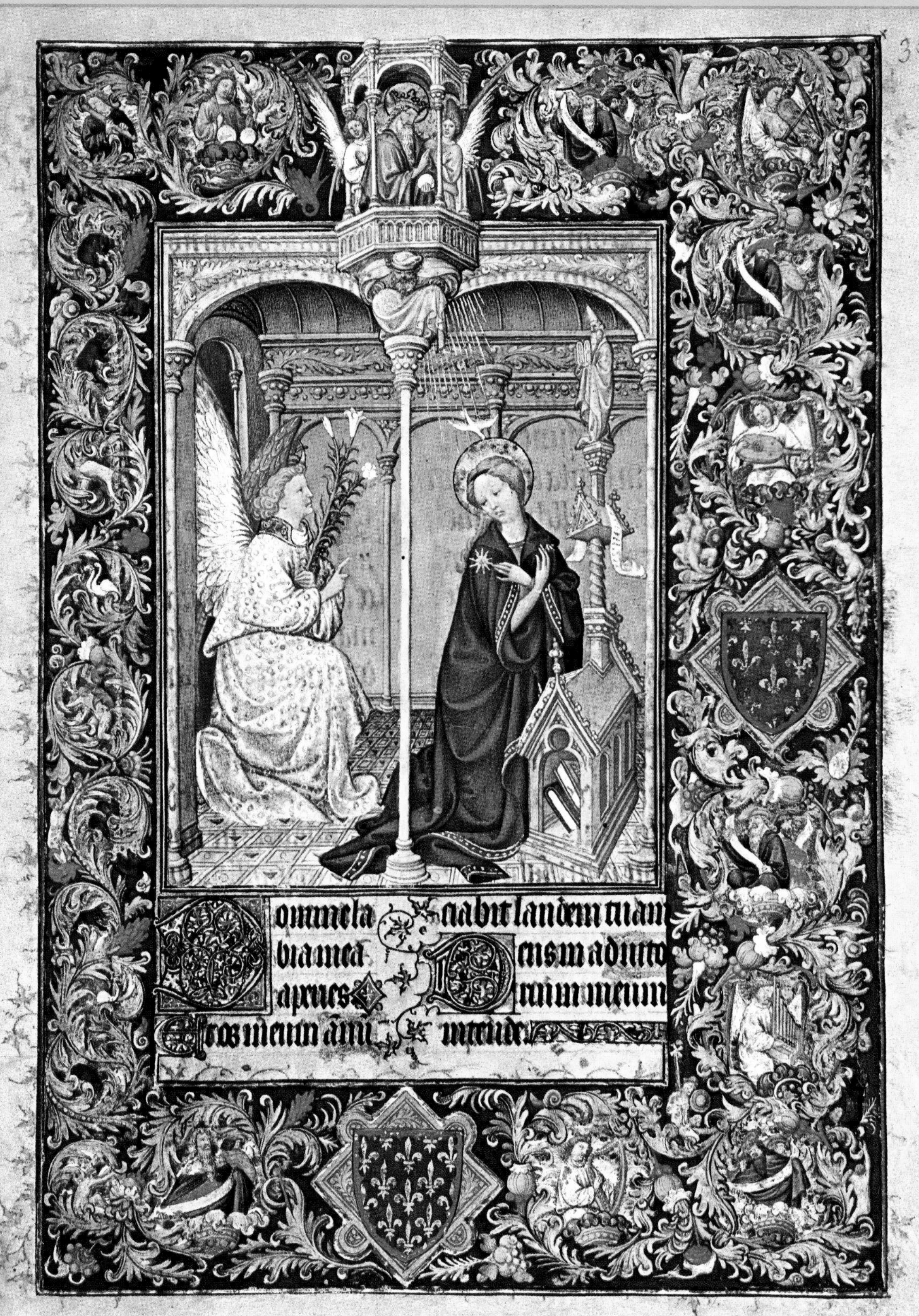
Domine la
bia mea
aperies
Et os meum anū
ciabit laudem tuam
Deus in adiuto
rium meum
intende

Domine la
bia mea a
peries.
Et os meum annũ
ciabit laudem tuam.
Deus in adiuto
rium meum
intende.

The Belles Heures of John, Duke of Berry

Use of Paris. France, Paris, 1408–10. 23.8 × 17 cm ($9\frac{3}{8} \times 6\frac{5}{8}$ in), 225ff. Calendar illustrations, 94 full-page miniatures, 54 column illustrations, initials, borders.

The Metropolitan Museum of Art, New York, The Cloisters Collection

62 **Annunciation** f.30

The Belles Heures is the only one of the Berry prayerbooks which is virtually complete and consistent in style.[1] It is one of two Books of Hours, the second being the *Très Riches Heures*, supplied to the Duke by the three Limbourg brothers who became his principal *ouvriers* during the last years of his life.

The Annunciation page at Matins in the Little Office of the Virgin is considered to be the work of Pol de Limbourg, the eldest and most accomplished of the brothers. Distinctly Italianate in style, it is also the sole page in which appears the rich border of acanthus sprays on a blue ground matching the Virgin's mantle. On an earlier page in this survey the superior quality of many Annunciation pictures in Books of Hours was mentioned: here is an example. Iconographically the miniature is fairly conventional, with the demure Virgin crossing her hands on her breast in the enclosed stillness of her chamber, into which the Archangel Gabriel enters through an open archway on the left. But there are several interesting details. The walls are painted in the pale green favoured by the Limbourgs for their interiors. The star of Bethlehem prominently displayed on the Virgin's right shoulder anticipates its appearance in the Nativity and Adoration of the Magi scenes, later in the manuscript, but may allude also to the Virgin's title of *Stella Maris* (Star of the Sea). The somewhat matter-of-fact Archangel carries a lily spray in the Italian manner; in northern Books of Hours this is more likely to be found in a vase placed on the floor. The slender column with a caryatid prophet(?) supports a balcony whence God the Father attended by angels sends the Holy Ghost in rays of light on to the Virgin's head. Her reading desk is surmounted by Moses, holding the tablets of the Law, a figure representing the Old Dispensation which was replaced by the New Dispensation symbolized in Mary and the Annunciation. In the elaborate acanthus border appear the Duke of Berry's coat of arms, angels playing musical instruments, prophets holding scrolls, and minute representations of the Duke's bear and swan emblems. The lasting impression of this beautiful page is one of a rich blue, the Virgin's colour.

THE BELLES HEURES is included in the 1413 inventory of the Duke of Berry, where it is described in considerable detail except for the basic omission of the names of the artists responsible for its decoration; they are mentioned only as being the Duke's *ouvriers*. But the miniatures are so close in style to those in the *Très Riches Heures*, specifically described in a later inventory as having been made by the three Limbourg brothers, that scholars have no hesitation in assigning the *Belles Heures* to the same source. Pol, Jean (Janequin) and Herman de Limbourg came from Guelders to complete their training in Paris and succeeded Jacquemart de Hesdin (who is thought to have died about 1409) as the Duke's principal *ouvriers*. Their *Belles Heures* is one of the most successful grander Books of Hours, displaying a masterly integration of text, miniatures and borders.

The manuscript is remarkable for the addition of several special picture cycles which considerably augment the traditional texts and illustrations. These cycles comprise the stories of St Catherine, St Bruno (founder of the Carthusian Order), the Emperor Heraclius and the True Cross, St Jerome, SS. Anthony Abbot and Paul the Hermit, and John the Baptist, patron saint of the Duke. There is a further sequence of four separate scenes from the Grand Supplication of St Gregory at the time of the plague in Rome, a remarkable subject treated again by the Limbourg brothers in the *Très Riches Heures* (*see* pp. 66–67). The addition of these cycles makes the *Belles Heures* as much a picture- as a prayerbook. It was to become a seminal work when the manuscript was acquired after the Duke of Berry's death in 1416 by his niece Yolande, Duchess of Anjou; through her it became known to the Rohan Master.

Until 1880, when it was purchased by Baron Edmond de Rothschild, it belonged to the Ailly family; hence its older name of the *Heures d'Ailly*. In 1954 the manuscript was acquired by the Cloisters Collection from Baron Maurice de Rothschild.

The Très Riches Heures of John, Duke of Berry

France, *c.* 1411–16 and 1485–90. 29 × 21 cm ($11\frac{3}{8} \times 8\frac{1}{4}$ in) *Musée Condé, Chantilly*

63 **Christ as the Man of Sorrows** f.75r

THE 'TRÈS RICHES HEURES' was unfinished when the Duke of Berry and the three Limbourg brothers, his principal artists or *ouvriers* at the time, all died in the same year, 1416. The decoration of the book was completed about seventy years later by the miniaturist Jean Colombe of Bourges for its then owners, the Duke and Duchess of Savoy. One of the first pages decorated by Colombe was for the Hours of the Cross, a fine example of his style. Christ as the Man of Sorrows stands in his tomb with the Cross dominating the immediate background. Facing him, the new owners of the book, Charles I of Savoy and his wife Blanche of Montferrat, kneel like donors, with hands folded in prayer beneath Gothic canopies. At the bottom of the page their coats of arms are supported by two blue-winged cherubs.

The opening words of text at the Hours of the Cross (*Domine labia mea aperies*, 'O Lord open thou my lips'), appear as if written on a partly opened scroll, but the general effect of the boldly designed canopies is of an architectural frontispiece. The Cross serves as a window through which one looks on to a beautiful landscape, which is perhaps a view of Lake Geneva with the castle of Ripaille on the left. It was from this castle, situated at Thonon above Geneva, and owned by the Dukes of Savoy, that the authorization of payment to Jean Colombe for completing the *Très Riches Heures* was issued. He must have worked on it between 1485, the year of the marriage of the Duke and Duchess, and March 1490, when Charles I died. In his miniatures a cloud of gold dust seems to settle upon architectural motifs and draperies, giving a sparkle to the pages. He is said to have been an impatient, hurried man; but he gives no sign of it in this serenely contemplative picture.

See pages 68–69 for commentary on the Duke of Berry's *Très Riches Heures*.

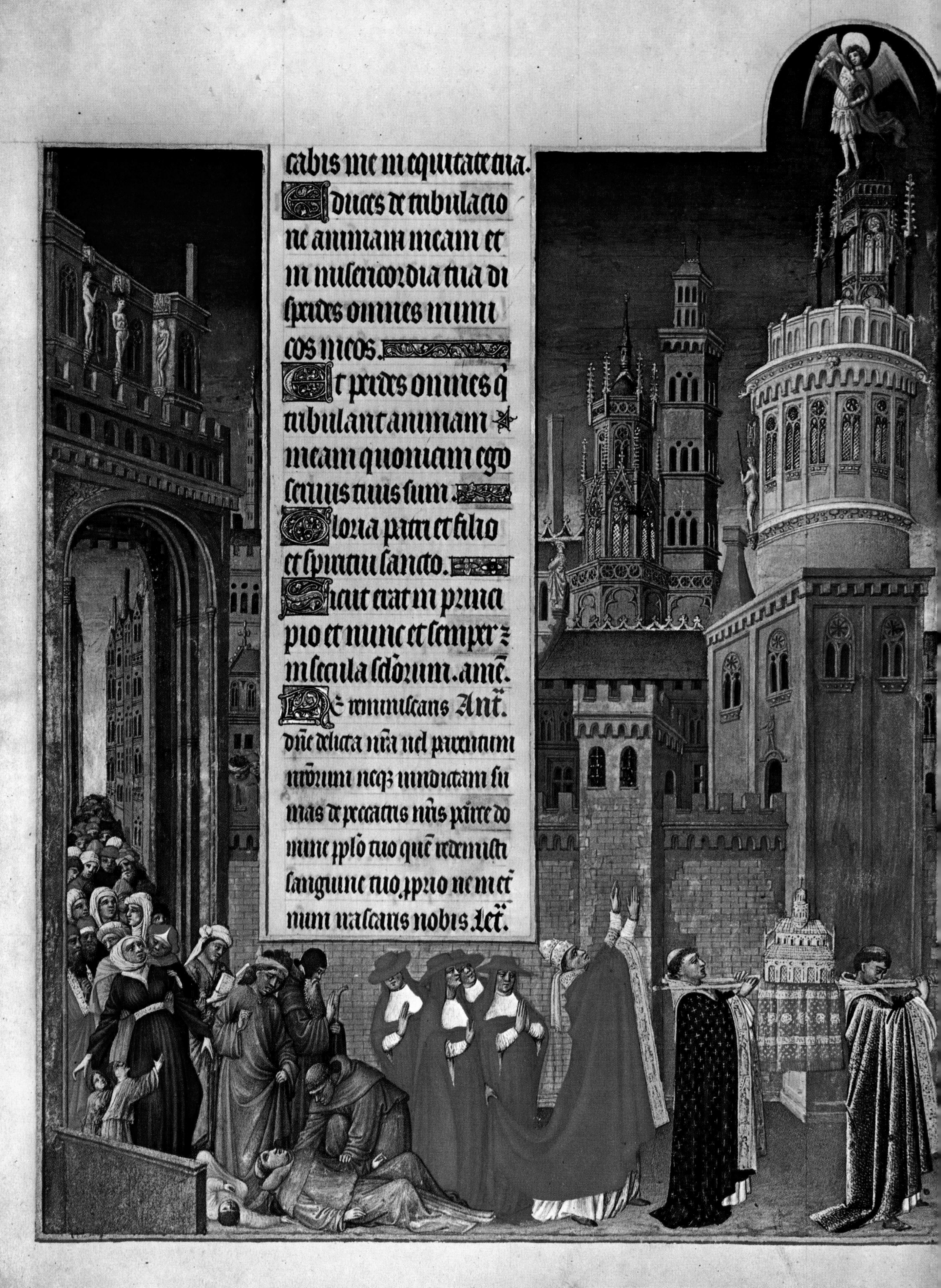

cabis me in equitate tua.
Educes de tribulatio
ne animam meam et
in misericordia tua di
sperdes omnes inimi
cos meos.
Et perdes omnes q̄
tribulant animam
meam quoniam ego
servus tuus sum.
Gloria patri et filio
et spiritui sancto.
Sicut erat in princi
pio et nunc et semper ꝫ
in secula sclo̅rum. amē.
Ne reminiscaris Ant̄.
dn̄e delicta nr̄a vel parentum
nr̄orum neqꝫ vindictam su
mas de peccatis nr̄is parce do
mine p̄plo tuo quē redemisti
sanguine tuo, p̄pro ne in et̄
num irascaris nobis. Lec̄.

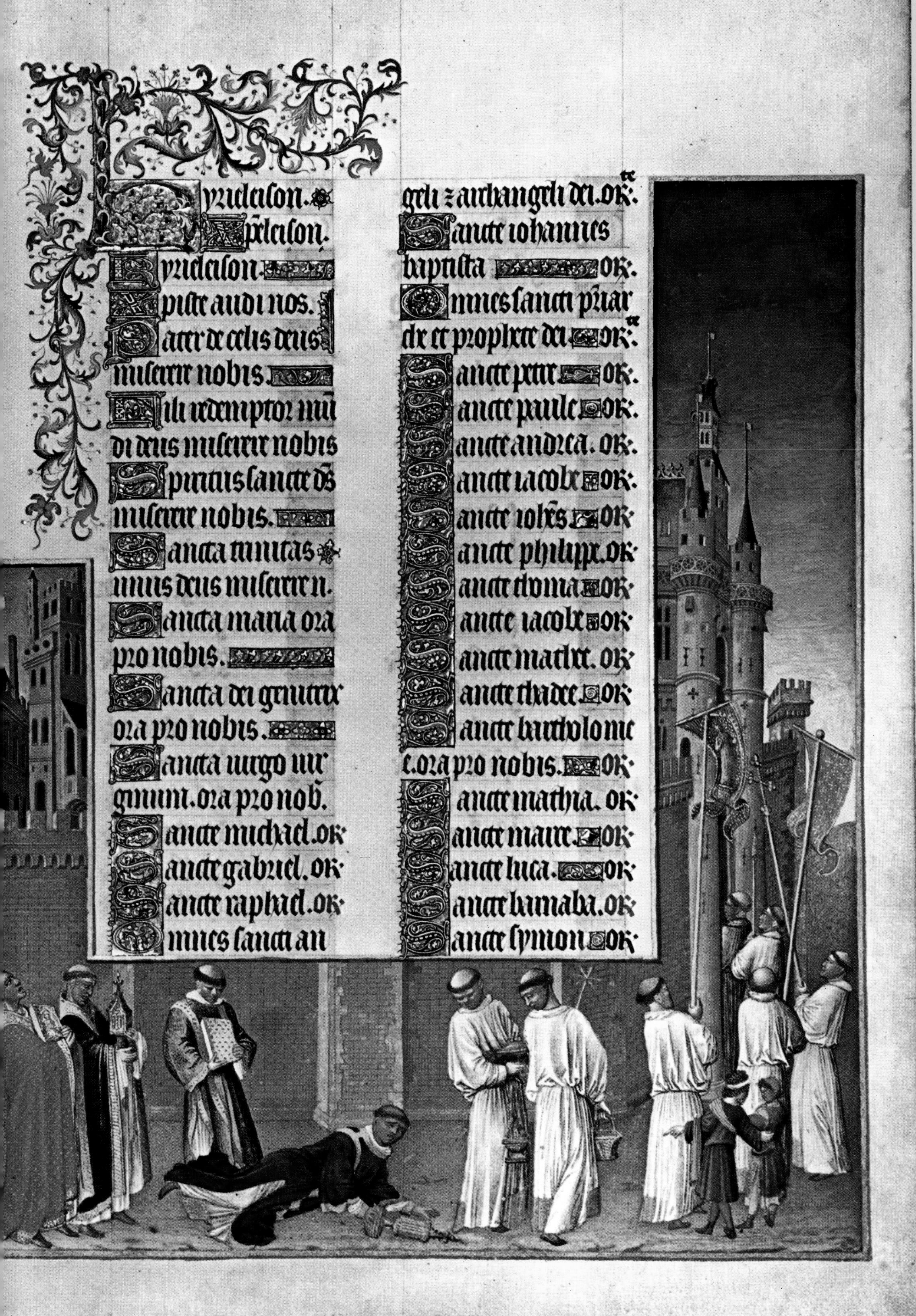

Kyrieleison.
Xpeleison.
Kyrieleison.
Xpiste audi nos.
Pater de celis deus
miserere nobis.
Fili redemptor mun-
di deus miserere nobis
Spiritus sancte ds
miserere nobis.
Sancta trinitas
unus deus miserere n.
Sancta maria ora
pro nobis.
Sancta dei genitrix
ora pro nobis.
Sancta virgo vir-
ginum. ora pro nob.
Sancte michael. or.
Sancte gabriel. or.
Sancte raphael. or.
Omnes sancti an-
geli et archangeli dei. or.
Sancte iohannes
baptista or.
Omnes sancti patriar-
che et prophete dei or.
Sancte petre or.
Sancte paule or.
Sancte andrea. or.
Sancte iacobe or.
Sancte iohes or.
Sancte philippe. or.
Sancte thoma or.
Sancte iacobe or.
Sancte mathee. or.
Sancte thadee or.
Sancte bartholome-
e. ora pro nobis. or.
Sancte mathia. or.
Sancte marce or.
Sancte luca. or.
Sancte barnaba. or.
Sancte symon or.

The Très Riches Heures of John, Duke of Berry

France, *c.* 1411–16 and 1485–90. 29 × 21 cm ($11\frac{3}{8} \times 8\frac{1}{4}$ in)
Musée Condé, Chantilly

66–67 **Procession of St Gregory the Great: the Great Litany** f.71v–72

The last page reached by the Limbourg brothers in the *Très Riches Heures* before their death in 1416 was probably the procession of St Gregory at the Litany (pp. 66–67). This double-page miniature was designed and partly painted by them but completed only many years later by Jean Colombe (all the faces are his). The subject was one seldom attempted in Books of Hours, perhaps because of design problems and the large number of figures involved. In the *Très Riches Heures* there were additional difficulties because the scene appears to have been inserted in consequence of a sudden change of plan. At the conclusion of the Penitential Psalms on f.71v, only the space normally filled by one column of text had been left blank for a miniature. This did not leave room for a large picture, but the Limbourg brothers found a solution by extending the procession scene right across the foreground of the double-page. St Gregory's procession had already been introduced into the *Belles Heures*, where it appears distributed among four separate miniatures. The subject appears again, in a double-spread, in the Soane Hours (p. 151); much later, the Procession of Corpus Christi in the Farnese Hours is disposed in similar fashion (pp. 166–67).

The procession was an historical event which occurred in AD 590, soon after St Gregory's election as unwilling Pope. A plague to which his predecessor Pelagius II had succumbed was then ravaging Rome. The new Pope assembled a procession from the seven districts of the city at the Basilica of Santa Maria Maggiore, which he then led to St Peter's imploring God's mercy for deliverance from the scourge. Jacobus de Voragine's *Golden Legend* records that as the procession passed Hadrian's Mausoleum the figure of the Archangel St Michael was seen on the summit in the act of replacing his sword in its scabbard. God had heard the Pope's prayer; the plague was spent. In memory of this miracle the Mausoleum was thenceforth known as Castel Sant'Angelo.

The reasons for inserting St Gregory's procession at the Litany of the *Très Riches Heures* can only be surmised. The Duke of Berry was over seventy years old and perhaps in failing health. At the beginning of the book is a miniature of the Zodiacal or Astrological Man, unique in manuscript Books of Hours, which is now known to have medical significance. It is sad but not altogether inappropriate that the 'Great Litany' or 'Supplication', as St Gregory's procession was later called, occurs on the last page reached by the Limbourg brothers in the *Très Riches Heures* before all three died suddenly in 1416, perhaps in an epidemic. Their patron the Duke of Berry himself died on 15 June and was buried with great solemnity in the Sainte-Chapelle he had built at Bourges. Nobody seems to have thought to place on his breast as he lay in state one of his Books of Hours, as was to be done on the death of his nephew Louis II of Anjou in 1417. Of all owners of Books of Hours the Duke of Berry most deserved this final recognition.

The most famous Berry Book of Hours is the *Très Riches Heures*, the Limbourg brothers' masterpiece, known especially for its Calendar.[1] The manuscript was begun about 1413 when the Limbourgs had succeeded Jacquemart de Hesdin as the Duke's principal *ouvriers*. All three were later appointed *varlets de chambre*, but the special esteem in which the Duke held them was expressed in more unusual manner by the gift of a large house in Bourges to the eldest brother, Pol de Limbourg, in 1411. It would be interesting to know whether this gift implied that the brothers had established their studio in Bourges rather than in Paris, but this remains an open question. If such were the case the Duke of Berry, who resided in Paris during the last years of his life, may have seen sample pages only of the *Très Riches Heures*, to which more than any other single item in his collections he owes his posthumous fame as an art patron.

At his death in 1416 the manuscript was unfinished and in unbound sheets. In the inventory of the Duke's possessions it appears as *plusieurs cayers d'unes très riches Heures, que faisoient Pol et ses frères, très richement historiez et enluminez* ('several gatherings of a very rich Book of Hours made by Pol and his brothers, very richly historiated and illuminated'). The Limbourg brothers themselves died suddenly in the same year, perhaps in an epidemic or accident. They were still in their twenties or early thirties and died as prematurely as Keats or Schubert. The brothers had just discovered Italy and lived long enough to incorporate motifs from Italian art with great delicacy and originality into the Franco-Flemish tradition of book painting in which they had been trained.

The immediate fate of the *Très Riches Heures* is not known. Towards the end of the fifteenth century it was acquired through inheritance or purchase by Duke Charles I of Savoy and his wife Blanche of Montferrat. Both were descended from the Duke of Berry through his daughter Bonne, who was briefly married to Amadeus VII of Savoy. Despite this early family connection it is now thought that the *Très Riches Heures* did not pass immediately into the possession of the House of Savoy on the death of the Duke of Berry but remained for some time in metropolitan France; miniatures and detailed motifs from it were copied into other French manuscripts in the decades following 1416.[2] The fourth-generation descendants of Bonne de Berry showed piety and pride in commissioning Jean Colombe, a painter from Bourges, to complete the decoration of their famous ancestor's prayerbook. The work was done at some time between 1485, the year of the Duke's marriage, and his death in 1490.

The later history of the *Très Riches Heures* presents problems to fascinate and tantalize those who find interest in the descent of art objects. From Duke Charles the book passed to his cousin Philibert of Savoy, the husband of Margaret of Austria, later Regent of the Netherlands. There is some evidence, unfortunately not quite conclusive, that the book may have been taken by Margaret to the Netherlands after her husband's premature death in 1504.

Whether or not the *Très Riches Heures* migrated to the Netherlands, the manuscript returned to Savoy; not this time, so far as is known, to the ducal house, but in unknown circumstances to the Spinolas, the famous military and banking family of Genoa who were staunch supporters of the Hapsburgs. In the eighteenth century the book was rebound in red leather with the Spinola arms impressed on the cover. By the early nineteenth century another Genoese family, the Marchesi of Serra, had added their armorial stamp to the binding.

The final owner was the Duke of Aumale, youngest son of the French King, Louis-Philippe, creator of the castle of Chantilly north of Paris. In the catalogue of the manuscripts at Chantilly he records that in December 1855 he left Twickenham, the home of the exiled Orleans family outside London, to visit his invalid mother Queen Amelia, the widow of Louis-Philippe, who was then staying at Nervi near Genoa. Before leaving England Aumale had been told by Anthony Panizzi, the librarian at the British Museum, that an important illuminated manuscript was on the market in Italy and could be seen in Genoa. The Duke finally traced it to a girls' school at the Villa Pallavicini in the suburbs. He immediately recognized, from the armorials and mottoes, the pictures of Vincennes Castle in the Calendar and other evidence, that he saw before him a Book of Hours which had once belonged to the Duke of Berry. Negotiations for the purchase of the volume from Baron Felix de Margherita of Turin and Milan, who had inherited it from the Serra family, were at once begun and promptly concluded. For the sum of 19,280 francs the Duke of Aumale acquired what is now the most celebrated of all Books of Hours.[3]

The Hours of Marshal Jean de Boucicaut

Use of Paris. France, Paris, *c.* 1405–08.
27.4 × 19 cm (10¾ × 7½ in), 242ff. 44 miniatures.
Musée Jacquemart-André, Paris, ms. 2

70 **Visitation** f.65v
71 **Flight into Egypt** f.90v

The Boucicaut Master, who illuminated this prayerbook for the distinguished soldier whose name it bears, was a landscape artist of genius who achieved effects of light and aerial perspective such as had not been seen before in book illumination.[1] The Visitation and the Flight into Egypt, at Lauds and Vespers of the Hours of the Virgin, are superlative examples of his style, complementing each other in design but lit in different ways. In the Visitation the light streams down from above the picture on to the heads of the Virgin and St Elizabeth. In the Flight into Egypt the rising sun, a golden orb within three orange rings, sends rays of light upwards into the blue sky. Symbolical interpretations could be devised for the light descending from an unknown source in the Visitation, and the rising sun ('I am the light of the world') in the Flight scene. In both pictures the heavens confer luminosity upon the earthly landscape.

The two pictures also show a favourite colour combination of the Boucicaut Master, a pure green accompanied by a vivid vermilion. Another feature of his work is the introduction of a curved strip of earth or pasture planted with little trees in the immediate foreground which sets the action back as if it were taking place on a raised platform. Each landscape shows shepherds with their flocks in the distance and swans (a favourite motif with this artist) upon the water.

The Visitation takes place in a hilly landscape, which fits the statement in St Luke's Gospel (1:39–45) that Mary 'went into the hill country' to visit her cousin Elizabeth. The two women of different ages are shown embracing. Each carries a child in her womb, and they thus share a common human condition. In Christian doctrine the Visitation carries a further meaning as the first encounter of St John the Baptist with Christ. Certain curious works of art from the late medieval period show the figures of Jesus and John in the wombs of their mothers, as if in embryonic X-rays, with Jesus making a gesture of blessing towards John.[2]

Mary is accompanied by two angel attendants, one of whom holds her train, the other her prayerbook. As if in anticipation of her Coronation, Mary has become a princess. Theologians explained Mary's ability to make an unaccompanied, hilly walk when pregnant to visit her cousin Elizabeth as a sign that she suffered none of the usual weariness or pains of ordinary motherhood. By giving her a train and attendants the simplicity of the brief Gospel narrative is replaced by a transcendental meaning. With haloes outlined against the blue lake, rays of light fall upon the two women as if suggesting a further descent of the Holy Spirit.

The miniature of the Flight into Egypt is as calmly composed but indicates movement. Joseph seems to be regarding a possible danger in the distance, perhaps the first glimpse of Herod's pursuing soldiers. Two angel attendants carrying provisions are aided in their task by a flying companion bearing a basket and a spray of fruit. A fourth, supernumerary, angel contemplates the Holy Family from behind a wattle fence. His lack of occupation implies adoration at its most profound.

As often happens with Books of Hours, we know little for certain about the artist, not even his name; but much about the owner. This was Jean le Meingre (or Maingre) de Boucicaut, Marshal of France, a successful soldier and administrator who died in England in 1421, six years after being taken prisoner at Agincourt. His early life, up to April 1409, is well documented in a biography by a close associate, perhaps his chaplain Honorat Durand, who presents the Marshal as a somewhat inflated version of Chaucer's 'very parfit gentle knight'.[3] His military prowess, respect for women, piety and austerity are constantly emphasized. As a personification of the chivalric ideal Boucicaut sounds a little too good to be true, but the facts of his career speak for his ability. He was also lucky in his private life. Not particularly well born himself, he had the good fortune to make a happy marriage above his station with Antoinette de Beaufort, daughter of the Vicomte de Turenne, to the lasting vexation of her father.

Boucicaut fought with the Teutonic Knights against the heathen in Prussia (as did Chaucer's knight), and took part in the crusade led by the Count of Nevers (later, as John the Fearless, Duke of Burgundy) which ended in catastrophic defeat by the Turks at Nicopolis on the Danube in 1397. The French army was taken prisoner and all those who could not pay large ransoms were brutally executed. Boucicaut escaped only because he had an influential friend in the Count of Nevers. In 1401 he was appointed Governor of Genoa, then under French protection, where he established a peaceful regime for some years before being driven out by a popular uprising.

Boucicaut is depicted by his admiring biographer as being almost inhumanly devout. He rose early, spent three hours in prayer, heard Mass twice daily however busy, fasted and wore black on Fridays, made pilgrimages on foot on Sundays and feast days, stopped his servants from swearing and 'every day without fail he says his Hours and many prayers, and suffrages to the saints'. This sounds exaggerated. But the fact that twenty-seven large miniatures of saints come at the beginning of the book, and have been selected with special relevance to Boucicaut's life, does indicate a rather special habit of devotion. The first to appear is St Leonard, patron saint of prisoners, who is shown chained to a pair of almost naked kneeling figures, a reminder of Boucicaut's narrow escape at Nicopolis.

Boucicaut's 'boast of heraldry', in these and other pages of his Book of Hours, is plausibly explained thus by Professor Meiss: 'contemptuous treatment by a father-in-law who despised his birth might have been one of the motives that drove the Marshal to the unprecedented display of arms and devices in his Book of Hours'.[4]

When the coats of arms do not appear like a tapestried background they are usually held up by angels who seem to be invoking or mediating help from the Virgin and the saints. Is their purpose perhaps more than mere embellishment and self-assertion? The psychology of heraldic thought is a subject which has never been adequately investigated, as Huizinga observed many years ago.[5] Boucicaut's book, in all its intricate artistry, is itself a prayer, with the heraldic symbolism indicating the owner's personality as much as his position in society.

When the book passed into the possession of Aymar de Poitiers (grandfather of Diane, the celebrated mistress of Henry II), he caused his own arms to be painted over most of the Marshal's shields and substituted his motto *sans nombre* ('Without Number') for Boucicaut's *ce que vous voudres* ('What You Will'). Aymar de Poitiers inherited the manuscript from his cousin Jean Le Meingre, a nephew of the Marshal. His tampering with the heraldry and, much worse, a measure of repainting in certain miniatures, have earned Aymar the admonitions of scholars. But what else could he have done if he valued his Book of Hours? Later possessors of Books of Hours frequently removed or updated ownership evidence in similar fashion. They might wish to ensure that divine favours, the answers to their prayers, should be directed to present, not deceased, owners. It is unreasonable to criticize them for not possessing a twentieth-century sense of scholarly and aesthetic niceties.

The market for illuminated manuscripts of all kinds was so great in Paris around the year 1400 that demand outran supply. In these circumstances it is strange that the Boucicaut Master apparently failed to obtain a court appointment. Professor Meiss lists more than fifty manuscripts with which the Boucicaut Master is connected. He further observes that the artist's failure 'to win for a period of years a great, sympathetic patron such as Jean de Berry or Yolande d'Aragon, Duchess of Anjou, is an accident of history that very probably has deprived us of masterpieces even more deeply contemplated than the Boucicaut Hours'.[6]

The Boucicaut Master disappears from Paris soon after 1420. He was identified by Count Paul Durrieu as long ago as 1905 with Jacques Coene, a painter from Bruges who settled in Paris. Professor Meiss has gone far to establish the validity of Durrieu's hypothesis. The Boucicaut Master is now firmly established in the select company of great French book artists of the later Middle Ages – Jean Pucelle, the Parement Master, Jacquemart de Hesdin, the Limbourg brothers, the Rohan Master, Jean Fouquet and his follower Jean Bourdichon. The Boucicaut Master is important, firstly, in his own right as 'the greatest pioneer of naturalism' (Panofsky), a phrase which sums up his understanding of space and perspective, fine observation of detail and ability to group figures harmoniously in landscape or interior settings; to these characteristics must be added his clear, luminous colour sense. Secondly, he is recognized as establishing a style, typically Parisian, which was adopted, circulated and diluted by book painters throughout the first half of the fifteenth century. His finest manuscript is one of the jewels of the Musée Jacquemart-André in Paris, where it gleams brightly among the distinguished bric-à-brac of that gloomy Second Empire mansion.

ego autem exercebor in mandatis tuis. Co
uertantur michi timentes te. et qui nouerunt
testimonia tua. Fiat cor meum immacu
latum. in iustificationibus tuis ut non co
fundar.

Defecit in
salutari
tuo. ani
ma mea
in uerbu
tuum sup
speraui. Defecerunt oculi mei in eloq
ium tuum. dicentes quando consolaberis
me. Quia factus sum sicut uter in prui

115

torium meum intende. ℟ Domine
ad adiuuandum me festina Gloria

The Hours of Giangaleazzo Visconti, Duke of Milan

Use of Rome. Italy, Milan, *c.* 1388–95; completed after 1428. In two sections: 24.7 × 17.5 cm ($9\frac{3}{4} \times 6\frac{7}{8}$ in), 151ff. (BR 397), and 25 × 17.9 cm ($9\frac{7}{8} \times 7$ in), 167ff. (LF 22). Miniatures and historiated initials with decorative borders.
Biblioteca Nazionale, Florence, BR 397 and LF 22

74 **David Blessing; Giangaleazzo Visconti** BR 397 f.115

75 **Creation of the Birds** LF 22 f.41

THIS, ONE OF THE MOST splendid Italian Books of Hours, was begun for Giangaleazzo Visconti, Duke of Milan, in about 1388, by Giovannino dei Grassi and completed around 1428 by Belbello da Pavia during the reign of Giangaleazzo's son Filippo Maria.[1]

The style of the first artist, Giovannino dei Grassi, is shown in the page here reproduced (p. 74) from the Psalter (not a usual feature of Books of Hours). It marks the beginning of the eleventh section (*caph*) of Psalm 119: 'My soul hath longed for thy salvation: and I have a good hope because of thy word. Mine eyes long sore for thy word, saying, O when wilt thou comfort me?' Above the miniature is a blank line probably intended for a rubric announcing the section, which is appointed to be said in the Divine Office at Sext on Sunday. Inside the initial *D* (*Defecit in salutari tuo anima mea*) the Psalmist King David sits beneath a canopy and raises his over-large left hand as if acknowledging God the Father, who peeps inconspicuously from behind the spiral frame filled with fleurs-de-lys. David's gesture may equally well be interpreted as drawing attention to the text or to the ubiquitous Visconti viper coats of arms in the corners of the frame.

In the margin below Giangaleazzo appears in profile, posed as in a medallion (or as in a modern studio photograph), and looking across and out of the page with a studied unconcern. In the top margin is his motto *A droyt*. Of equal interest are the finely observed animals at the bottom of the two golden trees. To the right is a group of deer as yet happily unaware of the two hounds who have scented them from the other side of the margin. Realistic animal portraiture is one of the most attractive features of both sections of the manuscript.

The decoration of the second part was completed by Belbello da Pavia in a style markedly different from that of Giovannino dei Grassi. Belbello's emphatic manner and strong colour range is seen in his embellishments of the Hours of the Virgin. Vespers opens with a large miniature of her death or Dormition, but the first lines of text on the facing page (*Deus in adjutorium meum intende. Domine ad adjuvandum me festina. Gloria*) are all but submerged in one of Belbello's most animated designs (p. 75). The subject is a Creation scene. A stern-faced Almighty hovers above a stormy sea filled with ships, but attention focuses on the creation of the birds in the lower border. Many are birds of prey, falcons and hawks in pursuit of cranes. On the ground is one of the commonest motifs in medieval animal art, the hawk on a duck, flanked by a solitary peacock and parrot. The other birds are shown in varied forms of flight. They balance the vigorous heraldic emblems in the upper half of the page, where clusters of angels raise up coroneted helmets with Visconti crests. On either side of the Creator is another Visconti emblem, a pink helmeted lion with feathered crest sitting in fire and holding a stick from which hang two buckets. As a further decorative accessory the Visconti arms of a writhing serpent devouring a child appear five times in this crowded page.

GIANGALEAZZO VISCONTI'S sudden rise to absolute power in the late fourteenth century was one of the sensations of medieval Italy. Born in 1351, he had a reputation in early life for studious tastes, a retiring disposition and delicate health. Seven years after the death of his father Galeazzo II in 1378, he showed his true character by audaciously overthrowing his uncle Bernabò and probably poisoning him shortly afterwards. In a few years he extended his rule over Verona, Pavia and other cities in a series of brilliant military campaigns. He crowned this success in 1395 by persuading or bribing the Holy Roman Emperor Wenceslaus to raise Milan (hitherto a mere county) to the status of an hereditary duchy vested in the Visconti family. After establishing his rule over Lombardy and the Romagna, he was on the point of occupying Florence and Umbria – with the mantle, crown and sceptre for a royal coronation already prepared – when Fortune's wheel caught up on him and he died suddenly on 3 September 1402, outside Florence, at the age of fifty-one. By this Act of God the unification of northern Italy was deferred for several centuries, as Macchiavelli prophesied.

Giangaleazzo's early marriage in 1360 to Isabelle de Valois, daughter of John II (*le Bon*), brought French influence and northern patterns of patronage to his court. Three sons of the marriage died in infancy, leaving only a daughter, Valentina, who was to marry Louis, Duke of Orleans, brother of Charles VI. After Isabelle's death Giangaleazzo married in 1380 his cousin Caterina Visconti (a daughter of the deposed and murdered Bernabò), but for eight years they had no children. Then two sons were born, Giovanni in 1388 and Filippo in 1392. Both were given the additional baptismal name of Maria in honour of the Virgin Mary for whom Giangaleazzo had a special devotion.

To commemorate the birth of Giovanni Maria, Giangaleazzo commissioned a magnificent Book of Hours from Giovannino dei Grassi, an architect and painter already employed in the building of the new Cathedral of St Mary in Milan and the Certosa at Pavia. The commission must date from before 1395, for the prayerbook contains no ducal emblems.

The book has several unusual features. The early part contains a complete Psalter, a reversion to the earlier type of Psalter-Hours. Also remarkable is the prominence given in the opening miniatures to the story of St Joachim and St Anne, a Biblical couple who waited long for a child: an allusion to Giangaleazzo and Caterina (cf. pp. 122–25, Marguerite de Foix).

Giovannino dei Grassi died in 1398, after decorating nearly half of the already written pages (a single scribe who signed himself on f.108 *frater Amadeus* appears to have written out the whole text). The completed section was bound as a separate volume, perhaps because it contained the Psalter and could be used for reciting the Divine Office. Embellishment was resumed in the reign of the second son, Filippo Maria, who succeeded his brother Giovanni Maria in 1412 and ruled until 1447. At about the time of his marriage to Maria of Savoy in 1428, Filippo Maria entrusted the work to Luchino Belbello da Pavia, one of the great names in Lombard book illumination.

The two parts acquired different owners. The Giovannino section passed to the Dukes of Visconti di Modrone, a cadet branch of the family. The second section, completed by Belbello, was eventually acquired by Baron Horace Landau (1824–1903) of Florence (who has a place in literary history as the original of Nissim Bernard in Proust's great novel *A la recherche du temps perdu*).[2] The heirs of the Baron's niece Madame Hugo Finaly (Proust's Madame Bloch) generously presented the book, known as the Landau-Finaly Hours, to the Biblioteca Nazionale after World War II. There, the two sections of the Visconti Hours finally came together under one roof in 1959.

Of the two artists employed, the work of Giovannino is the more attractive, with graceful figures posed in fanciful architectural settings (p. 74). Belbello introduces a more emphatic, harsher note. His strong tones of green, blue and purple, and his stocky, often ugly figures, suggest an aggressive reaction to the sweetness of the International style of Giovannino (p. 75). Both artists employ borders of assertive magnificence. Is it, perhaps, a sign of decadence in book illumination when our attention is so forcibly arrested by the borders before we look at the miniatures?

The display of heraldry is as lavish as in the Boucicaut Hours, but appears as an ingredient in a hectic decorative repertoire rather than in any rational sense. Few of the main pages are without the Visconti silver shield, bearing the *bisceglia*, a blue viper devouring a red child: on some the arms appear as many as ten times. Elsewhere the vipers escape from their shields and twine up the stem borders with terrifying effect.

Both artists show a keen interest in beasts and birds which reflects the movement towards naturalism which radiated from the feudal northern Italian courts around the year 1400.[3] The peacocks kept in the ducal park at Pavia appear on several pages, together with hawks and an engaging quartet of rabbits firmly confined in a barred and castellated hutch (BR 397, f.124).

Despite the bravura overall effect, the Belbello section leaves a disturbing impression, especially in the violent, often cruel emphasis given to the Old Testament scenes. This cycle of Old Testament pictures is unprecedented in a Book of Hours. Both the sons of Giangaleazzo (himself the best of a bad bunch) appear to have derived absolutely no grace or benefit from their second baptismal name of Maria; the horrific family life of the Visconti and other northern Italian despots was to provide an inexhaustible source for plots of sombre Elizabethan tragedies, and for early nineteenth-century operas (e.g. Bellini's *Beatrice di Tenda*).

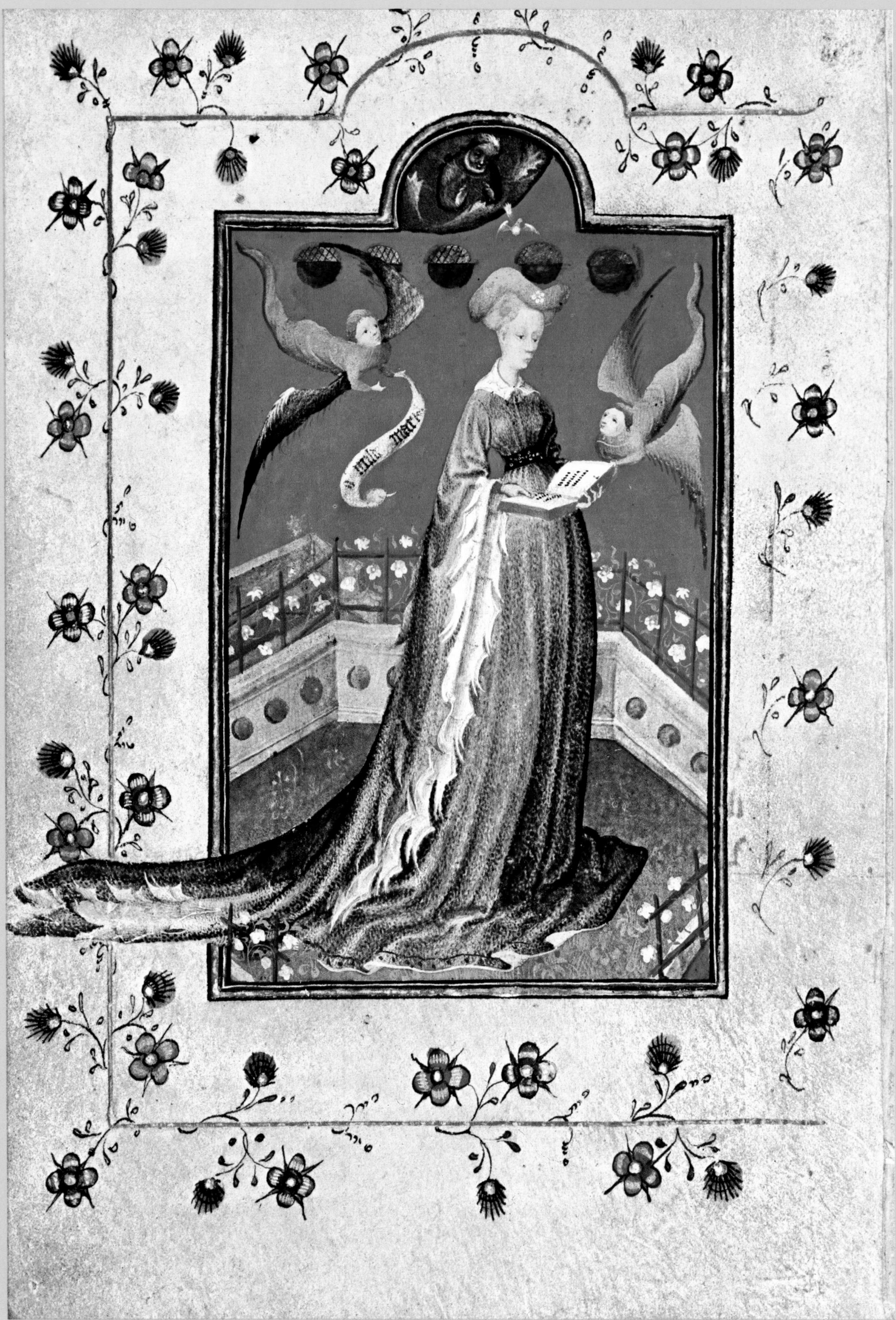

20
Heer ihesu criste
vmb dat wreeli
che anetasten dat
19

The Hours of Mary of Guelders

Use of Rome. German-Dutch border, Guelders. 1415. 13 × 19 cm ($5\frac{1}{8} \times 7\frac{1}{2}$ in), 482ff. 6 full-page and 86 smaller miniatures with stylized ivy-leaf borders.
Staatsbibliothek, Stiftung Preussischer Kulturbesitz, Berlin-Dahlem, ms. germ. quart. 42

78–79 **Annunciation (Mary of Guelders in a walled garden); Betrayal of Christ** ff. 19v–20

AT FIRST GLANCE the left-hand page reproduced (p. 78) looks like a Gothic fashion plate. An exquisitely robed lady whose train extends beyond the picture frame stands in a garden reading her Book of Hours, which an angel presents to her. It is only when we notice the rose-decked fence of the walled garden or *hortus conclusus* (a symbolic anticipation of Paradise), and the presence of God in the arched frame at the top despatching the Holy Ghost in the form of a dove, that we realize with some surprise that this is an Annunciation scene. A second angel carries a banderole on which, instead of the familiar *Ave Maria gratia plena* ('Hail Mary full of grace'), appear the German words *O milde Maria* ('O gracious Mary'). Has the inscription been altered? Does the elegant lady represent the Virgin Mary dressed in the height of fashion and wearing a smart bonnet of the type known as *bourrelet* or chaplet instead of a halo; or is she the prayerbook's owner personifying the Madonna? Unclear also is the significance of the five discs above her head.

We know from evidence elsewhere in the book that the owner was Marie d'Harcourt, Duchess of Guelders (Geldern or Gelderland, between Cologne and Utrecht), and that she had no children by her husband Reinald IV. God extends his blessing on the childless woman who seems to stand with lofty pride in the mystical garden of her patron, the Virgin Mary. The words 'O gracious Mary' could apply to both of them. Once we know about Marie's childlessness, the symbolic act of assuming the blue robe of the Virgin in a *hortus conclusus* attended by angels becomes less presumptuous. This is more than a picture of a pretty young woman in a garden. It combines religious belief with fashionable awareness in a manner rare in Books of Hours of this date.

To turn from this elegant lady in her garden to the Betrayal of Christ scene opposite (p. 79) is to become immediately aware that this double-page was not planned as a unit. The different sizes of the miniatures and the disparity of border decoration indicate that the Annunciation is an insertion. Why it should have been placed here, before the Hours of the Passion, rather than, more appropriately, at Matins of the Virgin or the *Obsecro te* prayer, is a mystery. The contrast is extreme between the elegant, French-looking lady and the stocky figures which make up a crowded scene in the Betrayal of Christ miniature. In such company the lady appears like a choice butterfly which has momentarily alighted in a strange habitat.

LIKE THE LATER Hours of Mary of Burgundy (pp. 110–13), this manuscript raises the question of fashion in dress as reflected in Books of Hours.[1] In both manuscripts the conventional little 'portraits' of praying donors customarily found in Books of Hours are replaced by ladies who wear their clothes not only with an elegance appropriate to their rank but with a new awareness of themselves. Like figures on a stage, they dominate their setting. They attract immediate attention, taking precedence over the subject matter of the miniatures in which they appear.

Professor Panofsky sees the 'extraordinary miniature' on f. 19v (p. 78), which identifies the Duchess of Guelders with the Virgin Annunciate, as a possible allusion to the Duchess's unfulfilled hope of having children.[2] This perceptive interpretation is confirmed by what is known about her life.

She was born Marie d'Harcourt, the daughter of John, Count of Harcourt and Aumale, who came of an old Norman family, and of Catherine de Bourbon. Her maternal grandfather, Duke Peter I of Bourbon, died on the battlefield of Poitiers (1356); her aunt Jeanne was the wife of King Charles V, the Wise, of France. She and her father shared the Valois taste for fine books, and belonged to the inner family circle which was in the habit of exchanging expensive gifts on 1 January of each year. Their correspondence with the Duke of Berry about such matters still survives.[3]

They were also well known to Louis, Duke of Orleans, who sought to rule France in the name of his brother, the intermittently mad Charles VI. Since 1400, if not earlier, he had worked to establish his influence in areas adjoining Burgundian territories so that he could harass and if necessary attack his relatives, the Dukes of Burgundy, who were his greatest rivals for control of the King's person and thereby effective rule in France. The ruler of Guelders was a desirable ally. His Duchy, situated between Cologne and Utrecht, immediately to the south of the Zuyder Zee, was the most northerly of a string of princely and ecclesiastical states, all nominally fiefs of the Holy Roman Empire, which flanked the Burgundian territories on the east along the rivers Rhine and Moselle.

The Duke of Guelders was persuaded to become a vassal of the French King. Reinald IV paid homage to Charles VI (then in one of his periods of sanity) on 29 April 1405, receiving in return monetary rewards and the hand of the King's niece by marriage, Marie d'Harcourt, maid of honour to the Duchess of Orleans, Valentina Visconti. The wedding was arranged and financed, for political reasons, by the Duke of Orleans, to the intense annoyance of John the Fearless of Burgundy.

To Guelders Marie d'Harcourt must have brought a welcome breath of French manners, modes and taste. The Annunciation page in her Book of Hours is so French in feeling and in such marked contrast to the other miniatures in this German-Dutch manuscript that its insertion must have been deliberate. But there is more in it than a nostalgic memory of her homeland. Her political role, and the need for heirs to confirm the adherence of Guelders to the Orleanist cause, are implicit in her marriage circumstances; and a large part of her dowry, some 30,000 *écus*, had been paid by the Duke of Orleans with the stipulation that it was to be returned in default of male heirs.[4] Other wives lacking sons invoked the aid of the Virgin and appropriate saints in their Books of Hours; Marguerite de Foix and Anne of Brittany are mentioned elsewhere in these pages. Mary of Guelders went a stage further in actually identifying herself with the Mother of Christ.

An inscription on f.410, at the Vigil of the Feast of St Matthew, records that the manuscript, the text of which is in Low German, was completed for the Duchess of Guelders on 23 February 1415 by Brother Helmich de Leev, in the monastery of Marienborn near Arnhem. This house belonged to the Windesheim Congregation of the Brethren of the Common Life, the branch of the Augustinian Order which initiated the movement for spiritual reform in the Northern Netherlands known as the *devotio moderna*. The most famous literary testimony of this movement is the devotional manual *On the Imitation of Christ* attributed to Thomas à Kempis.[5]

Whether a direct connection may be established between the *devotio moderna* and book illumination is a complex question which cannot be pursued here, but it is worth noting that the Bibles, Books of Hours and other religious texts written in the monasteries and lay houses of the Brethren of the Common Life are not usually as elaborately decorated as the Hours of Mary of Guelders. This must have been a specially commissioned work. Like some other important Books of Hours it contains a considerable portion of the Breviary (and is sometimes so described). This probably accounts for the number of saints included, 189 – many more than in the London Hours of René of Anjou (pp. 86–89) – arranged three to a page, and perhaps constituting a record in Books of Hours.

Both artistically and historically Mary of Guelders' Book of Hours is a challenging manuscript, which its fragile condition makes difficult to study. The source of the Annunciation page, whether or not it has been repainted or touched up to serve as a portrait of the Duchess, may never be traced. Perhaps it does not matter very much. Mary of Guelders died childless in 1425. In a picture which fuses aristocratic mannerism and mystical self-identification with the Virgin Mary, she has left an unforgettable portrait of herself as an ideal type of the grand lady reading her Book of Hours.

Ce que noe planta la vigne et but
du vin que lui mesmes planta.
Genesis ix. signifie ihesucrist qui planta les iuis et but de
mesmes le cep en la passion. Ce que ly uns des
filz descouvry noe et ly autres le couvry si-
gnefie les iuis qui descouvrirent la char ihesucrist
et ly crestien la recouvrirent.

Secundum marcum.
In illo tempore. Recu-
bentibus undecim di

Quiconques veult estre bien conseilliez de la chose dont il a

The Grandes Heures de Rohan

Use of Paris. France, *c.* 1420. 29 × 20.8 cm ($11\frac{3}{8} \times 8\frac{1}{8}$ in), 239ff. 11 full-page and 54 half-page miniatures, 470 smaller miniatures in borders. *Bibliothèque Nationale, Paris, ms. lat. 9471*

82 **St Mark; Christ drinks the cup of the Passion** f.23

83 **Christ in Judgment** f.154

THIS GREAT ANJOU PRAYERBOOK, which bears the name of Rohan through an accident of later ownership, is marked throughout by the powerful personality of the artist known to us only as the Rohan Master.[1] The miniatures in the Gospel Sequences which follow the Calendar are set in vertical panels occupying almost all the space normally filled by a column of text. Here the Evangelists appear in fantastic architectural settings open to the sky and culminating in pinnacles at dizzy heights. In these draughty surroundings they write their Gospels. St Mark turns from his tiered desk to caress his symbolic beast, the winged lion here superbly depicted in heraldic demi-rampant position. As it lays a paw upon the open page the beast seems to roar gently in encouragement.

Several books, casually displayed on the reading-desk and on a curious sloping shelf fixed to the wall above the Evangelist's head, furnish the room. At the top of the spindly desk, which appears to be adjustable to a vertiginous height, a blindfolded female figure, presumably representing the Synagogue, is precariously placed. This airy chamber is improbably surmounted by a corner of a medieval town from whose turrets flutter superadded Rohan banners, one of them even breaking out of the gold picture frame.

In the right margin the smaller panel contains a scene from a devotional work, the *Bible moralisée*. Christ raises the Cup of the Passion to his lips. He is supported by a Christian. In front of him three Jews in tall hats are watching with gestures of surprise or possibly insult. The mosaic background to this scene is repeated on the floor of St Mark's study. But it is the beautifully composed group of the Evangelist with his symbolic beast which makes this a memorable page.

The Last Judgment in these *Grandes Heures* occurs not at the Office of the Dead, as is customary, but at the Seven Requests. These invocations to Christ the Saviour, attributed to the Venerable Bede, are introduced by a prayer which if recited daily preserved the petitioner from sudden death without confession or in any other violent manner. Today sudden death is considered to be almost desirable. For our medieval ancestors it was a catastrophe, since it deprived them of the opportunity to make confession, however inadequately and at the last moment, for mis-spent lives, and to be shriven.

Christ is seated on a rainbow holding an upright sword to indicate that he is indeed a judge. He is shown as old, not young. The Rohan Master seems to have preferred age to youth, but may here also have been aware of the theological doctrine that the Last Judgment unites God the Father and God the Son, two persons of the Trinity, permanently into one. Christ appears to accept his dolorous task with distress. A quartet of angels announce the terrible event with blasts from primitive trumpets. Finely composed, they are curiously human in gesture and expression; unlike Christ they seem almost to relish their task. Representatives of fallen man crawl painfully out of their graves. On the left Eve appears to recognize Adam. The most arresting figure is the dark-haired man who crouches in an attitude of utter misery and despair. Does his clothed condition indicate, as has been suggested, that he symbolizes those alive on Judgment Day?

THE DUCHY OF ANJOU, in west France, adjoining Brittany, was alloted *en apanage* (*see* p. 53) three times by the medieval French kings. The First House included Geoffrey of Anjou, who founded the English Plantagenet line in the twelfth century. The Second House started in the thirteenth century with Charles, brother of St Louis IX, and King of Sicily (he lost Sicily to the Spaniards in the Sicilian Vespers of 1284 but retained Naples). His descendants, titular Kings of Sicily, picked up many crowns from the political débris of the Crusades while contending among themselves for possession of Naples. In 1360 the French male line failed, and a Third House of Anjou began with the second son of King John II of France (*le Bon*), Louis, who was also declared heir to Naples and the Sicilian title by his relative Queen Joanna I. He and his descendants were distinguished for their ambition, energy, charm and artistic tastes. His son Louis II of Anjou, who succeeded in 1384 at the age of seven, had the reputation of a 'just, learned and debonair prince'. He died in 1417, and his favourite Book of Hours, which had belonged to his grandfather King John II, was placed on his breast as he lay in state. His elder son Louis III (1403–34) spent most of his short life in Italy; his younger son was the famous *bon roi* René, two of whose Books of Hours are illustrated here (pp. 86–93). But it was Louis II's widow, Yolanda, daughter of John I of Aragon and known in her lifetime as the Queen of Sicily, who now became a major power in France.

After the death of Charles VI in 1422, seven years after the *débâcle* of Agincourt, the English temporarily reduced his son Charles VII (whom even his own mother, the disreputable Queen Isabella, reputed mistress of Louis of Orleans, called the *soi-disant* Dauphin) to a precarious existence at John of Berry's former capital of Bourges. During these years Yolanda came into her own; she married her daughter Marie to the King, and until her death in 1442 she was the real leader of the legitimist party in France.

Yolanda was unsuccessful in reconciling her own Houses of Anjou and Aragon, which fought for Naples, but showed great skill in detaching the French feudal vassals from the English alliance. She is never mentioned by the Burgundian chroniclers, because the Angevins supported the Burgundians' hated rivals, the Armagnacs.[2]

The *Grandes Heures* was almost certainly made for Yolanda or for one of her children; the masculine form of the *Obsecro te* and *O intemerata* is not conclusive evidence that the first owner was a man (even Anne of Brittany's *Grandes Heures* have these prayers unaccountably in the masculine form). It has been suggested that the illuminations reflect the atmosphere of the dolorous years between Agincourt (1415) and the miraculous restoration of French morale by Joan of Arc fifteen years later.

The Rohan Master is usually assumed to have been the head of a busy workshop, patronized by the House of Anjou and seemingly located at different times in Paris, Angers, Bourges, Troyes, Brittany, Provence and elsewhere. His influence in this manuscript is strong, but not all the full-page miniatures are thought to be entirely in his own hand; perhaps he himself was not a professional book-painter?[3] He seems to have known the work of the Boucicaut and Bedford Masters and of the Limbourg brothers. His mature style is nonetheless so compelling and peculiar that scholars have sought its sources not only in Paris but in Catalonia (the country of his patron Yolanda of Aragon), Provence, northern France and Germany, with a possible contribution from Bologna.

The eleven full-page miniatures which survive (the Adoration of the Magi and other illustrations essential in a Book of Hours are missing) endow the manuscript with its unique and mysterious character. Distortion and violence are combined with a disquieting pathos. Advanced in some respects, in others the Rohan Master was almost old-fashioned, showing little interest in perspective or naturalistic landscape; he was largely immune to the new influences from Italy current in Paris. In his depiction of traditional scenes and encounters the faces of the sacred cast are as anxious, melancholy and even ugly as those of the human participants. He was a painter of ideas: specifically, of religious ideas.

The religious component in works of art, as distinct from religious iconography, is a matter art historians seem unwilling to examine. Yet in periods when art was motivated by religion we sometimes encounter works which display a transcendental quality too emphatic to be explained by iconography, aesthetics or stylistic analysis alone. An experience may be defined as religious if it comprises three elements: a sense of awe in the face of the unknown, a feeling of uneasiness and often guilt with the inadequacy of our human endowment, and a desire for some kind of participation or identification with a greater reality.[4] All three are present in the work of the Rohan Master.

A final mystery is the later history of the *Grandes Heures*. On several pages the arms of the Rohan family of Brittany, seven gold mascles (or diamonds) on a red ground, appear to have been added. The *Grandes Heures* may have come into their possession through a dynastic link, just as another Anjou manuscript, known as the Hours of Isabella Stuart (pp. 114–17), probably passed to the House of Brittany in the 1440s. Or, as has been ingeniously suggested (there is no proof), the precious manuscript may have formed part of the enormous ransom paid by Yolanda's son René to Philip the Good of Burgundy in 1437: Philip's ally Antoine de Vaudemont, victor over René at Bulgnéville in 1431, had a daughter who married Alain IX, Viscount of Rohan. As so often with manuscripts and other books, one wishes that somebody had thought to add the briefest ownership note at a time when such information seemed too obvious to be worth recording.

The *Grandes Heures de Rohan* remains one of the most puzzling and forceful in religious expression of all Books of Hours. It is appropriate, since religion is itself mysterious, that there should be so many mysteries surrounding the book.

en dieu en soit

48
en dieu en soit
eus in adiutorium
meum intende.
omine ad adiuuã

The Paris Hours of René of Anjou

Use of Paris. France, *c.* 1410–20. 26 × 18 cm (10¼ × 7⅛ in), 148ff. 23 full-page and 37 smaller miniatures, decorative borders.
Bibliothèque Nationale, Paris. ms. lat. 1156a

86 **Portrait of René** f.81v
87 **Nativity (Holy Family)** f.48

The most celebrated member of the House of Anjou, the chivalrous poet-prince 'Good King René', appears before us in person in his Paris Book of Hours. Wearing Italian dress, a liripipe hood lying across his shoulder, his beard and hair likewise trimmed in the Italian manner, he is felicitously posed in front of a black curtain. To the right hangs a tapestry bearing his arms. Heraldry always explains history, and here we see in schematic form the constellation of realms and territories which came to him by inheritance and marriage. In the top left are the arms of Hungary, followed by Anjou-Naples, Jerusalem, Anjou-Duchy, Bar and Lorraine. The Cross of Lorraine on the Angevin eagle in the border is an allusion to René's first wife Isabelle, the Lorraine heiress. Immediately below the portrait, and repeated four times, is his emblem of a billowing sail bearing the motto *en Dieu en soit*. The sail appears again at the bottom of the page together with another emblem, three spiky nails or thorns. The meaning of René's devices and motto is obscure. Did he hope the winds of fortune would bear him safely to those several but distant realms, whose elusive crowns he wore by title only?

The second miniature reproduced from this Book of Hours is a more conventional subject, a charming Nativity scene from Prime, with Mary, assisted by Joseph and a maidservant, testing the temperature of the bath in which she is about to wash her new-born son. This domestic moment in the life of the Holy Family received weighty exegesis from theologians. If Christ was born perfect, his mother having suffered none of the usual pain and weariness of human birth, he needed no bath. An explanation for the bath tub, which reflects the humanization of Mary in Gothic art, was found in the belief that the water, so far from cleansing the infant Christ, was itself purified by him, becoming the effective vehicle for all future baptisms. The humble bath which Mary tests is the holy font from whose sanctified water all Christians derive hope of salvation at their baptism.[1]

King René's Paris Book of Hours is one of several produced in the workshop patronized by his mother Yolanda of Aragon, Duchess of Anjou.[2] It shows the unmistakable influence of the Rohan Master, but also borrowings from the Boucicaut and other Paris workshops. Among other motifs which are almost like a signature of his style is the pink dress with horizontal stripes worn by the maidservant in the Nativity miniature; a similar dress appears frequently in miniatures in the *Grandes Heures de Rohan*.

In an authoritative study published in 1875 Lecoy de La Marche presented René as a good man, an unlucky man and an artist.[3] In his family life and personal relationships René was kindly, outgoing and affectionate to a remarkable degree. He was less fortunate in his political career. It was in the arts and literature that his peculiar gifts found their most permanent expression.[4]

Concerning his paintings and illuminations there has been much dispute. At one time almost every panel painting of the Provençal School was attributed to his hand, as well as the illuminations in six or seven Books of Hours. The judgment of art historians then went to the other extreme, and René was denied anything more than a general influence upon *les peintres du roi de Sicile*, as his artists were called. Today, a middle position has been reached. The tradition, dating from his lifetime, that he had professional knowledge and practice of painting, acquired possibly from Jan van Eyck, is now again taken seriously and has been closely investigated by Dr Otto Pächt.[5]

Writing was a less eccentric activity, recognized as an acceptable princely diversion from the example of Charles of Orleans, René's cousin, who relieved the tedium of a long captivity in London after the Battle of Agincourt by writing ballades and *rondeaux* (which do not, however, appear to have been widely known or circulated during his lifetime). René's literary works are numerous and long. The three best known are the *Livre des tournois*, a treatise on tournaments, the pastoral poem *Regnault et Jeanneton* in which the loves of René and Jeanne de Laval, his second wife, are transparently described, and the *Livre du Cueur d'amours espris*, a dream allegory of love famous from the superlatively illuminated copy in the Nationalbibliothek, Vienna.[6]

Few men can have collected as many crowns and titles through the accidents of inheritance as René. When he was born in Angers in 1409, the second son of Louis II, Duke of Anjou, and Yolanda of Aragon, there seemed little prospect that one day he would become King of a galaxy of realms – Aragon, Hungary, Jerusalem, Naples, Sicily – with shadowy claims to Poland, Armenia and Cyprus – whose very names resound with echoes of medieval pomp and circumstance. He wore these diverse crowns by title rather than possession, and only in Naples held precarious estate for a few years.

The first title which came to him was the Duchy of Bar, between Champagne and Lorraine in eastern France, whose ruler, his great-uncle the Cardinal-Duke Louis, adopted René in 1419 and married him to Isabelle of Lorraine, eldest daughter and heiress of Charles II, *le Hardi*, so that one day René would inherit both Duchies. This happened in 1430–31 when he had reached the age of twenty-two. But his right to Lorraine was disputed by Antoine de Vaudemont, a nephew of the late Duke. Vaudemont was supported by Philip the Good, Duke of Burgundy, the most powerful man in France. René unwisely accepted a trial by battle. At Bulgnéville in Lorraine on a very hot day, 2 July 1431, he suffered a crushing defeat, receiving a wound on the lip which marked him for life, and was taken prisoner while his loyal companions died by hundreds.

The victor of Bulgnéville was cheated of his prisoner, whom he had to surrender to Philip of Burgundy. René passed into the power of the greatest enemy of his house. For nearly six years he was technically, and for many months in fact, Philip's prisoner in the Tour de Dijon, afterwards known as the Tour de Bar, in the Burgundian capital. It is to this period that belongs the legend, never quite proved or disproved, that René met and received instruction from Jan van Eyck.

While he lingered in close but perhaps not uncomfortable confinement, fresh crowns and titles descended upon the prisoner's head. In November 1434 his elder brother Louis III, Duke of Anjou, died childless in Italy, leaving René that Duchy, together with Maine and the County of Provence in the south. The following year, in February 1435, Louis was followed to the grave by Joanna II, Queen of Sicily, who also made René her heir. With no aptitudes for anything except love and intrigue she had unfortunately already promised Sicily to her sometime lover Alfonso of Aragon.

It must be strange to become a king while in prison, but despite this circumstance René's status among his fellow princes was at once greatly improved. A deal was made with his cousin Philip of Burgundy. On payment of an enormous ransom, estimated in the nineteenth century to represent a million pounds, which permanently crippled René's finances, he was finally set free in 1437. We need not follow the details of his six years' attempt to hold Naples against his rival Alfonso of Aragon. In the end René had to admit defeat. His second attempt at military glory collapsed, like the first, in failure.

After his return to France, he became the trusted counsellor of his brother-in-law Charles VII, whose wife was René's sister Marie. These may have been the happiest years of his life. After the death of Isabelle in 1453 he married the twenty-one-year-old Jeanne, daughter of Guy XIV, Count of Laval, a Breton nobleman. With his young wife, of whom he was greatly fond, the happy pattern of his personal life was resumed.

In contrast, the harmonious understanding with the French Court ceased when Charles VII died in 1461 and was succeeded by his son Louis XI. The new King sought neither to collaborate with his feudal vassals nor even to play them off one against the other, but to crush them altogether and reunite their territories with the French Crown.

René was not, however, immune to a new turn of Fortune's wheel. In August 1466 the Catalans offered him the Crown of Aragon by right of succession, as grandson, through his mother Yolanda, of John I. René, who could never resist a crown, accepted the new royal title for himself, sending his son John to occupy Barcelona as Lieutenant-General of Aragon. John died in December 1470, whereupon the Aragonese family resumed possession. As permanent record of his latest kingdom René retained no more than an escutcheon of pretence on his coat of arms showing the yellow and red vertical pales of Aragon; it may be seen in the magnificent terracotta roundel of his arms now in the Victoria and Albert Museum, London.

After this Spanish fiasco René retired to his favourite inheritance, the County of Provence. He died in his castle at Aix-en-Provence on 10 July 1480. In his last years he had wished only to be left in peace in his southern retreat and made but feeble attempts to delay his nephew's infiltration into Anjou, where Louis systematically established administrative control. At René's death the Duchy and Third House of Anjou effectively came to an end.

Sequitur Officiū Mortuorū

The London Hours of René of Anjou

Use of the Sainte-Chapelle at Paris. France, early fifteenth century. 22.3 × 16.8 cm ($8\frac{3}{4} \times 6\frac{5}{8}$ in), 154ff. 10 full-page miniatures and historiated initials in text, particularly in the Suffrages.
British Library, London, Egerton ms. 1070

90 **René as le-roi-mort** f.53r
91 **Adoration of the Magi** f.34v

THE OFFICE OF THE DEAD in this second Book of Hours owned by King René presents us with another portrait of the King in startling contrast to that from his Paris Hours reproduced on p. 86. Instead of the sleek, well-groomed man in the prime of early middle age we see a disturbing image of *le-roi-mort* which is at the same time an allegorized self-portrait of René. A three-quarter-length crowned skeleton standing behind a curtain on which are painted René's arms (with Jerusalem to the right) holds a scroll bearing the words *Memento homo quod cinis es et in sinere* [*?cinerem*] *reverteris* (approximately, 'Dust thou art and to dust thou shalt return'). It is as if René has looked into a mirror and seen a reflection of himself as King-in-Death. That this was not a transient image is shown by the commission given in 1450 to his artist Coppin Delft to paint a fresco similarly depicting him as *le-roi-mort* above a tombe René designed for himself in the Church of Saint-Maurice at Angers.

This striking portrait is one of five miniatures added, together with coats of arms and devices, to the manuscript when it came into René's possession sometime during the 1430s. Like other famous examples this Book of Hours was not made for the owner after whom it is now named but had an earlier and unknown history. Professor Meiss dates the book to Paris around the years 1409–10, which makes it contemporaneous with René's birth.

The style of the miniatures belonging to the earlier campaign of embellishment may be seen in the Adoration of the Magi picture reproduced on p. 91.

This miniature introduces, as is customary, the noontide Hour of Sext (called *Midi* in the rubric on the previous page). It is painted in the tradition of the courtly International style of the early fifteenth century which reached its climax in the work of the Limbourg brothers. The bedside chair adds a domestic note, while the stable for once seems to be a proper brick-built construction.

KING RENÉ'S LONDON HOURS was embellished, twenty years or more before he acquired it in unknown circumstances, by two anonymous artists who appear almost always to have worked together: the Egerton Master, a French miniaturist who takes his name from this manuscript (formerly in the Egerton Collection), and the Boucicaut Master (*see* pp. 70–73).[1] No reason for their collaboration is known. The late Dr Rosy Schilling, who christened the Egerton Master, surmised that the partnership could perhaps be explained by workshop practices current in Paris in the early fifteenth century, about which very little is known. The two artists may have been neighbours or partners, both of them under contract to one of the major purveyors or 'publishers' of manuscript books. That the partnership, however organized, was a long-term and successful arrangement is indicated by the curious fact that few manuscripts are known which are wholly the work of either the Boucicaut or the Egerton Master, though their degree of participation varies with different examples. In this Book of Hours the Egerton Master has the dominant role. The large miniatures are all from his hand or executed under his direction. Of the hundred or more smaller miniatures about twenty are from the Boucicaut workshop.

No evidence survives to identify the first owner of this Book of Hours, but a connection with the Valois court is indicated by references in the Calendar, Litany and Suffrages to the relics kept in the Sainte-Chapelle in Paris. A liturgical purpose is further suggested by two facts. The Hours of the Cross and of the Holy Spirit have an Office for every day of the week, while the Suffrages contain the astonishing number of ninety-nine saints and feasts. They are moreover arranged in liturgical sequence, beginning with St Andrew on the eve of Advent and continuing according to the

Church's year. It has been deduced from this evidence that the *Livre d'Heures de la Sainte-Chapelle*, as it is sometimes called, may originally have been made for use in the chapel royal in Paris; from the start it was certainly a *manuscrit de luxe*.

Its principal interest for us, however, is supplied by five extraordinary miniatures which René caused to be added after the book came into his possession. They date probably from the time of his imprisonment at Dijon and concern matters so personal to René that they must have been painted by somebody with intimate knowledge of his circumstances.[2] There is space here only for the briefest summary of these challenging miniatures: 1) a full-page heraldic achievement (f.4v), aptly described by Dr Pächt as a *nature morte héraldique*, which faces 2), a view of Jerusalem showing the courtyard and Church of the Holy Sepulchre with the Dome of the Rock beyond (f.5); 3) *le-roi-mort* already described (f.53); 4), the Miraculous Host of Dijon, a relic destroyed in the French Revolution, shown here supported by two angels painted in a markedly Van Eyckian manner (f.110); and 5), the Three Knights offering the Waters of Jerusalem to King David while in exile in Babylon (f.139). The latter unusual subject, taken from the *Speculum humanae salvationis*, can allude only to René's recent inheritance of the titular Crown of Jerusalem; like David in exile, the King in prison cannot assume possession of his kingdom.

These five miniatures have been succinctly described by Dr Pächt as a 'pictorial autobiography' of René's political career. Whoever painted them knew the King's state of mind and most pressing thoughts at a crucial moment in his life. Pächt sees the miniatures as an early work of the unidentified artist known as the Master of King René, who later illustrated the *Livre du cueur d'amours espris* now in Vienna. This artist was deeply influenced by Jan van Eyck's style. It is difficult to believe that René himself could have produced such accomplished paintings, even if, as seems likely, he received tuition of some kind in the graphic arts. Possibly, however, this dilettante royal 'Sunday painter' (Grete Ring) may have attained sufficient skill in drawing, an accomplishment most people can acquire, to make rough sketches for the extra pages in his Book of Hours which his artist worked up into finished pictures. This is supposition but restores to René a participatory role in the embellishment of this and other manuscripts without crediting him with direct authorship.

One artist in René's entourage, Barthélemy Deick, was in constant attendance upon him from 1447 to 1472, frequently accompanying the King and his second wife Jeanne de Laval on their journeys between Anjou and Provence. His name is spelt in documents in almost as many ways as Shakespeare's – de Cler, der Clers, Deick, d'Ecle, d'Eilz, d'Eyck. Did the legend of René's meeting with Jan van Eyck originate in a confusion between Jan and Barthélemy van Eyck? The authorship of the five added miniatures in the London Book of Hours may never be known for certain. But if the anonymous Master of King René was not the King himself, Barthélemy Deick becomes the most likely candidate, the faithful interpretor of the King's exalted ideas, an inseparable, discreet companion and the effective partner, perhaps, in joint artistic enterprises.

The importance René's 'prison' Book of Hours assumed for him is seen not only in the five famous miniatures but also in textual additions to the book. Between the Hours of Matins and Lauds a poignant prayer has been written on a largely blank page. This is truly a *cri de coeur*. In it René invokes God to protect him, an unworthy sinner (*peccatori famulo tuo*) from assaults and illusions of demons during the night as well as from 'all pollution of mind and body' (*ab omni pollutione mentis et corporis*), preserving him always in safety that he may praise God. It is a pathetic, very human prayer suggesting that René, a young man aged twenty-two suddenly parted from his wife and shut up in a tower, was suffering intense loneliness. On ff.43v–44 is another addition, a curious version of the *Commendatio animae* in which René compiles a catalogue of Biblical figures who escaped from perils similar to his – Elias from the beasts, Susanna from false accusation, Jonah from the whale, Peter from prison, Paul from dungeon, the three boys from the fiery furnace – concluding with the anguished plea: 'Free René from all straits and confinements. Free René': *Libera Renatu[m] de omnibus angustiis. Libera me Renatum*. These heartfelt cries bring René to life as vividly as his portraits.

Domine labia mea aperies.
Et os meum annunciabit laude
tuam.
Deus in adiutorium meum
intende

Hic incipit tercia beate marie
Deus in adiutorium meum intende.
Domine ad adiuvandum me
festina.
Gloria patri

The Hours of Philip the Bold, Duke of Burgundy

Use of Paris. France, Paris, *c.* 1370.
25.3 × 17.7 cm (10 × 7 in), 275ff. Calendar illustrations and 11 large miniatures with ivy-leaf borders. Historiated initials.
Fitzwilliam Museum, Cambridge, ms. 3-1954

94 **Annunciation** f.13v
95 **Angel and shepherds** f.199

THE FIRST OF THE FOUR Valois Dukes of Burgundy was Philip the Bold (*le Hardi*), brother of Charles V of France. He was an ambitious prince who held the fief from 1363 to 1404; it was inherited by three generations of his direct descendants, all of whom have left Books of Hours which are illustrated in this book. Stylistic features establish that his Book of Hours was made in Paris around the year 1370, a few years after he became Duke of Burgundy.[1] His ownership is confirmed by both heraldic and documentary evidence, though on the Annunciation page from Matins reproduced here (p. 94) the heraldry has been almost totally obliterated. A shield with traces of the blue and red Burgundian colours and the outline drawing of two supporting lions can still just be seen. The little figure kneeling beneath a gold curtain in front of a wall-hanging decorated with fleurs-de-lys in the initial *D* above, *Domine labia mea aperies*, may be identified as Philip himself. He is gazing upwards at the Virgin who appears in the miniature standing under a portico in a typical Gothic pose in front of a similarly patterned curtain. The Archangel Gabriel, making his entrance as usual from the left, points with a dramatic gesture towards God the Father and angels in the sky.

The miniatures in Philip's prayerbook are by two artists. The first, who painted the Calendar scenes and all but one of the eleven large miniatures, was identified by the late Eric Millar as the *Maître aux Boquetaux*, or at least a close follower in this artist's extensive circle. The second artist comes from the same workshop but is less skilful. The *Maître aux Boquetaux* takes his name from the clumps of parasol-like trees which are a distinguishing feature in his work. His miniatures are usually set in quadrilobe frames, with little scenes painted at the bottom of the page. These *bas-de-pages* are executed in a most delicate manner, with a great feeling for animals. In the margins the ivy-leaf tendrils are beginning to sprout from the bar borders, but with nothing like the luxuriant growth they reached in the following century.

In the second page here reproduced, typical examples of the Boquetaux Master's little spinneys appear in the steep landscape of the Angel and Shepherds miniature. The hockey-style clubs held by the two shepherds are their *houlettes*, implements used for gathering up stones and earth for throwing at refractory sheep when they stray too far (*see* p. 28). The dog, wearing a spiked collar to protect the flock and his masters from attack by wolves and other marauders, regards the Angel with suspicious attention.

VALOIS BURGUNDY was an historical concept rather than a geographical reality. In the south it comprised the Duchy (with the capital city of Dijon), a fief of the French Crown, and the adjoining County of Burgundy (Franche-Comté) which nominally belonged to the Holy Roman Empire. Ducal and countly Burgundy, the 'two Burgundies', formed one unit. In the north a second, less compact but even richer cluster of territories came to the Dukes by marriage, inheritance, enfeoffment, conquest and outright purchase. These included the Counties of Flanders, Artois and Hainault, the Duchies of Brabant, Limburg and Luxembourg, and in the north the rich agricultural, corn-producing lands of Holland, Zealand and Friesland. From this personal union of Burgundy and the Low Countries came the wealth of the Dukes. Their northern and southern domains were separated by the County of Champagne, which belonged to the French Crown, and the neighbouring Duchies of Bar and Lorraine, ruled after 1430 by the House of Anjou.[2]

The state in which the Dukes lived, the luxury and appointments of their court, their stupendous festivities, the fabulous art collections they amassed, their energy, ambition and political flair, awed contemporaries and continue to fascinate posterity. To them we owe such civilized habits as the use of forks at the dinner table; they were also the first food snobs since Roman times, considering wild game, venison and boar to be viands more appropriate for their high rank than ordinary butcher's meat. Politically powerful, immensely rich and endowed with cultivated tastes, their reputation is clouded for modern eyes by their blatant ambition and lack of patriotic sentiment.

That is, they lacked French patriotism; of Burgundian patriotism in the sense of dynastic presumption they had plenty, showing little hesitation in forming alliances with England, France's traditional enemy, to advance their family power. It is fair to add that economic considerations (with which this study is little concerned) explain successive Anglo-Burgundian alliances; the cloth trade in the Low Countries depended on imported English wool.

Despite their wealth and ability a fundamental anomaly bedevilled the political role of the Dukes of Burgundy. Were their ambitions best served by maintaining their position as the most powerful vassal with the requisite authority to govern France should the King be weak? Or was there a greater prize to be gained by uniting their lands outside France into a single sovereign state? It was their constant aim to establish, by dynastic rule and a centralized administration, permanent control over a vast area, that was already economically unified by the circulation of a common currency.[3] They very nearly succeeded, and it is tempting to speculate what might have happened in European history if the ancient Kingdom of Lotharingia had been successfully revived as a buffer state between France and Germany and independent of both.

Philip the Bold's prayerbook, the first in the sequence of five represented here, is connected with Paris not only artistically but also devotionally. Both miniatures and text contain references to the holy relics kept in the Sainte-Chapelle, built by St Louis and later to become a shrine of family piety and Valois mystique. On f.226 (*Mémoire de la couronne*), a young man in a pink robe, presumably Philip himself, kneels under gold curtains before an altar on which are displayed the Crown of Thorns (the relic which the chapel was built to house) and head reliquaries of a king and bishop. The connection is confirmed by the series of *Memorie* or Suffrages which begin on f.226 to the Holy Cross, the Crown of Thorns and other relics kept there. It is further emphasized by the votive Masses for the great feasts of the Church's year, beginning with that of the Virgin Mary in Advent, which occupy a sizeable proportion of the volume (ff.121–213). A similar series is found in the London Hours of René of Anjou and in the *Très Belles Heures* of the Duke of Berry. Books of Hours combined with portions of the Missal and Breviary are not uncommon in the closely related circles of the royal family; they could be used both for private devotion and liturgically in the Sainte-Chapelle. There, in contrast with the political rivalries which increasingly divided them, the different branches of the Valois family met in dynastic and spiritual unity.

Philip the Bold's prayerbook illustrates the devotional, as well as the status-symbolic and artistic, aspect of Books of Hours. On the page showing the Sainte-Chapelle relics, and on other adjoining leaves, impressions survive of religious medals and pilgrims' badges formerly sewn into the margins. These badges were souvenirs brought back by travellers from famous shrines. Made in base metals (a few precious-metal examples survive), they served not only as tokens of piety but to establish a stranger's credentials as a respectable person worthy of help and interest.[4] A more common practice was to substitute painted for real badges, as seen in the anonymous Soane Hours (pp. 150–53).

The Cambridge prayerbook is very similar in style and physical make-up to two other Books of Hours made for Philip the Bold and now in the Bibliothèque Royale, Brussels (ms. 10392 and 11035-7).[5] These three books appear to have been companion volumes with complementary texts, since there is no duplication of the contents of the Fitzwilliam manuscript. Ms. 11035-7 carries evidence, like the Fitzwilliam book, of religious devotions of a special kind. Two pictures of St Veronica holding up a cloth with the image of the Holy Face, and a beautiful crowned Madonna with Child on a crescent moon, have been added.[6] The latter picture shows signs of much fingering and kissing, an indication that the picture was venerated like an icon when the text on the facing page was read by the owner.

It is not easy to imagine the youthful hero of the Battle of Poitiers, the founder of the Burgundian state, later to be described by the poetess Christine de Pisan as 'a man of dark complexion, and ugly', kissing his Book of Hours. This able politician, intent on manipulating the affairs of the French Crown in his own interests, found time to hear Mass on most days and took his Book of Hours, rosary and portable reliquary with him wherever he travelled. By the annual gift of a new dress for the Virgin's statue in the cathedral at Tournai he popularized the custom, followed to this day in Belgian churches, of adorning wooden statues of the Madonna with festive robes on great occasions.[7]

The Hours of John the Fearless, Duke of Burgundy

Use of Rome. Flanders, probably Ghent, 1406–15. 13.8 × 20.1 cm ($5\frac{3}{8} \times 7\frac{7}{8}$ in), 252ff. 12 Calendar illustrations, 28 large miniatures with ivy-leaf and acanthus rectilinear borders. *Bibliothèque Nationale, Paris, ms. lat. nouv. acq. 3055*

98 **St Andrew** f.172v
99 **Pentecost** f.28v

John the Fearless succeeded his father Philip the Bold as Duke of Burgundy in 1404 and was murdered by the Dauphin's supporters on the bridge at Montereau in 1419.[1] His ownership of this Book of Hours is indicated by the presence of a small shield of the Burgundian arms which appears beneath the feet of St Andrew in the miniature reproduced first (p. 98).[2] St Andrew was the patron saint of Burgundy, and is here shown surrounded by Burgundian emblems. The carpenter's plane and mason's level flanking the saint (here nailed to his cross, not tied as is more usual) seem odd emblems for a great prince until we remember the circumstances in which they were adopted. During the period of bitter rivalry between the Dukes of Orleans and Burgundy to gain control of the ailing King Charles VI, and thereby the government of France, Louis of Orleans had adopted as his emblem a knobbly club, to announce his aggressive intentions, together with the motto *Je l'Enuie*, an expression taken from the game of dice and meaning 'I defy you.' John of Burgundy retorted with the carpenter's plane as a threat that he would shave off the knobs from the Orleans stick, the mason's level to humble and debase his rival and the Flemish motto *Ich houd* ('I hold').[3] Great importance was attached in this age to personal badges and mottoes, childish as we may think some of them to be. John the Fearless was so fond of the carpenter's plane that he wore it embroidered on his robes and ordered little models in gold and silver complete with gilt wood shavings as presents which he gave to his courtiers and servants, rich gifts indeed. In the St Andrew miniature the blue diapered background is filled with the same motif.

The second miniature contains a personal allusion of a different kind. The Pentecost scene (p. 99) is surrounded by a narrow blank frame, perhaps intentionally left empty of the scroll border design with little sunbursts found in the St Andrew miniature; so that at the bottom it might appear as sky behind the armed knight standing in a boat drawn by a swan. What is Lohengrin, son of Parsifal, doing in a Book of Hours? Where is his bride Elsa of Brabant? The answer lies close at hand in John the Fearless's own family.

In October 1406 his daughter Marie was married to Adolph II de La Marck, Count of Cleves. The rulers of Cleves claimed descent from the legendary Knight of the Swan, a hero of the romances of chivalry who appears in German tradition as Lohengrin. Since Marie was a child aged twelve at the time of her marriage to a husband already in his thirties who had lately buried his first wife, the appearance of the Swan Knight in her father's prayerbook may have been intended not only as a polite allusion to her future husband but also as a picture to delight a little girl. Because of dowry difficulties Marie remained at the Burgundian Court until 1415, her nuptials long delayed.[4] The significance of the Swan Knight helps to date the manuscript to some time after 1406, perhaps even to 1415–16 when John the Fearless finally delivered his daughter to the Count of Cleves.

These two miniatures come from a workshop at Ghent or Malines which produced a number of Books of Hours, described by Dorothy Miner as 'all characterized by abundant and vigorous foliage ornament, amusing drolleries and a competent, decorative painting style, still essentially Gothic'.[5]

John the Fearless's sinister reputation stems from the ruthless methods he adopted in furthering his cardinal ambition – the aggrandizement of himself and Burgundy.[6] A small, tight-lipped, cunning, touchy man without scruples, he arranged in an impulsive moment the murder of his rival, the frivolous, insouciant Duke of Orleans. Louis of Orleans was said to have made amorous advances to John's wife (as well as to the Queen); sexual jealousy may thus have been a component in John's hatred for his handsome cousin. John appears in a more attractive, if largely imaginary, role as peace-maker in the scene in Shakespeare's *Henry V* where the Duke of Burgundy brings the Kings of France and England together after the Battle of Agincourt. In a magnificent speech describing the unhappy state of France, where 'all her husbandry doth lie in heaps, Corrupting in its own fertility', the Duke asks the contending kings why

naked, poor and mangled Peace,
Dear nurse of arts, plenties and joyful births,
Should not in this best garden of the world,
Our fertile France, put up her lovely face.

Shakespeare condenses historical events for maximum effect, and wisely evades the real situation: the Duke of Burgundy's treacherous and simultaneous intrigues with Henry V of England, Charles VI of France and the young Dauphin, all of whom he sought to manipulate in his own interests.

Despite his absorption in politics and conspiracies John the Fearless found time and inclination to patronize music, the arts and books. His finest manuscript was the Breviary made for himself and his wife, Margaret of Bavaria (British Library, Harley 2897 and Add. ms. 35311), which he had with him at the time of his death. His Book of Hours is a relatively modest specimen comprising the usual elements, with Parisian and Flemish saints given equal emphasis in the Calendar. The Flemish element, however, predominates in the Litany. (John the Fearless was more interested in Flanders than his father had been.) Supporting the universal saints is an impressive muster of local saints – Amand of Maestricht; Bavon of Ghent; Wulfran, Apostle of Frisia; Josse of Ponthieu; Piat of Tournai; Eloy of Noyon; Gertrude and Aldegunde of Nivelles; the exotic-sounding Pharailde of Brabant and several more.

The Suffrages are remarkable for unusually long invocations to SS. Christopher and Leonard. These give the first clues to ownership, which the Burgundian heraldry in the St Andrew miniature confirms. The presence of St Leonard in a Book of Hours may imply a captivity endured at some time by the owner. After the defeat of the French Crusading army at Nicopolis in Hungary in 1397, John of Burgundy (then Count of Nevers) was taken prisoner by the Sultan Bajazet together with his companions Guy de La Trémoille and Marshal Jean de Boucicaut (*see* pp. 70–73). John's nickname alluded to his bravery during this disastrous crusade. All three companions in arms escaped with their lives by paying large ransoms. John the Fearless and Marshal de Boucicaut both gave prominence in their Books of Hours to St Leonard, patron of prisoners. St Christopher provided a more general, comprehensive insurance against life's hazards. A daily glimpse through a church door of his picture painted on the opposite wall was said to preserve the viewer from sudden death.

John the Fearless's most notorious political act was the murder, already mentioned, of his cousin and rival Louis, Duke of Orleans, in a Paris street on a November evening in 1407 when the Duke was returning to his lodging after visiting the Bavarian-born Queen Isabeau, his reputed mistress. Admitting his responsibility for the crime, and even boasting that he had been tempted to it by the devil, John the Fearless employed the best legal advice of the time to support his plea that he was acting in the interests of the French Crown. The Orleans-Armagnac party never forgave him. Some twelve years later he himself was murdered by partisans of the Dauphin on the bridge at Montereau, where he had unwisely come to consult with the heir to the throne about ways of ending the civil war in Paris between the Armagnacs and Burgundians. Already, in the second generation of the Valois Dukes of Burgundy, the irreconcilable conflict between their pretensions of being simultaneously loyal French princes and independent rulers of an expanding state outside France was taking its toll.

Heure de nonne

Deus in adiutorium me-
um intende Dn̄e ad ad-
iuuandum me festina
Gloria patri Sicut
Veni creator spiritus mentes
tuorum visita imple superna

312

Heure de midi

Deus in adiutorium meum intende Domine ad adiuvandum me festina. Gloria

Veni creator spiritus mentes tuorum visita imple superna gratia que tu creasti pectora Me

The Hours of Philip the Good, Duke of Burgundy

Use of Rome. Flanders, Audenarde, 1454–55.
27 × 19 cm ($10\frac{5}{8} \times 7\frac{1}{2}$ in), 374ff. 165 miniatures.
Koninklijke Bibliotheek, The Hague, ms. 76.f.2

102 **Adoration of the Magi** f.141v
103 **Presentation in the Temple** f.143v

AT LEAST TWO Books of Hours survive which belonged to Philip the Good, third Valois Duke of Burgundy; the first in the Bibliothèque Nationale, Paris (ms. lat. 10538), the second the Hague Book of Hours considered here. In size and bulk the latter approaches the *Très Riches Heures* of the Duke of Berry (*see* pp. 63–69). Containing, besides the Hours of the Virgin and other customary texts, an unusual quantity of extra prayers in Latin and French as well as a substantial portion of the Breviary, the book must have been specially commissioned and was probably not completed in a single campaign.[1]

Before looking at the miniatures here reproduced the script should be noted, for it is characteristic of books produced for Philip the Good. Known to palaeographers as *bastarda* (the *bâtarde bourguignonne*), it represents a hybridization (hence the name) of formal Gothic bookhands with the cursive writing used for everyday purposes. The slanted letter forms with looped ascenders and pointed descenders, together with the space left between words, made it an easy hand to read, unlike some of the more angular Gothic scripts. Aesthetically, the *bâtarde bourguignonne* may be criticized as being often out of scale with the proportions of a vellum page. Its size reduced the number of lines on the folios and necessitated the making of larger books; lengthy prose romances, chronicles and other secular works might run into more than one volume, as may have been the case with this large Book of Hours. The appearance of *bastarda* script and of texts wholly in a vernacular language in Books of Hours reflects the popular trend in devotion during the late Middle Ages. *Bastarda* was never used for the official service books of the Church, which continued to preserve the hierarchy of scripts established by monastic scribes in earlier periods.

The many extra texts included in Philip's Book of Hours explain why two scribes were employed. One was identified by Delaissé as Jean Molinet, the Duke's secretary and *varlet de chambre*. From other manuscripts he is known to have worked with Jean Le Tavernier, the artist responsible for the finest of the 165 miniatures in this Book of Hours. Le Tavernier's authorship of the miniatures is established by stylistic features and, though less certainly, by an order for payment dated 3 April 1455 in the Archives at Lille recording that the artist received payment of 75 *écus* 40 *gros* for work apparently done in this book.[2]

To these miniatures we can now turn. They are all painted in grisaille, occupying about half of the page without borders. Colour is provided by the red and blue initials with penwork in-filling and terminal extensions in the margins. The 'metallic sobriety of grisaille', as Delaissé described the technique of painting in white and black, is peculiarly suitable for book painting.[3] The pewter-grey shades suggest a sense of refined luxury appropriate to the Burgundian Court where such books were much in vogue during Duke Philip's reign.

The first miniature (p. 102) shows the Adoration of the Magi at None. Mary receives her visitors before a bed of state placed in the open air. The Three Kings have approached through a yard in which the only suggestion of a stable is the raftered tester of the bed and a lean-to shed against a wall in the background. Placing the scene in the stable-yard of a Flemish manor house gives ample space for the finely drawn and composed group. The young king on the left is dressed in the height of Burgundian fashion and stands in detached self-awareness as if modelling his costume.

The subject of the second miniature (p. 103) is the Presentation in the Temple at Sext (*Heure de Midi*). The Christ Child has been brought to the Temple by his parents, as described in the Gospel of St Luke (2:22–32); 'And when the days of her purification according to the law of Moses were accomplished, they brought him to Jerusalem, to present him to the Lord . . . And to offer a sacrifice . . . a pair of turtledoves, or two young pigeons.' Christ stands on the altar supported by the High Priest. Mary kneels before him, with the elderly Prophetess Anna holding a candle, a non-scriptural addition to the scene symbolizing Christ as the True Light. A female attendant follows with a basket containing the two doves. The turbaned man is Simeon, who had been told by the Holy Ghost that he would not die before seeing the Messiah. In the Gospel account he takes

Jesus in his arms and speaks the beautiful words of the *Nunc dimittis*: 'Lord, now lettest thou thy servant depart in peace, according to thy word: For mine eyes have seen thy Salvation.' The third man in the family group is St Joseph.

DURING THE LONG REIGN (1419–67) of the third Valois Duke of Burgundy, Philip the Good, the Duchy attained its zenith of prosperity and power.[4] In cultural matters the Duke's most enduring achievement was the expansion of the renowned Burgundian Library, founded by his two predecessors, of which the greater part survives today in the Bibliothèque Royale, Brussels. Though his personal intellectual endowment is somewhat uncertain (he seems not to have read Greek or Latin), Philip encouraged authors, scribes and illuminators to produce a constant flow of magnificently written and illuminated books. The authors appear in many miniatures offering on bended knee presentation copies of their works to the aloof, proud figure of the Duke invariably clad in ceremonious black.

His interest in books seems to have developed only in the decade following the Treaty of Arras (1435) with the English. Disengagement from active involvement with the affairs of the French monarchy, in part voluntary, in part the result of political pressures, enabled him to give more time and energy to books and art patronage on a lavish scale made possible by his great wealth. A constellation of chroniclers recorded his pomps and festivities – Jean de Wavrin, Olivier de la Marche, Georges de Chastellain, Jean Molinet. Among his illuminators were Simon Marmion, Guillaume Vrelant, Loyset Liedet, the Wavrin Master and Jean Le Tavernier. The last named was the artist responsible for some of the finest miniatures in Philip's Book of Hours, two of which are here reproduced. Described in documents as *peintre historieur et enlumineur*, Le Tavernier is recorded at Tournai in 1435, in Bruges in 1450, and finally in his birthplace at Audenarde. There he settled, once his reputation was made, to work for Philip the Good from 1454 until sometime after 1460. This patronage made him one of the most important and influential of Flemish illuminators. He specialized in grisaille, a technique of monochrome painting in shades of grey, to which light touches of colouring for faces, hands and drapery were sometimes added. This was a style which had been used with great effect by Jean Pucelle in the first half of the fourteenth century (*see* p. 42), but no other illuminator made such a speciality of the technique as did Jean Le Tavernier.

In style and magnificence the Burgundian Court of Philip the Good surpassed that of the French King. This display of conspicuous consumption served a political purpose in providing proof of the Duke's wealth and position both to his subjects and to the world at large. A similar motive lay behind the inauguration of the Order of the Golden Fleece during the festivities marking his third marriage, to Isabella of Portugal in January 1429. The name chosen for the new knightly order was a subtle allusion both to the staple wool trade of the Low Countries and to the classical myth of Jason's search for the Golden Fleece, though the knights were expected to emulate the virtues of Gideon (whose miraculous fleece attracted heavenly dew, prefiguring the Annunciation: Judges 6:37–40) rather than Jason's treacherous example.

In character Philip was both sensual and pious, combining these seemingly opposite temperaments in a manner not uncommon in his age. He appears in René of Anjou's *Livre du cueur d'amours espris* in the company of Hercules, Paris, Mark Antony, Tristan and others, as a modern exemplar of the great lover. This reputation seems to have been well merited. Besides three wives he was credited with thirty-three mistresses and twenty-six bastards. Like Louis XIV (whom he anticipated in several respects) he believed in the convenient doctrine that 'the royal blood does not sully', though his mistresses were not seen at court like those of the *grand monarque*.

In his lifetime Philip was known as *l'Asseuré* ('the Assured'); as *le Bon* only after his death. The custom of bestowing sobriquets or nicknames on princes and rulers after their death was explained by the French historian Etienne Pasquier (d. 1615) as a posthumous prize-giving or recognition of a ruler's life-style by his contemporaries.[5] In Philip's case *le Bon* may have carried associations of happier times, before the disasters which occurred in the reign of his impetuous son and successor Charles the Rash brought ruin to the proud Burgundian state. His Book of Hours dates from his autumnal days, the ownership attested by the Duke's portrait and motto *Aultre naray* ('I will take no other'), referring to his third wife, which appear on several pages.

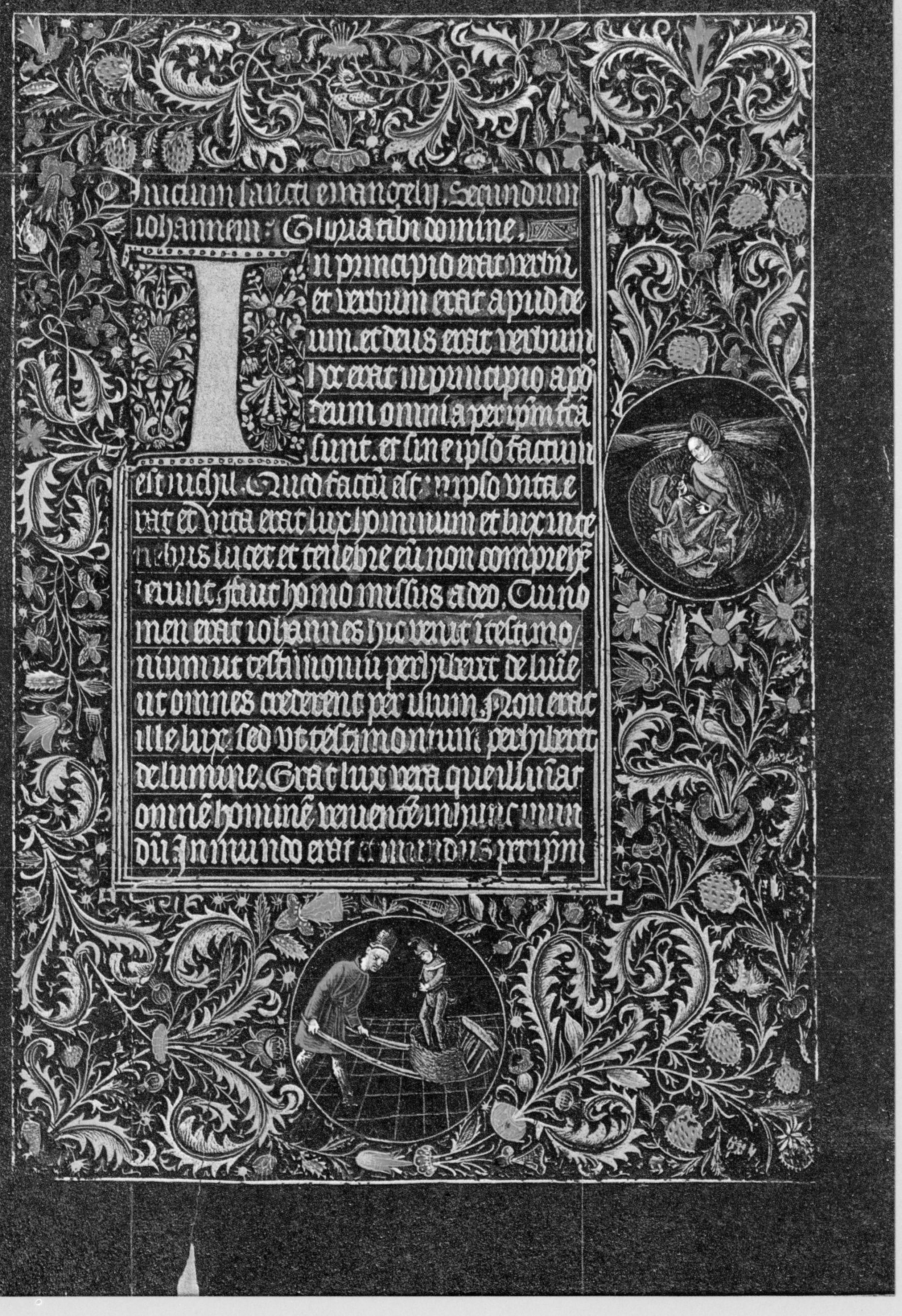

Inicium sancti euangelij. Secundum
iohannem: Gloria tibi domine.
In principio erat verbũ
et verbum erat apud de
um. et deus erat verbum
hoc erat in principio apd
deum omnia per ipm fca
sunt. et sine ipso factum
est nichil. Quod factũ est in ipso vita e
rat et vita erat lux hominum et lux in te
nebris lucet et tenebre eũ non comprehẽ
derunt. Fuit homo missus a deo. Cui no
men erat iohannes. hic venit i testimo
nium ut testimoniũ perhiberet de lu[m]ie
ut omnes crederent per illum. Non erat
ille lux sed vt testimonium perhiberet
de lumine. Erat lux vera que illuīat
omnẽ hominẽ venientẽ in hunc mun
dũ. In mundo erat et mundus per ipm

The Black Hours of Charles the Rash, Duke of Burgundy

Use of Rome (?). Flanders, Bruges, *c.* 1466–76.
25 × 18 cm ($9\frac{7}{8}$ × $7\frac{1}{8}$ in), 154ff. Calendar illustrations, 14 large miniatures, historiated and decorative initials, richly decorated borders with medallions.
Österreichische Nationalbibliothek, Vienna, Cod. 1856

106–07 **The Four Evangelists; St John in border** ff. 32v–33

The Black Hours now in Vienna represents an ultimate luxury in book decoration; it is the finest surviving example of a special category of Books of Hours which enjoyed a brief vogue at the Burgundian Court during the last years of the Duchy's existence as a powerful buffer state between Germany and France. Black or mourning Books of Hours are so called because the text is written in gold and silver letters on vellum leaves which have been stained black or purple. In the Vienna example the acid dye has damaged the vellum to such an extent that the leaves are now separately preserved between sheets of glass. Nobody can ever again handle or use the book in the manner intended when it was first made.

Only the most accomplished of artists could have overcome the limitations imposed by the black ground. Such was the anonymous Flemish artist known as the Master of Anthony of Burgundy, who illustrated this sophisticated prayerbook. The pages reproduced come from the Gospel Sequences near the beginning. The left-hand miniature shows the four Evangelists seated together in a long room with walls drawn in false perspective but giving a sense of space and recession. They are seen sharpening their quill pens or in the act of writing on their knees; their equipment is laid out on the table in the foreground. The roundels in the border show a hairy wildman riding a fantasy beast and a knight fighting a dragon. On the text page the first words of St John's Gospel, *In principio erat verbum*, 'In the beginning was the Word', begin with a large floral initial. At the side is St John on the Isle of Patmos, and at the bottom a man pushing a wheelbarrow in which a jester stands in a barrel, an illustration perhaps of a Flemish proverb. The borders on both pages have a rich, almost damascened appearance. Curling acanthus sprays like plumes on a helmet, flowers, fruits and birds stand out from the black ground in a dense pattern painted in tones of gold, silver, blue, green and cinnamon.

Charles the Rash or Bold, son of Philip the Good, reigned as the last Duke of Burgundy from 1467 to 1477.[1] He was associated with a considerable number of Books of Hours, and in particular with several 'black' or mourning examples, but his ownership of any surviving specimen of the latter type cannot be proved beyond doubt. His finest must have been the volume captured by the Swiss after the battle of Grandson in the fabulous Burgundian booty. This was described as being written in golden letters on purple vellum and bound in crimson, gold-embroidered velvet. But it is not to be found with the other booty now at Berne. In 1477 the book was offered for sale but found no buyers. Three years later the civic authorities sent it to Pope Sixtus IV as a *douceur* to secure his sanction for a third Jubilee to raise funds to complete the building of St Vincent, the cathedral church of Berne. The book appears never to have reached Rome and cannot now be found in the Vatican Library; it must be assumed to have vanished in or soon after 1480.[2]

Two black prayerbooks happily survive, both in Vienna. The first is the one considered here, usually called the *Schwarzes Gebetbuch* or, from later ownership, the Sforza Hours; the second is the Hours of Mary of Burgundy (pp. 110–11). Attempts have been made to identify each of them with a mourning Book of Hours known to have been presented to Charles the Rash in February 1466 by the Franc de Bruges, one of the Estates of Flanders, shortly after the death of his second wife Isabelle de Bourbon.[3] But the Hours of Mary of Burgundy is only partially a black prayerbook, since no more than the first thirty leaves are so stained, and from the description in the archives of the Franc de Bruges there are better grounds for believing that the present manuscript, now known as the Black Hours, is the one presented to Charles in 1466. The chief mystery about it, however, is its early if brief ownership by Galeazzo Maria Sforza, Duke of Milan 1466–76. At the beginning of the volume is a large Sforza *ex-libris*, which, though painted in a manner very similar to pages in the rest of the book, is considered to be an addition. If Charles gave the book to Galeazzo Maria as a present it did not remain long in Milan. In 1494 Galeazzo's daughter Maria Bianca married the Archduke Maximilian of Austria, ruler of the Netherlands, who had been a widower since the death in 1482 of his first wife Mary of Burgundy, the daughter of Charles the Rash. It was probably by this family route that the black prayerbook, which may once have belonged to Maximilian's father-in-law, returned to the north.[4]

These two black prayerbooks seem peculiarly appropriate for the saturnine young man who appears in the portrait by Rogier van der Weyden in the Berlin-Dahlem Museum. Intellectually he was the most gifted of the four Valois Dukes of Burgundy. He had a keen interest in music, was an excellent linguist, reading Latin easily (which his father did not) and knowing English. He worked incessantly at state affairs, again unlike Philip; his first nickname was 'the Industrious'. In marked contrast to his forebears, Charles was not a womanizer. His third marriage with Margaret of York, the 'Duchess Juno', sister of Edward IV and patroness of William Caxton, was a political match celebrated in Bruges with the greatest pomp and festivity in July 1468.

Charles was deeply religious, imposing strict rules in his court chapel. No whispering, grimaces, nods or mockery were allowed. A clerk or chaplain caught saying his private Hours when he should have been singing was fined. Egocentric, vain, proud and passionate, sometimes cruel, Charles had a withdrawn but violent temperament; his sensibilities make him appear curiously modern. Towards the end of his life a quasi-Freudian death-wish seems to have driven him as he embarked upon one rash enterprise after another until disaster overtook him outside the walls of Nancy. Here, while making a foolhardy attack on Duke René II of Lorraine, who had regained possesion of his capital from the Burgundian Duke with the help of Swiss allies, Charles the Rash was killed.

A page saw him fall from his horse beneath pike thrusts. The body was found several days later, naked in the snow and half-devoured by wolves. The doctors who examined the corpse recognized it from the fine hands and fingernails and from wounds received in former battles. Courtly Europe was shocked that the Duke of Burgundy should have been killed by soldiers of such an uncouth nation as the Swiss. But the passing of the paragon of chivalry, the mirror of princes and scourge of the French, was welcomed as a deliverance in many Flemish cities, which sought quickly to restore the local privileges which the Dukes of Burgundy had abolished in establishing their centralized state.

Charles was honourably buried in the Church of Saint-Georges at Nancy. Nearly a century later his descendant Philip II of Spain commissioned an impressive tomb for the Church of Notre-Dame in Bruges. Here the putative bones of Charles the Rash were re-interred, beneath a recumbent Mannerist effigy cast in copper, to lie beside the serenely Gothic figure of his daughter Mary. On the sides of both tombs their illustrious Valois, Bourbon, Portuguese and Plantagenet descents are recorded by emblazoned shields set in the gilt branches of a spreading family-tree.

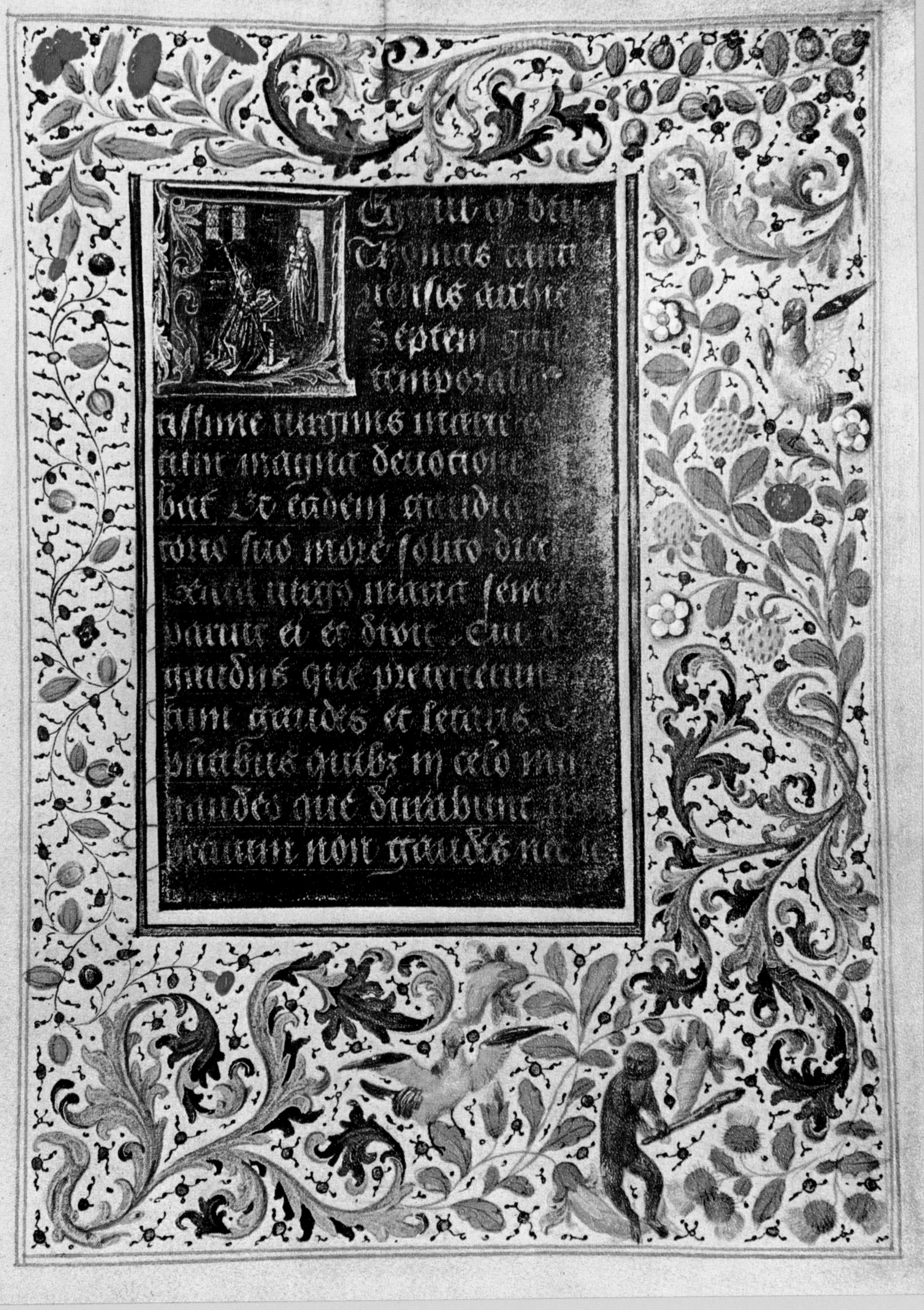

The Hours of Mary of Burgundy

Use of Rome. Flanders, *c.* 1477. 22.5 × 15 cm ($8\frac{7}{8} \times 5\frac{7}{8}$ in), 187ff. 24 calendar illustrations, 20 full-page miniatures, 32 small miniatures, historiated initials.
Österreichische Nationalbibliothek, Vienna, Cod. 1857

110–11 **Mary in church; St Thomas of Canterbury in initial** f. 14v.–15

THE FULL-PAGE MINIATURE shows a lady sitting at an open casement window which looks into the choir of a Gothic church. She is reading her Book of Hours with a pet dog on her lap and a veil, a gold chain with jewelled pendant, carnations and a vase of irises disposed along the sill beside her. Below the vase is a gold brocaded purse. The lady, we assume, is Mary of Burgundy, soon after the death of her father Charles the Rash in battle in 1477; but she is not dressed in mourning. She wears a robe of gold-brown velvet with steeple headdress and veil. Her prayerbook she holds with delicate care, one hand wrapped in the green *chemisette* binding, the other carefully marking with a finger the page at which the book is open. The prayer she is reading could be the popular *Obsecro te* ('I beseech thee') which is found in nearly every Book of Hours. The book is open at a page on which an initial O can be clearly seen.

In the church below is a group which could illustrate the prayer. In front of an altar with a gold reredos sits a blue-gowned Madonna with Child. Four angels holding candles sit at the corners of the carpet on which the chair is placed. To the left a lady wearing a gold-brocaded dress (perhaps Mary of Burgundy differently attired), and attended by three companions, kneels before the Virgin, a red prayerbook (?) tucked under her arm. On the right a young man in a red cope is swinging a censer. He has sometimes been identified as Mary's husband, Archduke Maximilian of Austria, but the absence of his coat of arms or initials make it unlikely he is represented here. Two men and a dog are in the background, and more spectators seem to be watching the scene from the ambulatory around the choir. The architecture is so carefully depicted that it seems to be taken from an actual church.

The miniature carries no text, but on the facing page begins the Seven Joys of the Virgin, a prayer attributed to St Thomas à Becket of Canterbury. It is announced by an historiated initial, the opening *L* (*Legitur*) of the rubric inside which the saint appears kneeling at a reading desk before a vision of the Virgin and Child. The scene inside the gold letter frame is painted in a grisaille technique which stands out in delicate contrast against the black panel of text written in silver. The achievement of painting a postage-stamp-sized scene in grey on black testifies to the virtuosity of the Master of Mary of Burgundy, whose identity is still a matter of dispute.

It is most unusual to find a large picture of the owner in a Book of Hours opposite such a secondary text and relatively uncommon prayer as the Seven Joys. The owner normally appears as a diminutive praying figure at Matins or at the *Obsecro te*. In the church below, towards which she does not look, the *Obsecro te* is, as we have seen, represented visually in a more elaborate version than usual. It is the same theme as in the historiated initial of the text page, but with the lady replacing St Thomas à Becket.

In relegating the principal scene to the background while focusing attention on the reading lady, the artist has reversed the usual arrangement. This is an accomplished feat, both devotionally and artistically, in which two planes of vision are combined. In the foreground is a 'real' picture of the reading lady with her still-life accessories, in the background an imagined devotional repetition of the same theme.

THIS BOOK OF HOURS shares with the Hours of Mary of Guelders a common characteristic in the stylish manner in which the respective owners are depicted. Preoccupation with fashion has seldom been developed to such extravagant lengths as in the courts of France and Burgundy between about 1380 and 1500. Ladies in particular were aware that their social place could be enhanced by the possession of a finely decorated personal prayerbook; what more fitting place could be found for inserting, if not a portrait in the modern sense, an idealized representation of themselves wearing their finest clothes as they prayed before the greatest lady of all, the Virgin Mary?

No inscription or coat of arms appears in the book positively to document the owner, but a combination of circumstances makes it almost certain she is Mary of Burgundy, only child and heiress of Charles the Rash. Indeed, it is impossible now to imagine anybody else as the possessor of this dazzling prayerbook which epitomizes the courtly Burgundian style in its most rarefied form. Mary was born in 1457 and inherited all the Burgundian territories outside France in the crucial days following her father's sudden death in January 1477 on the snowy battlefield of Nancy. A few months later she married the Hapsburg Archduke Maximilian of Austria, and she died in 1482 after a riding accident at the early age of twenty-five. She left two children, a daughter Margaret and a son Philip called 'the Fair'. Philip died young like his mother, but not before he had become father to the future Emperor Charles V. Mary was thus ancestress to many Hapsburgs.

The Hours of Mary of Burgundy is a black prayerbook, at least in part. The first thirty-four leaves have the text written in gold and silver letters on black panels surrounded by coloured borders painted on the natural white ground of the vellum. Was the intention, as these black pages suggest, to provide a mourning book after her father's death, for which a precedent existed in the family in Charles the Rash's Black Hours (see preceding pages)? Mary of Burgundy's Book of Hours was not, however, completed as seemingly intended. Perhaps the rapid approach of her marriage made a mourning Book of Hours inappropriate. From f.35 onwards the text as well as the borders appears on white pages. Two small blank shields held up by angels at the bottom of f.44v may have been intended to receive the arms of Mary and her husband, but must have been added as an afterthought and never completed.

The prayerbook is a major work of the Master of Mary of Burgundy, who executed this and a second Book of Hours now at Berlin. The latter was certainly made for Mary and her husband, since it contains the coats of arms and initials of both. The anonymous artist has variously been identified with Philippe Mazerolles, Alexander Bening, Nicolas van der Goes (a brother of the more famous Hugo) and Claes or Nicolas Spierinc who is chiefly known as a scribe. Claims for the latter have been persuasively argued by Dr Antoine van Schryver in the facsimile edition published in 1969. Much of the information in these paragraphs comes from this source, though not all specialists accept the conclusions and hypotheses of this absorbing commentary, the most detailed study of Mary's prayerbook yet to appear.[1]

Dr van Schryver distinguishes two artists as responsible for the Hours of Mary of Burgundy, whom he identifies as Claes Spierinc and Liétard van Lathem. Both had been held in high esteem by Charles the Rash, for whom they jointly provided a *Petites Heures* which survives in a private collection.[2] Whoever painted the reading lady in Mary's Book of Hours was a consummate master who introduced new concepts into book painting. He was the inventor of the 'view-from-a-window' theme, as it has been called, which added the illusion of space to the unity of ensemble in the miniature. The flat surface of the vellum page becomes a window opening on to a distant view, with the border representing the frame. Elsewhere in the artist's work flowers and insects casually placed upon the frame are seen in a single perspective with the vista: striking examples are found in the Hours of Engelbert of Nassau in the Bodleian Library, Oxford (ms. Douce 219–20). The text, when it appears, is limited to a few lines written in a large script and displayed, in Dr Pächt's happy phrase, 'like little posters picturesquely mounted on the page'.[3]

This *trompe-l'œil* approach leads us away from the Gothic two-dimensional world towards a future in which artists became increasingly preoccupied with problems of light, perspective and the optically accurate delineation of objects in space. But there can be few evocations of courtly-religious life in the expiring Middle Ages more beautiful than this picture of Mary of Burgundy as a young princess sitting in her oratory above a Gothic church as she recites her Book of Hours.

Oracio beate marie.
bsecro te domina
sancta maria

Quicunques veult e
stre bien conseillie
de la chose dont il a

The Hours of Isabella Stuart, Duchess of Brittany

Use of Paris. France, Angers, *c.* 1417–18.
24.8 × 17.8 cm ($9\frac{3}{4}$ × 7 in), 234ff.
Fitzwilliam Museum, Cambridge, ms. 62

114 **Isabella before the Virgin and Child** f.20
115 **Christ as Man of Sorrows; Christ in Judgment** f.199

attenuated body and loosely draped cloak outlined against a background of blue Cherubim. Instead of judging he looks down as if about to make the descent into Hell to rescue Adam and Eve and others of the Just who have been held there in captivity.

The three coroneted shields in the border, displaying the arms of Brittany and Scotland, appear to have been superimposed upon the flowing acanthus spray decoration.

ISABELLA STUART, the second daughter of James I of Scotland, was born about 1427. She married in 1442, as his second wife, Francis I, Duke of Brittany. Her ownership of a Book of Hours produced in the same workshop as the *Grandes Heures de Rohan* secures her a place among the select company of princely bibliophiles who are remembered for their superlative prayerbooks – patrons like the Duke of Berry, Yolanda of Aragon, her son *le bon roi* René of Anjou, and Anne of Brittany.

In the first page reproduced, wearing an heraldic skirt, Isabella kneels in the lower left-hand corner as she recites the *Obsecro te* before the Virgin and Child, to whom she is presented by St Catherine. Her petition *O Mater Dei memento mei* ('Mother of God, remember me') is on a scroll which links the two groups. In the corners of the page her coat of arms appears impaling the ermine of Brittany.

The second page reproduced contains two figures of Christ in his role of Redeemer at the Resurrection of the Dead. The text below the large miniature is the introductory prayer to the Seven Requests to the Saviour – *Quiconques veult estre bien conseillié* ('Whoever will be well counselled'). Of all the miniatures in this Book of Hours this page approaches most closely to the religious pathos found in the Judgment scene which introduces the same prayer in the *Grandes Heures de Rohan* (p. 83). But though the smaller picture in the border, of Christ seated on a rainbow, is reminiscent of the towering figure in the *Grandes Heures*, he here holds no sword and rests his feet upon the orb of the world instead of holding it. Compassion rather than judgment is conveyed by the inclined head and shoulders and in the upraised hands. The larger picture is a *Christ en douleur*, the Man of Sorrows, who contemplates with pity the dead rising from their graves. He stands with one foot upon an open tomb, his

BRITTANY, the ancient Armorica, dolmen-haunted, exposed to the buffetings of Atlantic gales, and populated by as many saints as Cornwall or Bavaria, has preserved through the centuries a separate identity not only of landscape but of ethnography, folk customs, institutions and art. Its Dukes asserted that their ancestors had ruled before Clovis became the first Christian King of France in the fifth century, and that they were subject only to the Pope. In the fifteenth century they minted their own money and claimed to rule by the Grace of God, a boast which neither Charles VII nor his crafty son Louis XI could accept from a vassal. Only the 'Most Christian' Kings of France, their rivals, the 'Most Catholic' Kings of Spain, and the English sovereigns, made such claims.[1]

Despite the evocative legends of St Ursula and Tristram and Iseult, Breton history is little known to modern readers. After Norman and Plantagenet rule the Duchy was contested by the rival families of Dreux, Penthièvre and Montfort in a series of tedious succession wars. By the late fourteenth century the Montforts emerged victorious, and it is with this family that we are concerned here. Eclipsed in fame by Burgundy and Anjou, their courts less brilliant, their prosperity dependent more on shipping and piracy than on such industries as brought great wealth to the Dukes of Burgundy through their inheritance of the Low Countries, the last Breton Dukes followed an ambivalent policy of hostility to, and short-lived rapprochements with, the French Crown, never certain whether their interests might not be better served by an English alliance.

Each of the fifteenth-century Dukes and Duchesses was a distinct personality; through their Books of Hours, of which several superb specimens exist today, they may be brought to life again in an unfamiliar context. These manuscripts are linked historically rather than artistically with

Brittany. The Duchy was an economic backwater and consequently produced no local school of illumination. The Dukes and Duchesses obtained their Books of Hours from Paris or Angers.

The Hours of Isabella Stuart is a product of the Rohan Master's workshop which supplied books to the court of Anjou (*see* pp. 82–101). The poignant figure of *Christ en douleur* (f.199, illustrated on p. 115), and two superb miniatures of the Madonna, standing in a Gothic hall (f.144v) and supported on a crescent moon between St Peter and St Paul (f.136v), are generally considered to be by the Rohan Master himself.[2] On many other pages his influence can be discerned, not least in the little golden clouds which so often fill the blue skygrounds of the miniatures with charming decorative effect.

The late Dr M. R. James, in a detailed catalogue description, counted no less than 528 separate miniatures in this manuscript, a staggering total accounted for by the fact that on almost every page a small oblong miniature is inserted in the vine-leaf decoration of the borders.[3] Within these little rectangles four distinct series of illustrations unfold: the Apocalypse of St John, followed by the *Three Pilgrimages*, a devotional work written about 1350 by Guillaume de Deguilleville, a monk of Chaarlis, comprising the separate pilgrimages of Jesus Christ, of Man's Life, and of Man's Soul. Thus, while turning the pages of this Book of Hours, two parallel themes occupy the eye and mind, both devotional. There is here none of the disparity of subject matter so often found in manuscripts of the thirteenth and fourteenth centuries, such as the Taymouth Hours, where drolleries and secular scenes of folklore or hunting in the margins accompany miniatures depicting the most solemn or tragic moments in the Christian story.

Isabella Stuart, Duchess of Brittany, though not the first, was certainly an early owner of the book.[4] Her coat of arms, 'or, a lion rampant gules within a tressure flory counter-flory', appears on many pages, usually impaling the ermine coat of Brittany. These Scottish arms seem, however, to have been added after the manuscript was finished. If it was not made for Isabella Stuart, who then was the first owner? The most likely candidate is her predecessor, the first wife of Francis I of Brittany. This was Yolande of Anjou, the sister of King René, and a daughter of the Duchess Yolanda, Queen of Sicily, who patronized the Rohan Master and probably commissioned the *Grandes Heures de Rohan*. It has been suggested that the book was presented to the younger Yolande by her mother when she married Francis in 1431. After her death in July 1440, at twenty-eight, Yolande's Book of Hours may have passed to Isabella Stuart.

Isabella had the reputation of being a devout princess, whose character comes vividly to life in a conversation preserved in contemporary records. While the negotiations for her marriage were going forward, her future father-in-law, Duke John V of Brittany, was much heartened by hearing his ambassadors report that she was not clever in conversation and seemed rather simple (*elle n'a pas grand discours en ses propos et semble assez simple*). 'Return to Scotland at once and bring her back with you,' was the Duke's prompt reply. He did not like blue-stockings (an expression not then current), and added that he considered a woman clever enough when she knew the difference between her own chemise and her husband's doublet – a *bon mot* later borrowed by Molière in *Les Femmes savantes* (act 2, scene 7).[5]

After her husband's death in 1450, Isabella's brother, now James II of Scotland, sent an embassy led by the Bishop of Galloway to negotiate for her return. The King complained that his sister was being badly treated by her brother-in-law, the new Duke Peter II. To this Isabella made a spirited reply, affirming that she was happy in Brittany and had no wish to return to Scotland. She added that she was feeble, ill and frightened of the sea. Her ill-health, if genuine, did not prevent her from living a further forty years or more. Defeated in his plans for marryng her to a Scottish nobleman, the King seems to have made no further attempt to persuade his sister to return home.

Isabella might well have strengthened her case for remaining in Brittany, although we do not know that she did, by affirming that she was happy to remain in the country of her ancestors. The first recorded Stuarts had been seneschals or stewards (hence their surname) in the eleventh century to the Counts of Dol in Brittany before settling in England where an Alain Stuart obtained favour and lands from Henry I. His son Walter went to Scotland and was appointed hereditary High Steward (or *Dapifer*) by King David I. His descendants married wisely and increasingly well, until another Walter became husband of Robert Bruce's daughter Marjorie. Their son succeeded as Robert II of Scotland in 1371, the first royal Stuart and great-grandfather of Isabella.

Concede nobis misericors
deus que tibi placita sut
ardenter concupiscere pru

De sancto michaele archangelo an.
Michael archangele veni in ad
iutorium populi. V In
conspectu angelorum

The Hours of Peter II, Duke of Brittany

Use of Nantes. France, Paris, completed 1455–57. 19 × 13 cm ($7\frac{1}{2} \times 5\frac{1}{4}$ in), 177ff. 50 miniatures, vignettes in borders.
Bibliothèque Nationale, Paris, ms. lat. 1159

118 **Peter II in prayer** f.27v
119 **St Michael; Mont Saint-Michel** f.160v

PETER II WAS DUKE of Brittany during the final period of the Hundred Years War, in which he played an important part in events which led to the final expulsion of the English from every corner of France except Calais.

On the first page reproduced he appears in full ducal attire, with coronet and red cloak lined and trimmed with ermine, kneeling beneath a canopy of estate. On the *prie-dieu* before him is a Book of Hours, closed. Instead of reading from it he gazes upward at a vision of God the Father who blesses him from within a circle of Cherubim. As in his sister-in-law Isabella Stuart's Book of Hours, banners of the Breton ermine coat of arms supported by angels are prominent in the border. The artist has given further emphasis to what seems intended to be an official portrait by adding a complete heraldic achievement with lion and griffin supporters, tournament shield, helmet, mantling and lion crest.

This portrait-page, for all its heraldic panache, comes in a sequence of prayers inserted before the Hours of the Virgin humbly invoking divine grace and acknowledging favours received. In one of these prayers, written in French, Peter gives thanks to God for bestowing on him the Duchy of Brittany, of which he is not worthy. He concludes with a supplication that God's grace may help him to rule for the salvation of his soul and the benefit of his people (*humblement vous supplie et requiers quil vous plaise me donner grace de my gouverner a vostres gloire et honneur, et au prouffit et sauvement de mon âme et au bien publique de toute la duchie et habitans en icelle. Amen*). It is probable that this fine prayer was composed by the Duke himself; it indicates Peter II's devout and simple nature.

The second page comes from the Suffrages and shows St Michael getting the better of the devil. Together with St George, the Archangel Michael was one of the major 'warrior saints', a role deriving from a passage in the Apocalypse: 'And there was war in Heaven: Michael and his angels fought against the dragon' (Revelation 12:7). The principal interest of the page, however, is topographical. In the bottom left corner is a charming view of Mont Saint-Michel with pilgrims arriving on foot, on horseback and in a large-wheeled cart of a type still used at low tide for crossing the sand. On this holy rock rising out of a sea-girt sandy peninsula in Normandy a chapel-crypt was built in AD 708 and dedicated to the Archangel following his appearance there to Authbert, Bishop of Avranches. St Michael made several memorable appearances in the Dark Ages. The first was in AD 492 in a grotto on Monte Gargano in Apulia, a setting repeated in the Normandy shrine. Another occasion was in AD 590 during the plague which afflicted Rome in the first year of the Papacy of St Gregory the Great (*see* pp. 66, 67, 151).

As a centre of pilgrimage, learning and book illumination Mont Saint-Michel was already famous in Carolingian and Norman times. Its significance for Peter II and his contemporaries was primarily as a symbol of resistance to the English. The fortress abbey held out against attack by sea and land, an event as miraculous as Joan of Arc's raising of the siege of Orleans. For Peter II, who had recaptured the Norman town of Fougères from the English in 1449, a picture of this symbolic stronghold was peculiarly appropriate in his Book of Hours.

THIS BOOK OF HOURS owes its special interest to several prayers and memoranda, all written in French, which have been added mainly in the Calendar and at the end.[1] In one of these memoranda we are told that *Monseigneur le duc* does not eat meat on St Stephen's Day (immediately following Christmas) nor on the Vigil of St Sebastian, while on Good Friday and on the Vigil of Our Lady he takes only bread and spiced water unless he be ill. This is followed by another note recording that he was born on 7 July 1418 and his Duchess on 9 May, St Nicholas' Day, 1427. On the last page (f.177v) is a warning that the Book of Hours belongs to the Duke but whoever finds and returns it will have a reward (*Cestes heures son au duc; qui les trouvera, si les renge, et il aura bonnes trouvailles*).

Peter de Montfort was second son of John V of Brittany and brother of Francis I, whom he succeeded as Duke in 1450. Isabella Stuart was thus his sister-in-law. The two main events of his brief reign (1450–57) were the ending of the Hundred Years War and the canonization of St Vincent Ferrer. To both these events allusion is made, by implication, in his Book of Hours. The memorandum about fasting on St Stephen's Day, already mentioned, specifically states that the vow was made at the siege of Fougères. This is of interest, for Peter's presence there in 1449 (when his brother Duke Francis I was still living) is a known fact. His personality becomes better defined when we know the circumstances of his vow.

A premeditated surprise attack by the English in March 1449 on the important fortified town of Fougères, on the Breton-Norman frontier, broke the official peace which had existed since 1444 between England, France and Brittany. Before departing to join the French in Normandy Francis I appointed his brother Peter Lieutenant-General of the Duchy and charged him with the recovery of the city. At the siege Peter seems to have acquitted himself well. He personally supervised the *bastilles fortes*, great wooden towers filled with archers and artillery, which were moved against the walls. Though handicapped by rain and disease, the Breton soldiers finally entered the much damaged town (where the inhabitants had been subjected to odious cruelties by the English) on 4 November 1449. Nearly 500 years later Fougères received another battering during the Allied invasion of Normandy in 1944, but the great castle, one of the most magnificent in western Europe, with its complicated system of water defences, great towers built to resist artillery, and legendary associations with Melusine and the Lusignan family, still stands.

Such was the background to the vow recorded in Peter II's Book of Hours. His recapture of Fougères was the opening campaign of the war which drove the English not only from Normandy but right out of France. A few years later on 17 July 1453 their valiant leader Talbot was killed in Guienne at the Battle of Châtillon. When Bordeaux capitulated the following October the English thenceforth had no foothold in France, except at Calais, which they retained only because it was surrounded by Burgundian territory.

Nobody, of course, knew at the time that the victory at Châtillon marked the end of the Hundred Years War. Peter was more likely to have been concerned with the final stages in the canonization of St Vincent Ferrer. This hypnotic Dominican preacher, who in open-air assemblies swayed vast crowds with remorseless reminders of the Last Judgment, was born in Valencia in 1350 and died at Vannes in Brittany in 1419, whither he had been summoned two years earlier by Duke John V. He is said to have spoken always in a Catalan dialect, but, like the Apostles after Pentecost, had the power through some personal magnetism of making himself understood wherever he went. His eloquence rivalled that of St Dominic himself, or even St Thomas Aquinas, though the printed Latin versions of his sermons which appeared many years later give only an occasional whiff of his compelling imagery.

Despite the preaching, eloquence, evangelization and miracles, it needed determined efforts by three Dukes of Brittany – John V, Francis I and Peter II – to secure Vincent Ferrer's canonization. He became an official saint of the Church on 29 June 1455. On 5 April of the following year, the thirty-seventh anniversary of his death, a great ceremony was held at Vannes, attended by the Duke and Duchess, in which the mortal remains of the saint were solemnly transferred into a new reliquary sealed with three locks of which the keys were separately held by the Papal Legate, the Duke and the Bishop of Vannes.

The inclusion of the new saint among the Suffrages in Peter II's Book of Hours indicates that the manuscript must have been completed sometime after 1455, during the last two years of the Duke's life. Though described as *un prince faible, mélancolique et superstitieux* Peter left his country rich and peaceful at his death in September 1457; it was facetiously said that his peasants supped off silver plates and the rich traders in the ports slept on silver beds. He was succeeded by his uncle Arthur III (reigned 1457–58), who is better remembered in history as the doughty Connétable de Richemont. As Constable of France, Richemont had for many years been the holder of one of the great offices of state under the French Crown. His soldierly skill and administrative ability in reorganizing the French army were largely responsible for the final expulsion of the English from France.

Neither Peter II or Arthur III left heirs. On Arthur's death the Breton throne was inherited by his nephew Francis of Etampes. We approach Francis II, last Duke of Brittany, through the Hours of his wife, Marguerite de Foix.

ns ad dona perveniat sem
piterna. Per xpm dominu
nostrum.
Amen.

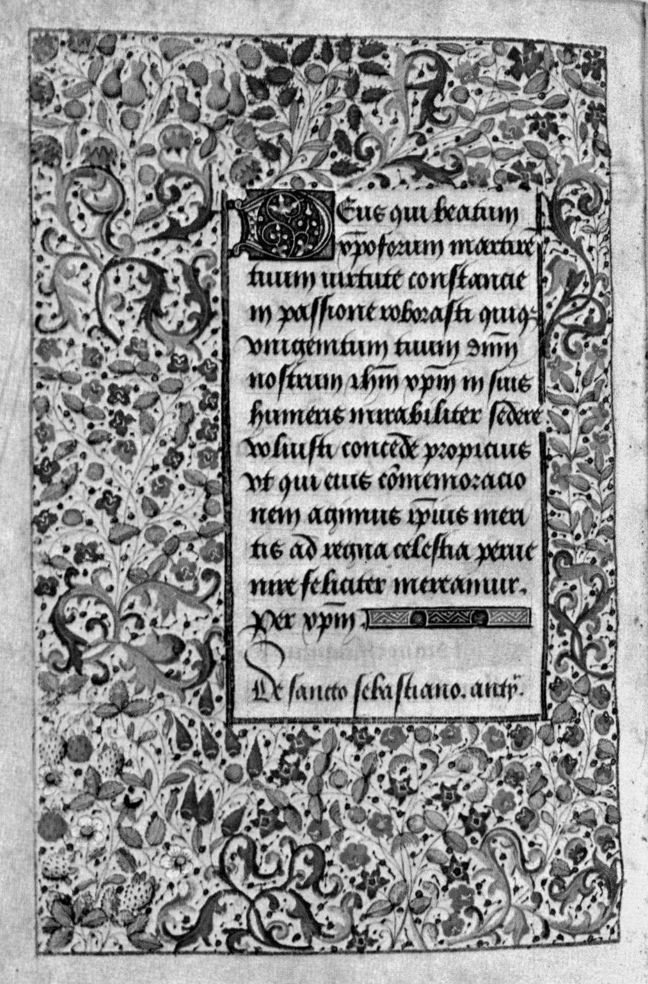

Deus qui beatum
xpoforum martire
tuum virtute constancie
in passione roborasti quiq;
unigenitum tuum dnm
nostrum ihm xpm in suis
humeris mirabiliter sedere
voluisti concede propicius
ut qui eius commemoracio
nem agimus ipsius meri
tis ad regna celestia perue
nire feliciter mereamur.
Per xpm

De sancto sebastiano. antr.

Quam mira refiul
sit gracia sebasti
anus martir in
clitus qui militie portans in

The Hours of Marguerite de Foix, Duchess of Brittany

Use of Paris. France, probably Paris, *c.* 1470–80.
17.6 × 10 cm ($6\frac{7}{8}$ × $3\frac{7}{8}$ in), iv + 288ff. 24 calendar illustrations, 12 large miniatures, 25 smaller miniatures.
Victoria and Albert Museum, London, Salting Collection no. 1222

122 **Text page: Flight into Egypt** f.83v–84
123 **Text page: St Sebastian** f.205v–206

MARGUERITE DE FOIX (d. 1486) was the wife of Francis II, Duke of Brittany, and mother of the great heiress Anne who, by marrying two successive Kings of France, united her Duchy with the French Crown, thus ending a long period of mutual rivalries and petty wars. Little is known about Marguerite except for a few references in contemporary chronicles and what may be learned from this finely illuminated Book of Hours.

The Flight into Egypt follows the end of None and introduces Vespers. Distant mountains, towers and a river landscape lead the eye down to the walled city of Bethlehem whence the Holy Family is fleeing. Immediately behind the mule an angel stands as if protecting the little group from the soldiers sent in pursuit by King Herod. Here a peasant, rather grandly dressed, is cutting corn, an illustration of the apocryphal Miracle of the Sower. According to this legend, Mary asked a sower to tell the soldiers that he had seen a family go past at sowing time. Thereupon a field of wheat sprang fully grown to conceal the fleeing family. On hearing the peasant's words the soldiers abandoned the pursuit in the belief that the refugees must now be too far away to be apprehended. It may be noticed that the peasant cuts off only the heads of wheat. This was the usual medieval practice, the stalks being left to dry out and then gathered into bundles for cattle fodder or for strewing on dwelling floors.

Below the panel of text written on the natural vellum, the Massacre of the Innocents is taking place in Bethlehem. Herod stands on the right pointing with his sceptre as the soldiers go about their work.

The Suffrage of St Sebastian which follows that of St Christopher shows the different type of border used in the last section of Marguerite de Foix's Book of Hours. On each page containing the miniature of a saint the border is painted against a solid matt gold field instead of the natural vellum. Against this rich background birds, animals, insects, snails and a few human figures and drolleries appear among the brightly coloured flowers and acanthus sprays. The natural vellum is retained only for the panel of text which appears below the miniatures like a caption.

Tied to a tree nearly in the centre of the picture, St Sebastian receives arrows at close range but, as customary in medieval art, shows few signs of suffering. In the *Golden Legend* he was said to have been pierced by so many arrows that his body resembled a hedgehog. His cult enjoyed an immense vogue in the Middle Ages, for he gave protection against the plague and epidemics. A curious feature of his iconography is his youthfulness: the saint usually appears as an attractive naked young man or even a boy. The original third-century soldier martyr was said to have been of mature age when he defied the Emperor Diocletian.

MARGUERITE DE FOIX's ownership of this Book of Hours is indicated by one prayer and two almost obliterated coats of arms. The prayer is written on some blank leaves at the end of the book. It begins with an appeal to Almighty God. A resumé follows of Biblical characters remarkable for their birth: the Patriarch Isaac, son of the aged Abraham and Sarah; the Prophet Samuel, born after many years to Hannah, wife of Elkanah the Ephraimite; John the Baptist, son of the aged Elizabeth; and the Virgin Mary, immaculate daughter of Anne. An invocation against sterility follows, backed up by a list of saints and martyrs of the 'Britannic Kingdom' whose relics are preserved and venerated in the Duchy of Brittany.

The prayer concludes with a specific mention of Francis II and his wife Marguerite; the wording implies that their daughter Anne, heiress of Brittany, was already born but that they hoped for a son to safeguard the independence of the Duchy, a forlorn hope as subsequent events proved. If this reading is accepted, the prayer must have been added at some time between 1477, when Anne was born, and 1486, when her mother died.[1]

The heraldic evidence for Marguerite's ownership appears on ff.21v and 227: two coats of arms supported by angels, which have been totally obliterated except for traces of black paint in the dexter and of gold and red in the sinister half of the shield. It is probable that the defaced arms were the black and white ermine coat of Brittany impaling the arms of Foix – three red pales (vertical bands) quartering two red cows, both on a gold field. If this is correct the manuscript belonged to Marguerite de Foix.

She was the daughter of Gaston IV, Count of Foix and Viscount of Béarn, who was a feudal magnate near the Spanish border. Her marriage with Francis II of Brittany took place on 26 June 1471 in the castle of Nantes, nearly two years after the death of his first wife, his virtuous and respected cousin Marguerite of Brittany, elder daughter of Francis I and Isabella Stuart. The marriage was part of a political deal in which Francis II joined a coalition formed in 1470 against Louis XI of France by the Dukes of Armagnac and Guienne, Gaston of Foix, Charles the Rash of Burgundy, King John of Aragon and sundry Italian allies. As usual, Louis XI emerged victorious.

Marguerite de Foix was the mother of Anne, Duchess of Brittany and twice Queen of France, who finally brought about the peaceful union of Brittany and France. A contemporary writer referred to Marguerite as fair, prudent and discreet (*une belle dame prudente et moult discrette*) and the Breton historian Argentré records her reputation for beauty and virtue in an equally conventional phrase: *laissant apres soy la réputation d'avoir esté une des plus belles princesses de son tems.*

If Marguerite de Foix makes only a brief and shadowy return to life in her Book of Hours, the personality of her husband Duke Francis II can still be felt across the centuries. He was the son of Richard, Count of Etampes, youngest son of Duke John IV of Brittany and brother to John V and Arthur III. Francis II, as a handsome man in his early twenties, entered Nantes in triumph in 1459, accompanied by his mother, the widowed Marguerite d'Orléans, Countess of Etampes, who emerged from her convent for the occasion. The debonair Francis, to use a favourite adjective of the time, was attractive, cultivated, open-hearted, fond of luxury and the arts. His motto was *Il n'est trésor que liese* ('There is no treasure but happiness'), which he had engraved on a garnet ring.

But by 1461 the shadow of Louis XI had begun to fall across the Duchy. For more than twenty years, Francis II followed a tortuous policy of short-lived alliances with any state which felt itself threatened by 'King Spider'. After the death of Charles the Rash of Burgundy in 1477, Brittany remained the sole great fief still independent of the French Crown. The final confrontation ended in disaster when the Breton army, supported by English, Spanish and German contingents, was decisively defeated by the French at the Battle of Saint-Aubin-du-Cormier on 28 July 1488. The Treaty of Vergers which followed in August ensured the ultimate absorption of Brittany into France, and the Duke himself, already ailing, died of chagrin and disappointment shortly afterwards on 7 September.

By his first wife Francis II had one son who died in infancy. Marguerite de Foix bore him two daughters, Anne and Isabeau, but the absence of a male heir was regarded as a sign of divine disapproval for his wanton ways. His first Duchess was said to have died of mortification at his neglect. It was believed, most unjustly, that the curse of sterility lay upon the second Duchess, whose two daughters were born only after the death of her husband's mistress, Antoinette de Maignelais, in 1475. We have here an interesting glimpse into the ambivalent attitudes of medieval subjects towards their rulers. Francis II of Brittany earned disapproval for too much gallantry; his contemporary Charles the Rash was criticized for a precisely opposite reason – his failure to lead the sexually self-indulgent life then expected of great princes. Both Dukes in fact offended in the same way: they fathered only daughters.

The poignant prayer added to Marguerite de Foix's Book of Hours is a reminder that the chances of a peaceful succession were slight. The example of Burgundy can have brought no comfort to Marguerite de Foix and her husband, as they waited in vain for a son. Their anxiety is vividly manifest in Marguerite's little-known Book of Hours, which, like so many others, reflects, no less validly than economic and nationalistic developments, the tensions of the times in which these men and women lived.

·SVRGE·ACCIPE·PVERV̄·ET·MATRĒ·EI·ET·FVGE·

The 'Grandes Heures' of Anne of Brittany, Queen of France

Use of Rome. France, Tours or Paris, *c.* 1500–08. 30 × 19.5 cm ($11\frac{3}{4} \times 7\frac{5}{8}$ in), 238ff. 12 calendar illustrations, 49 full-page miniatures, 2 pages of heraldic devices, over 300 borders, many decorated initials.
Bibliothèque Nationale, Paris, ms. lat. 9474.

126 **Flight into Egypt** f.76v
127 **Anne with Patron Saints** f.3
See also pages 130–31

Anne of Brittany was the heiress daughter of Francis II, the last independent Duke, by his second wife Marguerite de Foix. She married two successive Kings of France, Charles VIII and Louis XII, and died in 1514 leaving behind her a reputation for piety, patronage of the arts and love of luxury. Her *Grandes Heures* confirms these aspects of her character. The book (discussed on pp. 132–33) was commissioned from Jean Bourdichon around 1500; it is one of the most magnificent Books of Hours ever made.

The Flight into Egypt at Vespers displays the sweetness of Bourdichon's style. The suave features of the Holy Family, even the Christ Child's precocious expression as he holds an apple, may appear inappropriate to the scene; but in a devotional picture such as this, the contrast between the serene family and the turmoil behind them presents an appropriate theme for meditation. The picture, moreover, is faultlessly composed and iconographically instructive. In a setting of blue Leonardo-esque rocks the Miracle of the Sower takes place in the background. It is given less prominence than in the Hours of Marguerite de Foix (p. 122) and is treated in a more sophisticated manner. Herod's troopers look in every direction except towards the Holy Family as they disappear behind a protruding rock. The text at the foot is that of the angel's instruction to Joseph: *Surge, accipe puerum et matrem ejus et fuge* ('Arise, and take the young child and his mother, and flee', Matthew 2:13).

Early in the manuscript Anne is portrayed in prayer, wearing a gold robe with sleeves edged with fur and a Breton cap. Anne is more comely here than in other portraits; Bourdichon seems to have intended a quasi-state portrait of the Queen in her most benign aspect, with her Book of Hours, the edges richly gauffered and the two clasps open, lying before her. This page is half of a diptych: opposite in the manuscript is a Deposition scene with the dead Christ lying in the lap of his mother, who turns her tear-stained face towards Anne. The Queen is being presented by her patron saints. On the left is the elderly St Anne, mother of the Virgin, the most fitting person to make the presentation, which she does with her arm round Anne's shoulder. Next to her stands St Ursula holding an arrow, emblem of her martyrdom, and a banner bearing the arms of Brittany. On the right is St Helena, mother of the Emperor Constantine and discoverer of the True Cross, a replica of which she holds in her right hand. She is dressed even more richly than Anne of Brittany, in an ermine sideless surcoat and a cloak lined with the same material.

It is dismaying to contemplate Anne's situation in September 1488 after her father's death. She was an orphan not yet twelve years old. Except for her younger sister Isabeau (who died in 1490) she had no close relatives. As Duchess of Brittany she was the greatest heiress in France. Whoever married her would gain the last great feudal fief independent of the French Crown.[1]

The child at once showed her mettle. Among several ambitious suitors of varying ages she seriously considered only Maximilian of Austria, her father's favourite candidate. The thirty-one-year-old heir to the Empire had been a widower since the death in 1482 of his wife Mary of Burgundy (see pp. 110–13). Having acquired the Burgundian territories in the Low Countries by his first marriage, it now seemed that he might achieve another dynastic coup by marrying the second great heiress of the century. Anne's guardians considered Maximilian to be the best guarantee against a French occupation of Brittany. They accordingly embarked upon a policy of the utmost hazard by arranging a proxy marriage at Rennes on 19 December 1490. In the evening after the ceremony a handsome young German envoy, Wolfgang von Polheim, chamberlain at Maximilian's court, went through the ceremonial fiction of inserting his naked leg up to the knee inside Anne's bed. This ritual aroused ridicule among the French spectators, but it was fortunate for all parties that Maximilian (then in difficulties with revolts of his subjects in Flanders and distant Hungary) could not be present to be married in person to his child bride.

This rash proxy marriage had immediate grave consequences. The Treaty of Vergers (1488) expressly prohibited the heiress of Brittany from marrying without the knowledge or consent of the French King. Charles VIII replied by invading the Duchy, while Anne and her guardians shut themselves up in Rennes. Both sides settled down to a long siege, but a solution was now becoming clear: marriage between Anne and Charles. Such a marriage, with proper safeguards for Breton rights and customs, would end the war in Brittany, remove from France the menace of Hapsburg encirclement, and provide Anne with a husband suitable to her age and station. Though she complained of Charles – 'Am I so unfortunate as to marry the man who has treated me so badly?' – she finally yielded. Her proxy marriage with Maximilian was quickly annulled, and on 6 December 1491 she married the French King at Langeais in Touraine. She was fourteen and he twenty-one.

To the French court Anne brought a prestige lacking in the reign of the dowdy Louis XI. In person she was somewhat small and slightly lame, pleasant-looking rather than pretty, determined if not obstinate in mind, pious, well-educated, intelligent, and very proud of her position. She lived from 1477 to 1514, a short life-span of thirty-seven years which marked a transition from the medieval to the modern world. During her lifetime Columbus discovered America, while the printing press, matchless new instrument of enlightenment, became established in most European countries including her native Brittany.

On 8 April 1498 Charles VIII died suddenly at Amboise, from concussion after striking his head violently on a low doorway (which can still be seen) while hurrying to watch a tennis match. Anne had no surviving children and reverted to her former status of Duchess of Brittany. Her marriage contract with Charles VIII had stipulated that if she remarried it must be to the next successor to the French throne or to his heir. The new king was Louis XII, born in 1452, son of the poet-duke Charles of Orleans. At the earliest opportunity he paid a ceremonial call on the widowed Queen in her heavily draped apartments. After the mourning period was over she set out on a leisurely progress to her native Brittany. At Nantes she received a second visit from Louis XII, who entered her territory as a suitor and not as a conqueror like her first husband. She had known him since childhood, and may have had personal as well as political reasons for welcoming him as a suitor. On 8 January 1499, a fortnight before her twenty-second birthday, she became Queen of France for the second time. Her marriage contract established the precise succession rights of her children, daughters as well as sons, and reaffirmed that the union of Brittany with France was personal to the Duchess-Queen.

From a run of pregnancies during her second marriage only two daughters survived. Increasing doubts of a Dauphin yearly raised the hopes of the Orleans-Angoulême family, the next heirs to the throne of France. The heir-presumptive was the young Francis of Angoulême, for whose mother, Louise of Savoy, Anne developed an acute personal antipathy.

It gradually became clear that the political imperative which had forced Anne into marriage with Charles VIII would operate again in the case of her elder daughter Claude (born in 1499). On 9 January 1514, a few days before her thirty-eighth birthday, Anne died at the castle of Blois. On 18 May following, Claude was married at Amboise to Francis of Angoulême, an event her mother had always dreaded and perhaps happily did not live to witness. In June the ageing Louis XII married the buxom Tudor princess Mary, sister of Henry VIII of England, perhaps in the last hope of fathering a Dauphin. He died a few months later, on New Year's Day 1515; within less than a year of Anne's death her daughter Claude took her place as Queen of France beside the new King Francis I.

Anne was buried in the royal abbey of Saint-Denis, but her heart was sent back, on her instructions, to rest in Brittany. Enclosed in a silver heart-shaped urn, this last mortal relic of the Duchess-Queen was placed inside the sepulchral monument to her parents which she had already caused to be erected in the cathedral of Nantes. This fine example of late Gothic sculpture happily survives. Anne's herald-at-arms prepared an account of her death and funeral which was circulated in manuscript copies under the title *Trépas de l'hermine regretté*. The Breton ermine which she symbolically incarnated virtually died with her.

See pages 132–33 for commentary on Anne of Brittany's *Grandes Heures*.

·ÃNVCIO·VOBIS·GAVDIṼ·MAGNṼ·QÃ·HODIE·NAT'·E

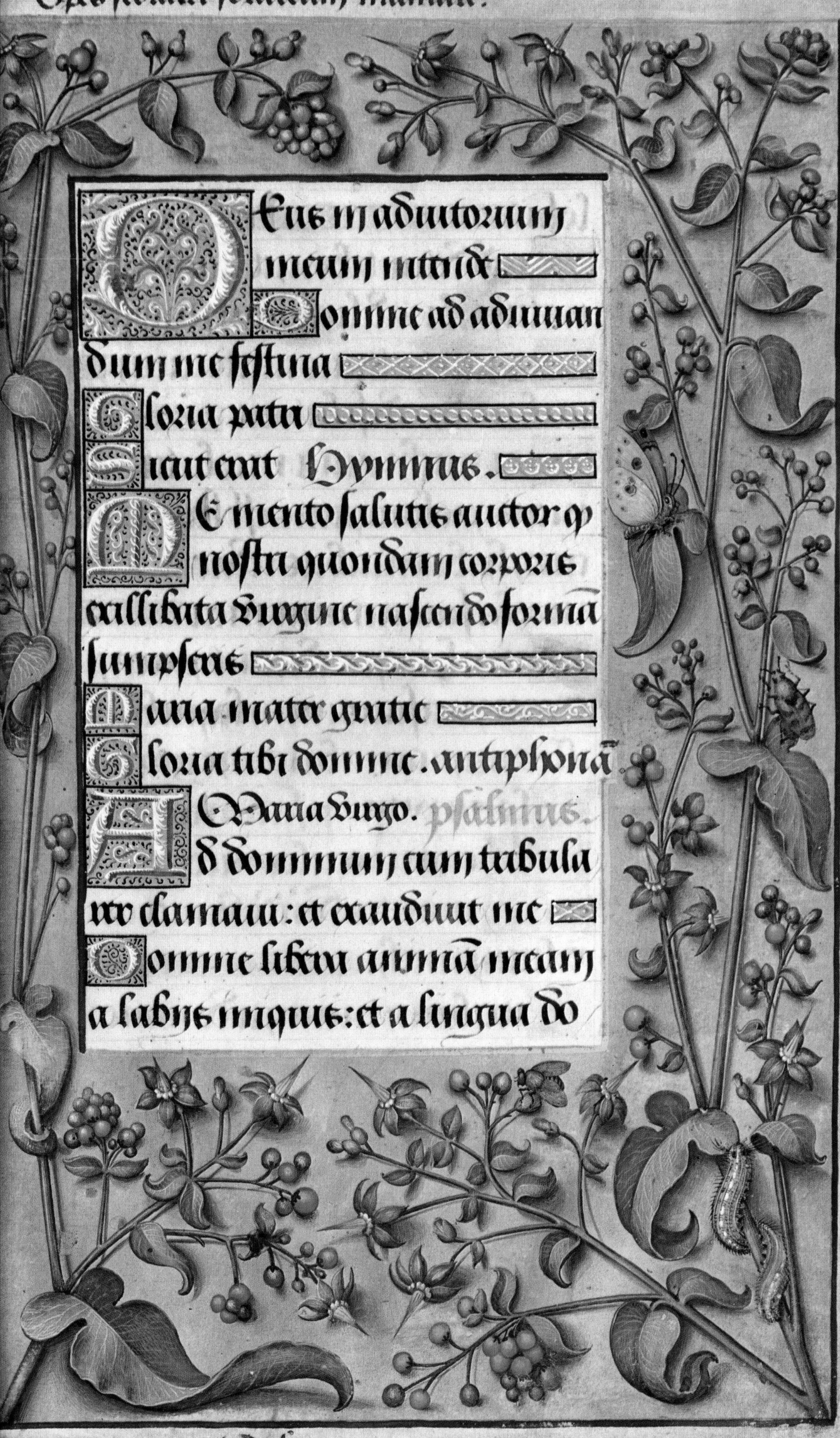

Deus in adiutorium
meum intende
Domine ad adiuuan
dum me festina
Gloria patri
Sicut erat Hymnus.
Memento salutis auctor q
nostri quondam corporis
ex illibata virgine nascendo formã
sumpseris
Maria mater gratie
Gloria tibi domine. antiphonã
O Maria virgo. psalmus.
Ad dominum cum tribula
rer clamaui: et exaudiuit me
Domine libera animã meam
a labiis iniquis: et a lingua do

De la cerquer

The 'Grandes Heures' of Anne of Brittany, Queen of France

Use of Rome. France, Tours or Paris, *c.* 1500–08. 30 × 19.5 cm ($11\frac{3}{4}$ × $7\frac{5}{8}$ in), 238ff. 12 calendar illustrations, 49 full-page miniatures, 2 pages of heraldic devices, over 300 borders, many decorated initials.

Bibliothèque Nationale, Paris, ms. lat. 9474

130–31 **The Angel's announcement to the shepherds; floral border** f.68v.–69

See also pages 126–27

The Angel's Announcement of Christ's Nativity to the Shepherds, at Prime in the Hours of the Virgin in Anne of Brittany's great prayerbook (p. 130) is one of the most ambitious night scenes in any Book of Hours. The contrast between the red glow from the fire in the foreground and the distant blue landscape heightens a dramatic moment. Two shepherds have been keeping watch while their companions doze by the fire. In the far distance is a second fire, an inspired touch, with a seated shepherd repeating the gesture of the bagpiper in the foreground. Only the angel appearing in a light-filled break in the clouds is a stereotyped figure; but his finger pointing at sleeping Bethlehem, where the Christ Child lies, connects him directly with the tense scene below. Even the sheep are imaginatively portrayed; some seem disturbed, others resume their grazing in automatic reflex. This is one of Jean Bourdichon's great pages, which establish him as a master.

Bourdichon's full-page miniatures, with their *trompe-l'œil* gold frames instead of borders, and their virtual exclusion of text, might easily be panel paintings; and the inscriptions – in this case *Annuncio vobis gaudium magnum, quod hodie natus est*, 'I bring you good tidings of great joy . . . for unto you is born this day . . .' – look like titles written on the frames. The miniatures are open to the often-repeated charge that they fail to function as book decoration. (The same criticism is, most oddly, never levelled at Romanesque book illuminations, which often suggest wall paintings reduced to the proportions of the vellum page.) It must be remembered, however, that Bourdichon's illuminations were never intended to be seen – much less reproduced – in isolation. They illustrate and complement texts and borders on adjacent pages, and appear quite differently when seen in this context.

A very special feature of the *Grandes Heures* is the botanical accuracy with which the flowers are depicted in the borders and given both their Latin and popular French names. On the broad gold borders of the last page shown are placed sprays of a plant with a potato-like flower. It is labelled *Sp[eci]es scolatri solatrum mam[m]ale* in red letters at the top, *De la cocqueree* at the bottom. This is *Solanum dulcamara*, sometimes known in French as *morelle douce-amère* and in English as bittersweet or woody nightshade. According to the botanist Decaisne, who made a catalogue of the plants in Anne's Book of Hours for the Curmer facsimile of 1861, *solatrum* is a corruption of *Solanum atrum*. Usually only one plant is shown, as here, in each border of the *Grandes Heures*. Though less bold than the fruits and flowers shown on many pages, the delicate branchings, mauve flowers and red berries are effectively disposed on the page; shadows and a few exploring insects increase the life-like effect.

The *Grandes Heures* illuminated for Anne of Brittany by Jean Bourdichon in 1500–08 ranks with the *Très Riches Heures* of the Duke of Berry among the most celebrated of all Books of Hours.[2] But because it belongs to the final period of book illumination, it is sometimes dismissed as an over-ripe or even boring example in comparison with Romanesque or early Gothic manuscripts. This is basically a question of historical perspectives. Anne of Brittany would have regarded the Taymouth Hours (pp. 46–47) as childish and indecent.

Bourdichon's manuscript displays a clarity of organization which makes it a Renaissance as well as a Gothic book.[3] The narrow rectangular frames of the large miniatures emphasize the proportions of the vellum page. At the principal divisions of the Hours the miniatures are balanced in scale and often colour by the wide floral borders which entirely surround the text page opposite.

Bourdichon's figures are solidly defined in space, beautifully composed against landscape or interior settings, and given additional brilliance by fine brushwork strokes of gold, a stylistic feature derived from Fouquet, applied to robes, armour, hair and wings. The stately, poised individuals display sweetness, serenity, grace, suavity of expression and occasional amplitude of form, qualities not now fashionable in art. By their dignified presence the sacred cast – figures from the Old and New Testaments, archangels and saints – induce a state of preparation for devotional exercises.

Despite their finished style and impeccable technique, the miniatures yield in interest, for many connoisseurs, to the borders. Bourdichon was much influenced by the *trompe-l'œil* 'strewn borders' made fashionable by the Ghent-Bruges school of illuminators. But he achieved a new effect by greatly increasing the number of plants represented and by painting them as if for a *florilegium* or herbal. Unlike the Flemish illuminators he often showed whole plants, complete with roots or bulbs, and labelled each with its Latin and French name. The flowers and fruits are accompanied by insects, snails and small mammals which crawl over and around them, in an intimate relationship as if neither could live without the other. One may speculate that the plants were copied from specimens grown in the royal gardens at Amboise and Blois in Touraine, to which Anne gave much attention. The total number represented is estimated to be 337. The work of collecting, identifying, painting and labelling them all is one reason why the book took several years to complete.

Bourdichon's career is well documented. He was born probably in 1457 and is thought to have entered Fouquet's studio at Tours when very young. He became one of the busiest and most successful artists of his time, an achievement which has earned him reserved evaluation from some art historians. Whether or not official success blunts an artist's integrity and independence of mind is irrelevant to Bourdichon's time. During his long life (he died in 1521 aged over sixty) he not only supplied the court with portraits, paintings, illuminations, banners, and designs for coins, stained glass and painted furniture, but also acted as stage-manager whenever an elaborate *décor* was required for ceremonial occasions. One of his last assignments was in 1520 to provide tents for the Field of the Cloth of Gold, where Francis I and Henry VIII of England met with their queens, in full panoply of state at Guines near Calais.

By then Bourdichon had served four French kings as well as Anne of Brittany. After carrying out minor commissions for Louis XI he had been appointed in 1484 *peintre en titre* and *varlet de chambre* to the young Charles VIII. He continued in these posts under Louis XII and Francis I. Payments in the archives record that the mule on which he travelled on business of all kinds for the court was fed and housed in the royal stables.

Bourdichon's authorship of the illuminations in Anne's *Grandes Heures* is established by the order for payment, which has luckily survived the centuries. It was discovered in Lyons, among a collection of old papers, in 1868. The name of the alert antiquarian, André Steyert, who identified this precious record (now in the Bibliothèque Nationale, Paris) should be remembered. The order for payment is the basic document for every study of Bourdichon's work.

Dated from Blois on 14 March 1507/8, in the name of the Queen of France, it orders her treasurer to pay her 'well-beloved' Bourdichon the sum of 1,050 *livres tournois* for 'richly and sumptuously illuminating' her great Hours: *à nostre cher et bien aimé Jehan Bourdichon, Peintre et Varlet de chambre de Monseigneur la some de mil cinquante livres tournois ou six centz ecuz d'or . . . pour le recompenser de ce qu'il nous a richement et somptueusement historie et enlumine une grans Heures pour nostre usaige et service.* Despite the appreciative manner in which the King's 'varlet' Bourdichon is mentioned he may not have received his money for another ten years. By this time Anne was dead and a new order was issued by Francis I in 1518 authorizing payment to Bourdichon of 600 *écus d'or* for work done before the King's accession and for supplying a *Grandes Heures*.

As a royal book of devotion Anne of Brittany's *Grandes Heures* is supremely successful. Only its size and weight make it more appropriate for the chapel rather than for a private room. On her frequent journeys and for daily use Anne provided herself with smaller Books of Hours. Several survive: a *Petites Heures* (Bibliothèque Nationale, Paris, ms. lat. nouv. acq. 3027), probably illuminated by a follower of Bourdichon; a *Très Petites Heures* in the Pierpont Morgan Library, New York (M.50), measuring 12 × 7.7 cm; and another, even smaller *Très Petites Heures* (Bibliothèque Nationale, Boisrouvray Donation) which measures only 6.6 × 4.6 cm. Anne of Brittany owned not only one of the biggest Books of Hours but also two of the smallest which have survived.

AVE MARIA GRACIA PLENA DOMINUS

O·MATER*DEI MENTO*MEI*AVE MARI GRACI PL
PENSON EN DIEV

The Primer of Claude de France

Primer. France, *c.* 1505–10.
26 × 17.5 cm ($10\frac{1}{4} \times 6\frac{7}{8}$ in), 14 pp. 2 full-page miniatures, 37 smaller miniatures in borders.
Fitzwilliam Museum, Cambridge, ms. 159

134 **Claude with patron saints** p.1
135 **Claude with patron saints** p.14

A Primer is a child's first book; and for hundreds of years that first book was a prayerbook. In England the term 'Primer' was often used to designate a full Book of Hours; but a true Primer was a shortened and simplified text suitable for use as an elementary reading manual. The Primer of Claude, elder daughter of Louis XII of France and Anne of Brittany, is a charming example. The text begins with the ABC and proceeds with the Lord's Prayer, the Creed, Grace before Meals, the Creation Story, Adam and Eve, the Hail Mary, Nativity and Adoration of the Shepherds and other basic religious matters. Mottoes appear over these texts, and at the beginning and end are portraits of the owner.[1]

On the first page the child princess appears before her patron St Claude, Bishop of Besançon. She is shown kneeling before him with her hands on a closed book resting on a *prie-dieu* covered with a cloth powdered with fleurs-de-lys and letters A, the initial of her mother and of St Anne, mother of the Virgin Mary. The latter stands behind her, with arms embracing both Claude and the youthful Virgin (the divine personages are recognized by their haloes).

On the last miniature these roles are reversed. Now St Anne sits before Claude, with an open book in her lap from which she instructs the Virgin Mary, who turns as if to bring Claude into the lesson. St Claude presents his protégée to St Anne and the Virgin. The *prie-dieu* covering bears his initial C (and Claude's) instead of the A. In contrast to the first miniature, the princess now has her hands upon an open book. On the arch above her is written in blue and red the words *O Mater Dei memento mei* (Oh Mother of God, forget not me). The meaning is clear: the young princess has now learnt to read.

Claude de France, born in October 1499, was the elder of the two daughters of Anne of Brittany by her second husband Louis XII. Her mother gave much thought to the future of her only surviving child, as Claude was for several years, and hoped to arrange a Hapsburg match for her. Negotiations for the marriage of Claude with Maximilian's grandson the Archduke Charles (the future Emperor Charles V) began when both infants were scarcely out of their cradles. But Louis XII, on recovering from a serious illness in 1505, insisted that his daughter must marry the next heir to the French throne, her cousin Francis of Angoulême, and officially betrothed the two children the following year. The art- and pleasure-loving Francis was to become one of his country's most flamboyant kings (reigned 1515–47).[2]

Claude's wedding took place in May 1514, when she was fourteen, a few months after her mother's death. Court mourning was not lifted for the occasion. As her mother's eldest child she had already become Duchess of Brittany. Less than a year later, her father's death made her Queen of France. Her marriage to the new King ensured that the Duchy of Brittany would not be separated from the Crown, and Francis later persuaded his wife to make over all her rights to him. This gentle woman, who was slightly lame like her mother, played no part in politics but was cherished by her consistently unfaithful husband. She bore him seven children, one of whom was later to succeed as Henry II. In 1524 she died, exhausted one may think by frequent child-bearing, before reaching her twenty-fifth birthday. Her memory survives in charming fashion in the name *la reine-claude*, given to the greengage, a fruit which was introduced into France from the East at this time and first cultivated for her.

Dating from about 1505, Claude's Primer is now in the Fitzwilliam Museum, Cambridge. This child's Book of Hours was superseded when Claude became Queen of France by another of the utmost refinement. Written in Roman script by Geoffrey Tory and embellished with exquisite miniatures by an unidentified artist, this minute book (8.6 × 5.5 cm), now in the H.P. Kraus collection, New York, is almost as small as the *Très Petites Henres* of Claude's mother. By the early nineteenth century it had somehow reached England, where it was seen by Thomas Frognall Dibdin and described by him as 'a jewel of calligraphy, and illumination fit for the book boudoir of such a fairy queen as Shakespeare's Titania'.[3]

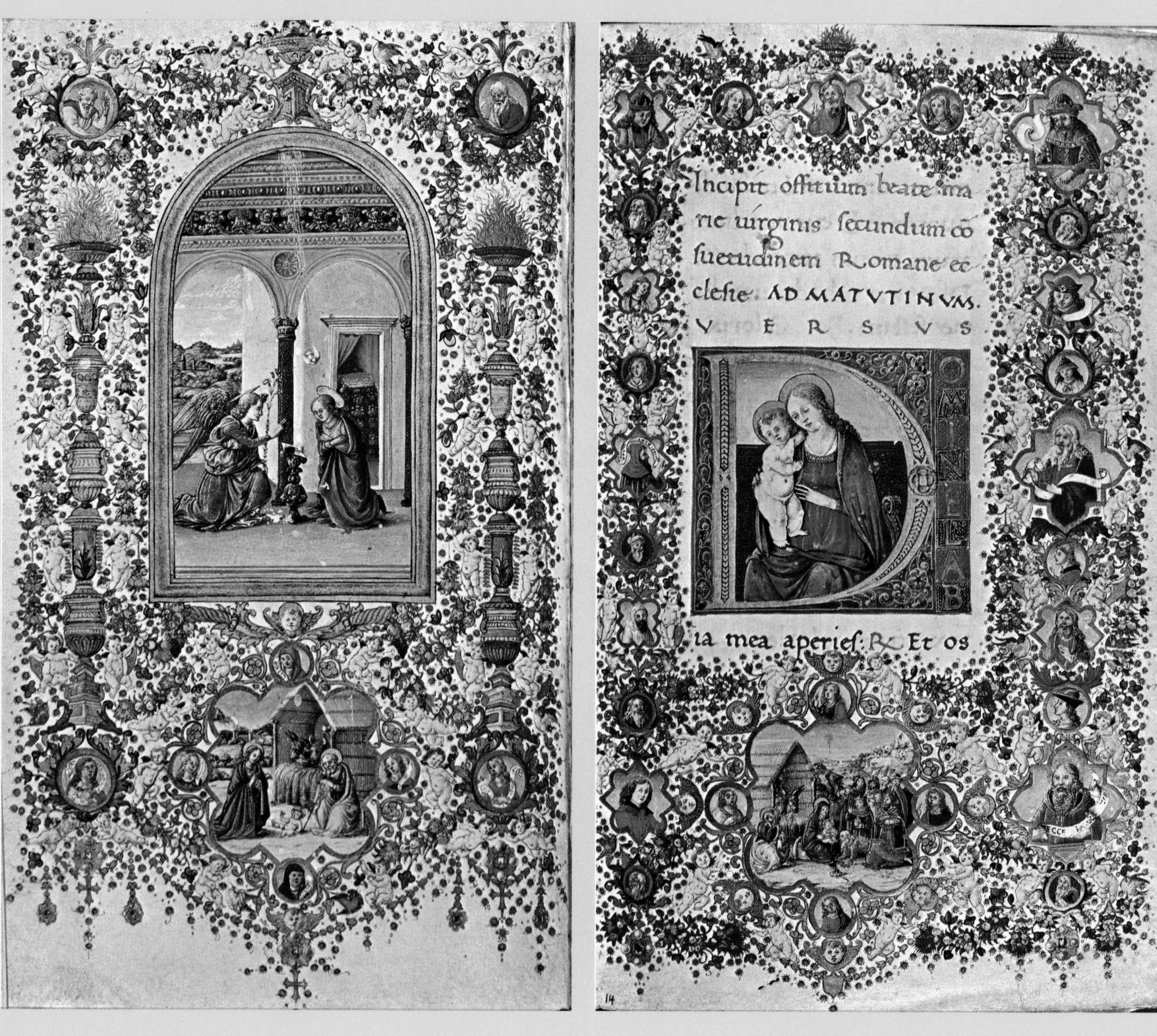
Incipit offitium beate ma
rie uirginis secundum co
suetudinem Romane ec
clesie. AD MATVTINVM.
V E R S V S
DOMINE LAB
ia mea aperies. R Et os
14

Incipiunt septem Psalmi
penitentiales. Antiphona.
NE REMINISCARIS
PSALMVS
furore tuo arguas me: neq.

The Hours of Lorenzo dei Medici, the Magnificent

Use of Rome. Italy, Florence, 1485. 15.3 × 9 cm (6 × 3½ in), 233ff. Calendar illustrations, 9 large miniatures with decorative borders.
Biblioteca Mediceo-Laurenziana, Florence, ms. Ashburnham 1874

138 **Annunciation; Nativity; Virgin and Child in initial: Adoration of the Magi** f. 13v–14

139 **David in Penitence; David enthroned in initial** ff. 162v–163

The Book of Hours of Lorenzo the Magnificent is a choice example of Florentine book illumination embellished in the style of Francesco d'Antonio del Cherico, who had been the favourite miniature painter of Lorenzo's grandfather Cosimo the Elder.[1] The beginning of the Little Office of the Virgin, at Matins, is indicated, as so often in Books of Hours, by a miniature of superlative quality. As customary at this place in the text, it is an Annunciation scene, here shown in a typically Florentine setting with a view of an enchanting distant landscape whence the Archangel Gabriel has come to confront Mary in the enclosed privacy of her bedchamber. In the quadrilobe medallion beneath, the Nativity is depicted; and on the facing page the Madonna and Child inside the initial *D* of the familiar opening words of Matins, *Domine labia mea aperies*; below the latter is a corresponding medallion showing the Adoration of the Magi. The Annunciation scene is flanked by two large candelabra surmounted by flaming braziers. On the opposite page these are replaced by medallions of prophets holding scrolls and the heads or busts of other, more youthful figures.

The Penitential Psalms of David, prefaced by the antiphon *Ne reminiscaris* ('Remember not, Lord, our offences'), begin with Psalm 6: *Domine ne in furore tuo arguas me* ('O Lord, rebuke me not in thy wrath'). In Lorenzo the Magnificent's Book of Hours they are introduced by a miniature conventional in theme, David in Penitence, but made memorable by its exquisite landscape background. The old man, here given a halo, kneels before God as he plays his psaltery. In the initial *D* of the facing page he appears again, this time as a younger man wearing a diadem and seated on a throne. He appears to be singing praises to the Lord and ignores the prophet who stands before him holding a scroll. The borders of both pages are as densely packed with decorative and emblematic ornaments as in the Annunciation scene. One notices a shield in the lower margin which should surely bear the Medici arms? It is surrounded by a chain of diamond rings, which are a Medici emblem more commonly encountered in the form of three interlaced rings. The unidentified cast of old and young personages in the medallions which are such a prominent feature of the borders appear to regard with varying attention the scenes displayed in the miniatures.

The artist who painted the densely packed borders of these pages, with their diminutive sunbursts, flowers, winged *amorini* and occasional birds, miraculously avoids any sense of crowded fussiness: the miniatures seem rather to rest upon a carpet laid upon the white vellum leaves.

The Medici were a family of bankers who reached and maintained a position of near-absolute supremacy in the republican government of Florence during the fifteenth century while remaining technically private citizens. They owed this achievement to their natural abilities, great wealth (from 1414–76 they were bankers to the Popes in Rome), success in gaining the support not only of the trade guilds but of the general populace of Florence, and to their reputation as patrons of literature and the arts on a scale which seemed to contemporaries and posterity to have restored a Golden Age. Despite several serious but temporary political set-backs, they finally attained an unassailable position in 1530 when the Holy Roman Emperor recognized them first as Dukes of Florence and soon afterwards as hereditary Grand Dukes of Tuscany, over which country they ruled until 1737.

One of them became recognized during his lifetime as the embodiment of the Italian Renaissance in its peculiarly Florentine manifestations. This man was Lorenzo dei Medici (1449–92), head of the third successful generation of his family. He was posthumously known as *il Magnifico*, an epithet applied to other Italians of lesser worth but meaning something more than personal panache. 'Magnificence' was a virtue of the rich, recognized by lavish expenditure on patronage, architecture, hospitality and public festivities in an almost Roman manner.[2] Constant in his pursuit of beauty, outgoing in friendship but ruthless when circumstances demanded, Lorenzo seems to approach the Renaissance ideal of the universal man.

What concerns us here, however, is what may be called his medieval inheritance. He enjoyed tournaments and jousts, most un-Florentine activities, in which he took part with his younger brother Giuliano. He was, moreover, a Christian as well as being a Neo-Platonist. Part of the fascination of Lorenzo's enigmatic character resides in this acceptance of his medieval inheritance simultaneously with the adoption of a pragmatic approach to political life which makes him one of the first truly modern men. 'The Renaissance,' Oswald Spengler observed, 'had ever the strong faith of the Gothic at the back of its world-outlook ... When Savonarola stood up, the antique trappings vanished from the surface of Florentine life in an instant.'[3]

This celebrated Book of Hours was written and dated for Lorenzo by the scribe Antonio Sinibaldi in 1485. Its miniatures and decoration are so typical of Francesco del Cherico's style that he is usually credited with their execution, though it is now known that he died a few months previously, on 28 October 1484. One of his followers may therefore have been responsible for a manuscript which has been described as a jewel of Florentine book illumination.

It is a small book. The miniatures are painted in a refined, delicate style which recalls the sweetness of Fra Angelico. They are surrounded by wide borders filled with a mass of tightly packed but lucidly disposed ornament – flowers, leaves, fruits, stars, heads in medallions and minute *putti*. Against the white vellum pages the whole ensemble sparkles with a refined vivacity. Despite the appearance in the borders of Renaissance accessories such as candelabra, *putti* and pearls, the books preserves a 'Gothic' character in which religious sentiment is not overwhelmed by the decorative opulence characteristic of much Italian book illumination in this period.

Francesco del Cherico (active 1454–84) was the leading Florentine miniature painter of his time, in whose workshop a generation of illuminators grew up which culminated in Attavante degli Attavanti and the brothers Gherardo and Monte del Fora in the last quarter of the fifteenth century. During this period Lorenzo il Magnifico was adding books and manuscripts to the library founded by his grandfather Cosimo the Elder. When the Medici temporarily lost power in 1494, only two years after Lorenzo's death, their library was for a time in considerable danger of dispersal or even destruction by the followers of Savonarola. The greater part was later removed to Rome by Pope Leo X, Lorenzo's son, but was returned to Florence at the direction of the second Medici Pope, Clement VII (reigned 1523–34). It was Clement (the illegitimate son of Lorenzo's brother Giuliano) who commissioned Michelangelo to design a library building in the cloisters of the Church of San Lorenzo in Florence. Thus began the Biblioteca Mediceo-Laurenziana, one of the great libraries of the world.[4] Lorenzo's Book of Hours is unlikely to have been among the collections when the library was first opened to the public in 1571. It had at some time migrated to the Low Countries where it was in the possession of the De Merode family during the seventeenth century. In the nineteenth century it was acquired by the brilliant bibliographer and book-thief Guglielmo Libri, whose library was subsequently bought by the fourth Earl of Ashburnham. After the latter's death in 1878 the Italian government commendably purchased the Ashburnham-Libri collection, and with it Lorenzo's sparkling little Book of Hours returned to its rightful home.

INRI

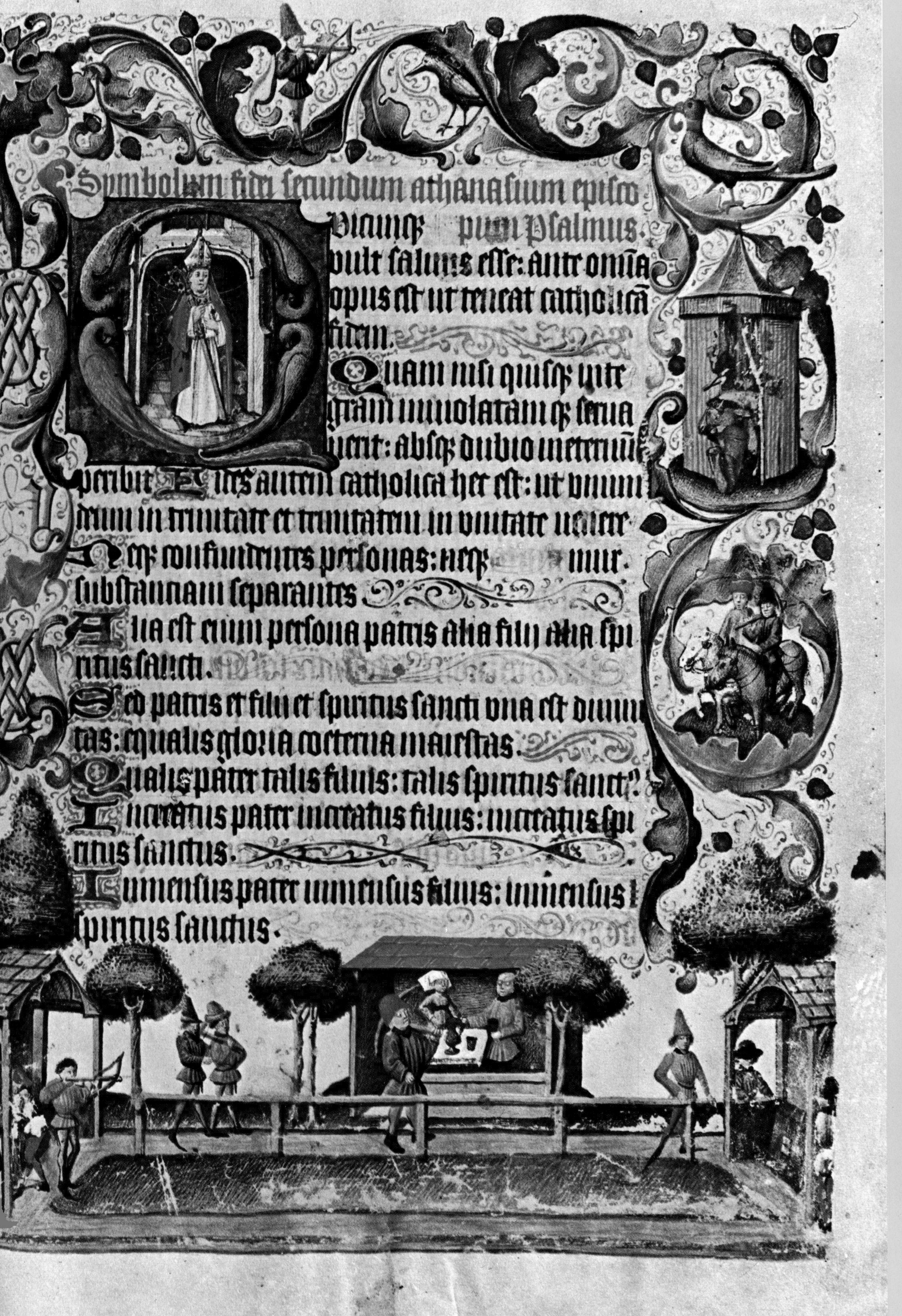
Symbolum fidei secundum athanasium episco
Quicunqz pum psalmus.
vult salvus esse: ante omnia
opus est ut teneat catholicam
fidem.
Quam nisi quisqz inte
gram inviolatamqz serva
verit: absqz dubio in eternum
peribit. Fides autem catholica hec est: ut unum
deum in trinitate et trinitatem in unitate venere
Neqz confundentes personas: neqz mur.
substantiam separantes.
Alia est enim persona patris alia filii alia spi
ritus sancti.
Sed patris et filii et spiritus sancti una est divini
tas: equalis gloria coeterna maiestas.
Qualis pater talis filius: talis spiritus sanctus.
Increatus pater increatus filius: increatus spi
ritus sanctus.
Inmensus pater inmensus filius: inmensus
spiritus sanctus.

The Hours of Yolande de Lalaing

Use of Rome. Netherlands, *c.* 1450–60.
21 × 15 cm ($8\frac{1}{4} \times 5\frac{7}{8}$ in), 123ff. 5 large miniatures with smaller miniatures in borders, many illuminated initials.
Bodleian Library, Oxford, ms. Douce 93

142–43 **Crucifixion; tournament in border; St Athanasius in initial; crossbowmen and nobles in border** ff.100v–101

YOLANDE DE LALAING'S Book of Hours is profusely embellished with heraldry, emblematic devices, and pictures showing the favourite occupations of the aristocratic class to which she belonged.[1] Born about 1422, she married Reinaud II of Brederode, a castle near Haarlem. Her brother Jacques de Lalaing was a famous jouster, known internationally as a tournament champion. A possible allusion to his prowess may be discerned in his sister's Book of Hours.

The *Symbolum* or Creed of St Athanasius on f.101, beginning with the words *Quicumque vult salvus esse* ('Whosoever will be saved'), is illustrated on the facing page by a large Crucifixion miniature with tournament scenes in the border. The iconography of this Crucifixion is unusual. St John supporting the swooning Virgin on the right forms a part of a familiar group, but opposite him is a crowned and haloed female figure riding a lion with a cross and banner in her left hand. She symbolizes *Ecclesia*, the Church, and holds in her other hand a chalice which receives the blood from Christ's side which the Church mediates to the world in the sacrament of Mass. Behind the lion close inspection reveals an ox, angel and eagle. These are the four creatures of the Evangelists, whose presence here at the Crucifixion is without precedent in a Book of Hours.[2]

This remarkable religious imagery is accompanied in the border by a tournament. Armoured knights emerge from their tents on caparisoned horses, ready to break lances in the lists below. Watched from boxes by their ladies, while heralds blow trumpets, the knights are seen at the bottom of the page in the crucial moment of encounter. These vivid, realistic scenes in the border appear to have no connection with the miniature.

On the page facing the Crucifixion are more sports. Below the text an archery contest with crossbows is in progress before a lady and her lord (Yolande and her husband?) who take refreshment in a pavilion. In the border at the sides are more knights and crossbowmen on horseback, and two Brederode emblems already seen in the border opposite: a knot, and a device of two crossed and flaming sticks beneath a boar's head. It is almost a surprise to be reminded, by the figure of St Athanasius in the historiated initial, that these borders accompany a religious text.

THIS BOOK OF HOURS finds a place in this anthology not only because the manuscript is a fine Dutch example but for a more specific reason. It presents Books of Hours in a new aspect which reveals how profoundly chivalric ideals permeated the religious sensibility of the knightly class.

We cannot know the thoughts of Yolande de Lalaing as she turned the pages of her Book of Hours, but she belonged to a family which made a profession of chivalry. The Church had at first greatly disapproved of chivalry and considered tournaments as assemblies which provided opportunity for committing all seven deadly sins at once. A more realistic view prevailed when the feudal knights became the strong arm of *Ecclesia*, a role which owed much to the Crusades. However frequent and lamentable were the lapses of the knights in practice, the ideal values of their chivalric code thenceforth assumed a Christian character.[3]

The converse is also true. Religious language often used the imagery of chivalry. In a number of medieval texts and lyrics Christ himself is boldly evoked in the guise of a knight. The poet-author in Langland's *Piers Plowman* (Passus xviii) sees in a dream Faith hailing Christ outside Jerusalem 'like a herald proclaiming a knight who comes to the tournament', where Christ, clad in armour and riding in Piers' doublet 'that no one here may know him as Almighty God', will joust against Satan. An even more specific instance of the Christ-Knight allegory occurs in *Le Livre du*

Chevalier (and its German version *Der Ritter vom Turm*) written by Geoffroy de La Tour Landry between 1371 and 1374 for the instruction of his daughters. The story tells how a girl wrongly accused by a false knight, whose advances she had rejected, of poisoning a child was about to be burnt at the stake for lack of a champion willing to take on her accuser in single combat. At the last moment a knight called Patrides appeared and fought on her behalf, killing the false knight, but himself sustaining five mortal wounds. While dying he sent the girl his shirt, pierced in five places, which she kept all her life, praying daily for the soul of her rescuer. This act of deliverance and sacrifice is explicitly linked at the end of the story with Christ's death upon the Cross and his five wounds.[4]

This tale from the *Livre du Chevalier* belongs to the category of *exempla* (exemplary stories) much used in the Middle Ages to illustrate religious teaching and to point the moral lesson in sermons. With such a correlation between knightly champions and the Crucifixion we can look again at the page from Yolande de Lalaing's Book of Hours with a new insight. To what extent the owner and artist were conscious of the *exemplum* is uncertain but it is as a 'chivalric' book that we consider it here.

Yolande and her husband belonged to the nobility of Hainault.[5] Their families were closely connected with the Burgundian court, where the ceremonial rites and fictions of chivalry enjoyed a sunset glow of the utmost splendour. The best-known was Yolande's eldest brother, Jacques de Lalaing, known as *le bon chevalier*, who made jousting a glamorous profession. He toured Europe displaying his expertise in tournaments with such legendary success that his deeds were recorded in a fifteenth-century best-seller, *Le Livre de faicts du bon Chevalier Messire Jacques de Lalaing*, attributed to the Burgundian chronicler Georges Chastellain.[6]

In 1452 the young Charles de Charolais (later Duke Charles the Rash of Burgundy) encountered Lalaing in his first tournament, much to the consternation of his Portuguese mother, who sought vainly to have the rules relaxed before her only son encountered the best jouster of the age. This dangerous initiation passed off without accident, but the next year Jacques de Lalaing, Knight of the Golden Fleece and *écuyer* (esquire or groom) to the Duke of Burgundy, was killed before the castle of Poucques outside Ghent fighting in the attack launched by his master against the rebellious city. He was then at the height of his fame, having captured the imagination of his age with the fervour accorded in our own day to successful footballers or Olympic champions. His death by cannon-shot, a new-fangled invention which chivalric opinion regarded as unsporting, was a sign of changing times.

As the sister of this latter-day Paladin, Yolande de Lalaing would have been familiar from her earliest years with the practice and mystique of chivalry. The knights fought in tournaments under the eyes of their ladies, whose favours they wore. The rarefied, idealizing cult of women fostered by chivalry was a secular counterpart of the devotion to the Virgin Mary which transformed religious thought in the later Middle Ages. The two cults developed simultaneously, though neither can be claimed as the cause of the other. They were rather two manifestations of a contemporary change of attitude towards women. While the theologians were defining Mary's role, the new Eve, as man's principal intercessor with God, the knightly classes were invoking her protection in the rituals which conferred knighthood. Yolande's Book of Hours was a reminder that she prayed daily before the greatest Lady of all.

And what of the anonymous artist who seems to have possessed such insight into the minds of his aristocratic patrons? He is known as the 'Master of Gisbert de Brederode' from another Book of Hours (now in the University Library, Liège) which he decorated for a younger brother of Yolande's husband who was Bishop of Utrecht. In addition to the Oxford and Liège Books of Hours the Brederode Master is known to have executed at least two more, one in Berlin, the other at Cambridge. His Books of Hours are characterized by a lively colour sense, unusual borders and, on occasion, remarkable miniatures which conflate chivalric ideals with devotion to the Virgin Mary and Christ's sacrifice upon the Cross.

Commemoracio de sc̄a
katherina
Gaude uir
go kathe
rina . qua
doctores
lex diuia
traxit ab erroribus
Gaude pro qua tenebro
sis . carcer fuit luminosꝯ
flagrans ex odoribus
Gaude conuertens regi
nam . cernens rotarū rui
nam . plebis ī discrimine .
Gaude tu que flagella
ris . et post preces decolla

Ad terciaꝫ
Deus in ad
iutoriū me
um inten
de . Domine
ad adiuuandum me fe
stina . Gloria pr̄i ꝯ
Memento salutis au
ctor quod nostri quon
dam corporis ex illibata
uirgine nascendo formā
sumpseris . Maria mr̄
gracie . mater misericor
die . tu nos ab hoste pro
tege in hora mortis sus
cipe . Gloria tibi domine

Incipit officiũ uigilie mo
rtuorũ: an: placebo. ps:
Dilexi qm ex
audiet dns
vocem orati
onis mee. Quia incli
nauit aurem suam michi
et in diebus meis inuocabo.
Circumdederunt me dolo
res mortis: et pericula infer
ni inuenerunt me. Tri
bulationem et dolorem in
ueni: et nomen domini i
nuocaui. O domine libe
ra animã misericors dns

The Simon Marmion Hours

Use of Rome. Franco-Flemish School, 1475–81. 11 × 7.6 cm ($4\frac{3}{8}$ × 3 in), 250ff. 1 full-page miniature, 12 miniatures in arched frames within full borders, matching borders on facing pages (except f.154), 7 additional borders.
Victoria and Albert Museum, London, Salting Collection no. 1221

146 **Martyrdom of St Catherine** f.15v–16
Angel and shepherds; pastoral scenes in borders f.85v–86

147 **Last Judgment; Paradise and Hell** f.152v–153
Raising of Lazarus; Judgment scenes in borders ff.153v–154

Simon Marmion (*c.* 1425–89) directed a workshop in Valenciennes from 1458 or earlier until his death, but had connections as well, the details of which are not precisely known, with the Bruges workshop of Guillaume Vrelant. Both artists specialized in the production of Books of Hours, for which Bruges was a centre.[1] The presence of miniatures from the Vrelant workshop in Simon Marmion's later Books of Hours suggests that his manuscripts may have been completed, or at least sold, in Bruges.

The first miniature in the so-called Simon Marmion Hours in the Victoria and Albert Museum (p. 146 *above*) is an example.[2] Stylistically it is a product of the Vrelant not the Marmion workshop, and the only such specimen to appear in the manuscript. The miniature and borders of the double-page are painted in grisaille technique with gold and white acanthus sprays upon a solid grey background. The subject is the martyrdom of St Catherine. The double-wheel of her torture breaks under blows from a tiny mallet held by the angel hovering in the sky above, but the exasperated executioner is about to decapitate the saint. In the background the Emperor Maximian (or Maxentius) and his attendants are spectators of the wretched scene.

Marmion's style is seen in the next miniature reproduced, the Angel's Announcement to the Shepherds, at Tierce in the Hours of the Virgin (p. 146 *below*). The dominant colouring is here red and green. Pastoral scenes, a lady spinning, a yokel playing his pipe and a wolf carrying off a lamb, appear in the borders. Also to be noted is the initial *D* of the text page, painted in gold with a silvery pattern on a black ground.

The Last Judgment scene, before the Office of the Dead, differs from the other miniatures in the book in facing not a page of text but another miniature, an arresting full-page picture without borders (p. 147 *above*) depicting the contrast between Paradise and Hell. In the background is an inviting, wooded landscape with the Fountain of Life. Lower down are rocks, and a river spanned by a narrow bridge over which naked souls are perilously crossing towards an angel waiting to receive them on the shore of Paradise. Several stumble or are pulled off by devils into the water which carries them down into Hell-Mouth in the foreground. Marmion's Hell scene anticipates in uncanny manner the apocalyptic visions of Hieronymus Bosch, nearly a century later.

The Last Judgment scene itself is surrounded by a green border in which two angels sound the Last Trump while others pick up skulls. Christ sits on a golden arc, displaying his wounds, with saints and the Elect beside him. Beneath the court of Heaven the dead rise from their graves; one of the saved is already being lifted up by his guardian angel. These remarkable pages illustrate Marmion's skill in depicting landscape and distance, his characteristic use of a bird's-eye view and his ability to convey atmosphere in the luminous cloud of light which surrounds Christ.

Immediately following the Last Judgment and Hell-Mouth comes another striking miniature, the Raising of Lazarus, which introduces the text of the Office of the Dead (p. 146 *below*). In this miniature the faces of the people who witness the miracle are subtly differentiated. Once again Marmion paints the scene as viewed from above. Of special interest are the matching borders of the two pages. The foliage ornament is painted in gold on a black ground, which gives an effect of sombre depth fitting the subject matter of the miniature. In the group of Death seizing a maiden, and in the skilfully executed figures of devils carrying off naked souls, we see the first steps in the Dance of Death encountered so often in the borders of printed Books of Hours.

The Simon Marmion Hours is a choice example of the vogue for very small manuscript prayer-books during the last quarter of the fifteenth century. Dating from the immediate post-Burgundian period, it is a fine but not a 'princely' Book of Hours. We do not know who first owned it; there is evidence of a negative kind to suggest that it was made for stock and not commissioned. If this were so it is nonetheless strange that whoever was fortunate enough to acquire such a delicate *bijou* Book of Hours, perhaps a member of the prosperous bourgeoisie of northern France, the Low Countries or England, resisted the temptation to add his or her ownership mark.

A preliminary glance at the writing shows that Gothic script has here been abandoned in favour of a rounded Italianate hand which, like the various types of *bastarda*, was more up to date as well as being easier to read. The principal divisions of the text are marked by large decorative initials painted in gold or silver on black grounds which produce a metallic or damascened effect. 'Black' prayerbooks were fashionable, as we have seen, at the Burgundian court; here the black decoration is confined to initials, except in the border around the Raising of Lazarus miniature at the Office of the Dead, which is appropriately painted on a black ground.

The variety of borders is an interesting feature of the manuscript. The familiar acanthus sprays which originated in French illumination in the early fifteenth century are no longer painted invariably upon the natural vellum. Instead, solid monochrome backgrounds often of strong colours – red, blue, green, matt gold or occasionally black – are introduced upon which the acanthus sprays are painted in graduated tones of gold, blue and white. Identifiable flowers accompanied by fruits, animals, insects and realistic figures and drolleries obtrude among the acanthus.

The first indication that the book was not commissioned occurs in the Calendar, which contains a number of Bruges as well as northern French saints and cannot be definitely localized; it is sparsely filled, and the absence of pictures showing the occupations of the months and the zodiacal signs, as well as of decorative borders, suggests that the Calendar's embellishment was never completed for a client.

It is immediately followed by a prayer to the Holy Face (*Salve sancta facies*, f.13), with a rubric concerning the indulgence granted by Pope John XXII. This page is framed by a border complete except for a blank shield held by two kneeling angels in a vernal landscape at the bottom of the page. No owner's coat of arms appears ever to have been inserted. Following this indulgence prayer comes the Suffrage to St Catherine, with a miniature opposite of her martyrdom (p. 146 *above*). This miniature, from the workshop of Guillaume Vrelant of Bruges, is blank on the reverse, which indicates that it is an insertion. It is possible that there were once other Vrelant pictures in the book, for at least seven miniatures are now missing from their customary places in the text. The unusual position of the isolated St Catherine miniature suggests that the book may have belonged to somebody named Catherine.

Simon Marmion came from the area now known as French Flanders, which for much of the fifteenth century belonged to Duke Philip the Good of Burgundy. He was born around 1425, probably at Amiens where his father was a painter. By 1458 he had moved to Valenciennes where he married, acquired property and established a workshop. He was primarily a book illuminator but also produced panel paintings. At Valenciennes he died in 1489. Towards the end of his life he had business relations with Bruges, the centre of a prosperous trade in Books of Hours both for home consumption and for export abroad to England. Some of his manuscripts appear to have been 'made up', with miniatures and borders produced in different workshops. For these and other reasons it is difficult to know whether to describe Marmion as a French or Flemish painter.

His reputation outlasted his death; he was described in 1503 as a *prince d'enluminure* in 'Couronne margaritique', a poem written by Jean Le Maire, secretary to Margaret of Burgundy (daughter of Mary and Maximilian), to console her on the premature death of her husband Philibert of Savoy. Le Maire couples Marmion's name with that of the celebrated Jean Fouquet, who illuminated the now dismembered Chevalier Hours at Chantilly. Despite this testimony of fame, no signed or otherwise documented picture or illuminated manuscript survives. Marmion's name occurs several times in the Archives of Valenciennes, but it is exasperating that these entries (relating mainly to property) cannot be used positively to identify any of the works attributed to him. The painted shutters, now divided between the National Gallery, London, and the Berlin-Dahlem Museum, from a sculptured retable of gilded silver (destroyed in the French Revolution) formerly in the Abbey Church of Saint-Bertin at Saint-Omer, are generally accepted to be by his hand; but no signed Book of Hours is known.

Dr Hoffman has reconstituted Marmion's artistic personality and identified twenty-five manuscripts connected with the workshop of this major artist.

The Soane Hours

Use of Rome(?). Flanders, Ghent-Bruges School, *c.* 1500. 10.5 × 7 cm ($4\frac{1}{8} \times 2\frac{3}{4}$ in), 179ff. 78 miniatures in decorative borders.

Sir John Soane's Museum, London, ms. 4

150 **Baptism of Christ; cleansing of Naaman** f.27v–28

St Sebastian; pilgrim badges in border; Christ and St Mary Magdalene; objects of devotion in border f.112v, 115v

151 **Assumption; Coronation of the Virgin** f.97v–98

Procession of St Gregory ff.136v–137

THE FIRST DOUBLE PAGE shown from this anonymous Flemish volume (p. 150 *above*) presents one of the clearest examples of Biblical typology to be found in any Book of Hours. Specific events and individuals in the Old Testament were regarded by theologians as 'types', prefiguring New Testament scenes and persons ('antitypes') in which the Christian dispensation was later fulfilled. The left-hand page shows the Baptism of Christ in the River Jordan (Matthew 3). On the right is the Old Testament prefiguration: Naaman being cured of his leprosy in the same river. Naaman, captain of the army of the King of Syria, was a 'mighty man in valour, but he was a leper' (II Kings 5:1). Through the intervention of the Prophet Elisha, the Syrian captain was persuaded to dip himself seven times in the waters of Jordan; 'his flesh came again like unto the flesh of a little child, and he was clean' (5:14).

There are subtle pictorial differences in the manner in which the artist shows Christ's Baptism and Naaman's immersion. The legs of both men below the water are marvellously depicted, but the different treatment of their loincloths and gestures, Christ with hands folded in prayer and head bowed before John the Baptist, while Naaman washes himself, differentiate the parallel events. In concentric circles of light the Holy Ghost hovers above Christ while an angel holds his clothes; Naaman is attended by his comrades in arms. Christ's Baptism occurs in a timeless setting, but Naaman's plunge is fixed in an historical time indicated by the Flemish fortified manor house which appears behind him. The Grace of the Holy Ghost (*gratia sancti spiritus*) is specifically mentioned in the Biblical inscriptions of both pictures and appears vividly in Christ's Baptism. The dark blue columbine in the margin on the other page symbolizes, in its petals shaped like doves or *columbae*, the sevenfold gifts of the Holy Spirit.

At the Suffrage of St Sebastian, the saint's near-naked body, tied to a tree planted in a grassy platform, is pierced by many arrows from the bows of four archers (p. 150 *below left*). In the background the Emperor Diocletian and his train watch the scene as if it were a court spectacle. The main interest, however, of this page is the border filled with pilgrims' souvenirs on a mauve ground. The most obvious are the St Veronica Cloth or *Sudarium* with the Holy Face; the Holy Coat or Tunic of Christ, a relic kept at Trier, which appears three times as a small roundel; and the medal of St Michael at the bottom of the border.

The Suffrage of St Mary Magdalene opens with a striking picture of Christ showing himself to the Magdalene, the first person to see him after the Resurrection. This is the scene called the *Noli me tangere* ('Touch me not', John 20:17). It is seen here (p. 150 *below right*) against a luminous background. A slender tree divides the two participants in this memorable event. To accommodate the text the figures are cut off at waist level. The border appears to be close to the spectator; we look through it as if it were a window-frame.

A choice collection of religious objects is depicted on shelves in the border. Their twentieth-century equivalents may still be seen at famous pilgrimage churches, such as Einsiedeln, near Zürich, in Switzerland.

In another ravishing double-page from the Soane Hours we see the Assumption and Coronation of the Virgin at the Hour of Compline (p. 151 *above*). On the left-hand page Mary is carried to Heaven by angels. The vernal landscape beneath contains no empty, flower-filled tomb, but above her Christ appears already holding her crown. On the right-hand page her Coronation (by the Holy Trinity, a feature not found in Books of Hours before the fifteenth century) is shown in a grand but basically simple scene. God the Father and God the Son, identically crowned figures wearing red robes, share a green-draped throne over which hovers the Holy Ghost, a replica of the figure already seen in the Baptism miniature. The blue sky is here rolled back at top and bottom like a curtain to show that the event is taking place in a celestial sphere. A link with the earth is nevertheless preserved by the flower-heads strewn on the gold border, which are all white in homage to the immaculate purity of the Virgin.

The Assumption of the Virgin into Heaven, and her subsequent Coronation, have no scriptural authority but were elaborated in apocryphal writings and popularized by St Gregory of Tours in the sixth century. There is a distinction between the Assumption of her *soul* at death, known as the Dormition or Sleep of the Virgin, and the Assumption of her *body* (leaving a tomb full of flowers to amaze the Apostles). The Eastern Church recognizes, in its doctrine and its art, only the Dormition; the Roman Catholic Church had already believed in the bodily Assumption for many centuries when Pope Pius XII proclaimed it as a dogma in the Holy Year of 1950. To quote Mrs Jameson, the author of *Legends of the Madonna*, 'Of all the themes of sacred art there is not one more complete and beautiful than this, in what it represents, and what it suggests.'

An opening from the Litany of the Saints (p. 151 *below*) shows an elaborate medieval procession which records an historical event: the same one which is shown in the *Très Riches Heures* (pp. 66–67). In February AD 590 a plague had reduced Rome to a city of the dead and dying. The newly elected Pope, St Gregory the Great (590–604), led a sevenfold procession to St Peter's praying for the withdrawal of the plague, and the Archangel Michael appeared at the summit of Castel Sant'Angelo, sheathing his sword as a sign that the Pope's prayers had been answered.

On the right-hand page the Pope, carrying an image of the Virgin Mary, seems to gaze in some astonishment at the apparition. He is followed by a group of hooded flagellants. Immediately behind them comes a group of clerics bearing candles beneath streaming banners. The miserable inhabitants of Rome bring up the rear, while their dead or dying fellow-citizens lie prostrate on the grass in the left foreground.

No whiff of the Renaissance appears to have reached the northern artist. There is no attempt to reproduce any of the classical buildings of Rome. Castel Sant'Angelo is a Gothic castle (though the castellated wall in the background may possibly represent the fortified passageway from the Vatican along which Clement VII fled in 1527; cf. pp. 167–68). The frame-borders of the miniatures are strewn with heads of flowers, a characteristic feature of the Ghent-Bruges School of the late fifteenth and early sixteenth centuries. This striking scene accompanies the text of St Gregory the Great's Litany, beginning *Kyrie eleison* ('Lord, have mercy upon us'), in which prayers of supplication are addressed to a long list of saints.

THIS EARLY SIXTEENTH-CENTURY Book of Hours displays features typical of the late Ghent-Bruges school of book illumination.[1] The miniatures depend from Flemish panel paintings by artists such as Memling, Hugo van der Goes and Gerard David, and are executed with a high degree of technical finish. The borders show the pervasive influence of the Master of Mary of Burgundy (*see* p. 110–13) in the frequent appearance of cut heads of flowers and the charming but unbotanical practice of making acanthus sprays terminate in roses, daisies, carnations, pansies and other flowers. This indulgence is something the more scrupulous Jean Bourdichon never allowed himself in the exactly contemporaneous *Grandes Heures* of Anne of Brittany (p. 126–33). The *tour de force* of painting script or foliage as if seen through the transparent wings of a dragonfly (a trick with which illuminators in this period liked to show off their skill) is also found. A preponderating background influence is the Grimani Breviary (Venice, Biblioteca Marciana), one of the last and grandest manuscripts of the Flemish School.

This rich and mellow style of book illumination appealed to the taste of early nineteenth-century connoisseurs. The book was bought at the Edward Knight Sale in 1821 by the Duke of Buckingham and Chandos for the sum of £105. In 1833 it was acquired by the architect Sir John Soane for his Museum in Lincoln's Inn Fields, London.

It is disappointing that nothing is known of the first owner, but the later history of the manuscript is not entirely blank. Two inscriptions on the first leaf, one in Latin, the other in German, record that the book was given by Wolfgang Wilhelm, Count Palatine (*Pfalzgraf*) of Neuburg, to the Duchess Johanna of Villenosa, a German-born lady living in Spain.[2] The Count (1578–1653) became a Catholic in 1614, partly for political reasons since he had claims to inherit Cleves and Jülich from his mother, the last Duchess. The fact that he refers to the Duchess of Villenosa as his 'mother' perhaps implies that she may have been his sponsor or godmother at the time of his conversion.

For centuries the Soane Hours seems to have remained in Spain. Another inscription in a Spanish hand dating from the eighteenth century certifies the orthodoxy of the manuscript. How it reached England is not known; presumably in the upheavals of the Napoleonic Wars when so many treasures were looted by the occupying armies.

Incipit officiũ beate Marie uirgis
secundum cõsuetudinẽ Romane cu
rie. Ad matutinum. uers.
Domine labia mea aperies
Et os meum annũciabit la
udem tuam. ℣ Deus in adiutoriũ
meum intende. ℟ Dñe ad adiuuan
dum me festina. Glã pri et filio. Sicut
Inuit. Aue Maria gra pl. Dñs tec.
Venite exultemus domino in

The Serristori Hours

Use of Rome. Italy, Florence, *c.* 1500.
21.3 × 14.5 cm ($8\frac{3}{8} \times 5\frac{3}{4}$ in), 189ff. 4 fully decorated pages with miniatures in circular frames, 14 historiated initials and decorative borders.
Victoria and Albert Museum, London, L. 1722–1921

154 **David with the head of Goliath** f.108v

THIS IS A LATE EXAMPLE of Florentine book illumination dating from around the year 1500 and surviving in a contemporary gold-tooled binding. Heraldic evidence establishes that the book was made for the Serristori family, but for which specific individual it is impossible to determine.[1]

The Penitential Psalms (f.109) are introduced by a circular miniature of the boy David standing triumphant in a stony field, one hand resting on a sword, the other on his hip, with the huge head of Goliath lying at his feet. The figure depends from Donatello's and Verrocchio's bronze figures of *David*, two statues well known by the time the Serristori Hours was written. The young David was a favourite subject in Florentine art. He symbolized the republic's heroic resistance to the Visconti and other tyrannical enemies.

At the bottom of the page is a medallion bearing the Serristori arms – Azure, a fess argent accompanied by three gold mullets and in chief the Angevin label of four red points with fleurs-de-lys in between. The other medallions on the page contain Serristori mottoes and emblems. The ornamentation of this and the three other decorated pages in the manuscript is somewhat unusual. Pink and blue foliage sprays are symmetrically disposed in the corners of the narrow rectangular frame. With additional colouring, and painted on a speckled, irregularly shaped lozenge pattern, they form a wreath surrounding the circular miniature.

THE SUBJECTS OF THE THREE other large miniatures are: 1) the Three Living and Three Dead at the Office of the Dead (f.57v); 2) the Visitation at the Gradual Psalms (f.125v); and 3) St Jerome in the wilderness introducing his so-called Psalter (f.134v). The miniatures in the Serristori Hours have been attributed to the School of Boccardino, except for the St Jerome which is by another hand, possibly Monte di Giovanni.[2]

The Serristori Family came originally from Figline in the Valdarno and made their fortune by trading in wool and silk. They became one of the patrician families of Florence, acquiring pictures and statues for their palaces near Santa Croce and on the Lung'Arno. The first notable member was Ser Ristori di Ser Jacopo di Ser Lippo, notary in 1383 to the Signoria. He drew up the articles of peace between the Florentine Republic and Charles of Anjou, King of Naples, for which service he may have been granted the right to use the Angevin label in his arms. At the time when this Book of Hours was written, around the year 1500, the most important representative of the family was Averardo Serristori, ambassador from Florence to the Pope in 1498. Another prominent member was Ristoro di Antonio di Silvestro Serristori, who held the offices of Prior and Gonfaloniere of the Republic at various times between the years 1460–85. A Maddelena Serristori married Jacopo di Pazzi in 1446, for which occasion a terracotta medallion showing the arms of the two families was commissioned from Luca della Robbia.[3] After the failure of the Pazzi conspiracy in 1478 Jacopo was executed, his property was confiscated and his wife retired into a convent.

Despite this connection with the Pazzi, the Serristori family appear to have been supporters of the Medici party and on friendly terms with Lorenzo il Magnifico. At a slightly later date a Giovanni Serristori was a member of the convivial *Compagnia della Cazzola* (Society of the Trowel) to which belonged the sculptor Giovanni Rustici, the painter Andrea del Sarto and members of the Medici family.[4] Pope Leo X regarded the Serristori with special favour, granting them a further augmentation of arms in the form of the letters L.X., after himself. Since this augmentation does not appear in the version of the arms shown in the Book of Hours now in the Victoria and Albert Museum it cannot be later than 1513, when Leo became Pope.

At the very end of the Medici period a Serristori was one of the four executors of the family's last representative, Anna Maria dei Medici, the widowed Electress Palatine, Florence's greatest benefactor, who died in 1743 bequeathing the fabulous Medici treasures in perpetuity to her native city.

The Hours of Alfonso of Aragon, Duke of Calabria

Use of Rome. Italy, Naples, *c.* 1480. 26.5 × 18 cm ($10\frac{3}{8} \times 7\frac{1}{8}$ in), 411ff. 13 large miniatures mostly with full-page borders of white vine interlace, 14 smaller miniatures, 21 historiated initials with partial borders.

Victoria and Albert Museum, London, Salting Collection no. 1224

155 **Annunciation** f.14

ALFONSO, DUKE OF CALABRIA, was a soldier prince who shared the family love of learning and added many books to the renowned Aragonese Library in Naples. His coat of arms, which shows the quarterings of Calabria and Aragon, appears in the laurel wreath at the bottom of the Annunciation page; but it is unlikely that Alfonso was the first owner of the manuscript.

The Annunciation miniature which introduces the text of Matins (the first Hour of the Office of the Virgin) is shown taking place inside a colonnade or loggia, a favourite setting for this scene in Italian painting (p. 155). The brilliant appearance of the page owes as much, however, to the triple border as to the miniature. In a dense white-vine interlace on coloured ground, a crew of lively *putti* play with rabbits, other animals and peacocks. These white-vine interlace borders came into fashion in the early fifteenth century as a decorative auxiliary to the newly developed humanistic script. Both were deliberately adopted as alternatives to Gothic styles of writing and illumination. At first they were used exclusively for classical and humanistic texts; only towards the end of the fifteenth century is the white-vine interlace found in liturgical and devotional texts as seen here. The vine stalks bear only vestigial leaves or flowers, and for this reason the interlace is sometimes described as worm-like (*vermiculato*).

THE BOOK OF HOURS of Alfonso of Aragon, Duke of Calabria, is primarily interesting as a stray volume from the library of the Aragonese Kings of Naples. The first of the dynasty, Alfonso I, the Magnanimous (reigned 1435–58), the victorious rival of René of Anjou (*see* p. 89), founded the library which made Naples a centre of Renaissance learning. His grandson, the Duke of Calabria, became King as Alfonso II, after the death of his father, Ferrante I, and reigned from 25 January 1494 to 23 January 1495, when he abdicated as the troops of the French King Charles VIII were invading his country. A few months later Charles (who claimed to have inherited René of Anjou's titles to Sicily and Naples) entered the capital, but like René did not maintain his position for long. Spanish rule was re-established in 1505.

The Aragonese library was an early casualty of the French occupation. Most of it is now divided between the Bibliothèque Nationale, Paris, and the Biblioteca Universitaria, Valencia. But many single volumes escaped elsewhere. The Hours of Alfonso II arrived at the Victoria and Albert Museum in 1910 via the Spitzer and Salting collections.

It is a large book, containing not only the customary Hours but also a number of additional Offices and quasi-liturgical prayers including the Office of the Trinity (f.336). The large miniatures have been attributed by De Marinis to Matteo Felice, who is recorded in the library's archives from 1467–93. Alfonso's coat of arms (p. 155) is painted over the arms of a previous owner, probably the 'Galiaccio' (Galeazzo) whose name occurs in this form twice in the special prayers. Alfonso's arms are one of several versions adopted before his brief reign over Naples in 1494–95.

The lavish patronage of the Aragonese kings attracted artists to Naples from other parts of Italy, Spain and even distant Flanders. They based their style on the Italian manuscripts which arrived in the Aragonese library. It is ironical that the interlacing white-vine decoration of their works was adopted by the humanists in the mistaken belief that it represented a style of illumination practised in classical Antiquity. The Renaissance interlace derived, in fact, from the Carolingian and Romanesque manuscripts of the despised 'Goths', though it was enriched by the addition of *putti*, parrots (an indication of Neapolitan provenance), pearls, candelabra and other items from the repertoire of Renaissance ornament.

The Aragonese library in Naples has been reconstituted, book by book as it were, in a magisterial study by Tammarino de Marinis.[1] Here are listed and described 479 manuscripts formerly in the library and painstakingly identified from documents and inventories. Among them is Alfonso of Aragon's Book of Hours.

The Hours of Reynalt von Homoet

Use of Utrecht. Germany, Cologne, 1475.
18 × 13 cm ($7\frac{1}{8} \times 5\frac{1}{8}$ in), 362 pp. 13 miniatures in elaborate frames.
Wallraf-Richartz-Museum, Cologne

158 **Reynalt before St John the Baptist** p. 150
159 **Crowning with Thorns** p. 102

THIS IS A RARE EXAMPLE of a posthumous Book of Hours. The manuscript was apparently commissioned by Reynalt's widow, Sophia von Bylant, some years after Reynalt's death in 1459, from the so-called Bartholomew Master of Cologne. The Homoets and Bylants belonged to the nobility of Guelderland or Guelders (Geldern), a duchy between Utrecht and Cologne on the lower Rhine; and they announce their status by a bold display of heraldry. But since this is not a wedding Book of Hours, one of the partners being dead when it was written, husband and wife are shown on separate pages.[1]

Reynalt von Homoet kneels before his patron St John the Baptist in an undefined setting indicated only by a gold brocade curtain in the background with blue sky above (p. 158). Both men are portrayed in an individual manner, suggesting portraits painted from life, but with a difference of scale. Reynalt, an elderly man with grey hair and trim figure dressed in a tunic of gold and black brocade, kneels on a blue cushion before a *prie-dieu* draped in black, on which rests his Book of Hours in its *chemisette* binding. Above his head is suspended a red shield bearing a silver fess nebuly, the arms of the Homoet family, with a lion-head crest and flowing red mantling.

The larger and younger figure of St John the Baptist is elaborately dressed in a lion skin and slashed undershirt girdled by a white cloth and with a bright red cloak slung over his shoulder. He ignores his suppliant but gazes lovingly at the Lamb of God nestling in his left hand, towards which he points with the other hand in explanation of the crinkled scroll above his head which carries his own words (John 1:29): *Ecce agnus Dei, ecce qui tollit peccata mundi* ('Behold the Lamb of God, which taketh away the sin of the world'). In the broad gold border, fantastic birds flit and perch among foliage sprays belonging to no known botanical species. Two angels hover in space, one playing music, the other praying to show that Reynalt is in their care.

The Crowning with Thorns at the Mocking of Christ (p. 159) is a scene of the utmost cruelty. Christ's hands are bound up in his sleeves, from which protrudes the reed given him in mockery of a sceptre. Pilate stands on the right directing operations, which three torturers perform with obvious relish. Half kneeling in front of Christ is a jester-like figure, dressed in yellow trousers and a long green outer garment lined with red (the colours of hatred, jealousy and sexuality), who makes an obscene gesture. In the background a woman (Pilate's wife?) and other people watch the scene through an open window.

The rectangular border framing the miniature is painted in matt gold over which are placed vivid, unpleasant scenes of the strong triumphing over the weak. At the top is a scorpion with raised tail, flanked by a crane-like bird of prey attacking a smaller bird and, on the left, an eagle devouring a limb torn from a bleeding lamb. Below is a centaur with a very human face and cap carrying off a naked child. At the bottom of the page Reynard the fox has got Chanticleer by the neck; an owl, sinister bird of evil, is being mobbed by smaller birds; and a pine marten or similar creature robs a nest of eggs. In the margin on the right an evil-looking serpent-woman or mermaid completes the parade of malevolence.

THE HOMOET HOURS, like the Hours of Mary of Guelders (pp. 78–81) and Yolande de Lalaing (pp. 142–45), belongs to the northern region where German and Netherlandish cultural influences met in the fifteenth century. A succession of artists produced, for patrons living in this area, Books of Hours charged with a realism which makes many contemporary French examples seem anaemic and mannered by comparison. In quasi-chronological sequence the most distinguished of these artists are: the Master of Mary of Guelders; the Master of Zweder of Culemborg (so called after a Bishop of Utrecht); the Master of Catherine of Cleves; the Souldenbach Master (who takes his name from a Canon of Utrecht); the Master of Gisbert de Brederode, who supplied Yolande de Lalaing with her Book of Hours; and the Bartholomew Master, who illuminated the Hours of Reynalt von Homoet.

This Book of Hours, like some other works of the northern schools, distils a religious sensibility paralleled in France only by the Rohan Master. The Bartholomew Master is chiefly known as a panel painter. His name comes from the large altarpiece of St Bartholomew (now in the Alte Pinakothek, Munich) which he painted for the Church of Sankt Kolomb in Cologne. Little is known about him except that he studied in Utrecht and worked in Cologne from 1470 to *c.* 1510 for the Carthusian Order. Two of his altarpieces, the *Thomas-Altar* and the *Kreuz-Altar*, were made for Carthusian churches in the city.

The Bartholomew Master's large altarpieces were painted without assistants, and he left no followers. This isolation has been explained by the hypothesis that he may have been a Carthusian himself, either a lay brother or perhaps a monk of this strictest and most self-contained of the religious orders. His highly individual style, agitated, dynamic but at the same time deeply pondered in a manner which makes him immediately recognizable as 'a painter of ideas', was not developed in monastic seclusion but derived from Utrecht, where he may have been born.

This is one of his early works, produced in 1475 if this date on the Scourging miniature applies to the whole book. Though a *manuscrit de luxe*, its impact is quite different from that of, say, the Berry Books of Hours. Here is displayed a suffering, not an elegant, religious sensibility. The miniatures and borders of the Passion scenes are filled with a concentration of realistic detail which forces the viewer to identify himself directly with Christ's physical sufferings in the Flagellation, Crowning with Thorns and Crucifixion. In the Middle Ages people identified themselves with the Passion of Christ in a manner difficult for us to understand or share today; in the Mystery Plays, the spectators were closely involved with scenes which gave dramatic form to the essential paradox of the Christian religion – the sacrifice of the innocent victim, the only man not fallen from a state of grace, for the salvation of all mankind.[2]

The 'pathetic' quality in northern art was early recognized. Michelangelo is reported by Francesco d'Ollanda to have said of Flemish painting that 'it will generally satisfy any devout person more than the painting of Italy, which will never cause him to drop a single tear, but that of Flanders will cause him to shed many; this is not owing to the vigour and goodness of that painting, but to the goodness of such devout person; women will like it, especially the very old ones, or very young ones. It will please likewise friars and nuns, and also some noble persons who have no ear for true harmony.'[3] It would be interesting to know the reactions of patrons when they received such disturbing works as those of the Bartholomew Master.

DEVS·IN·ADIVTORIV
MEVM·INTENDE
DOMINE·AD·ADIVVA
NDVM·ME·FESTINA

The Hours of Cardinal Alessandro Farnese

Use of Rome. Italy, Rome, completed 1546.
14.5 × 10.5 cm ($5\frac{3}{4} \times 4\frac{1}{8}$ in), 114ff. 28 miniatures with historiated borders.
Pierpont Morgan Library, New York, M. 69

162–63 **Visitation of the Shepherds; Fall of Man**
f.27v–28
See also pages 166–67

WITH THE HOURS of Cardinal Alessandro Farnese we enter the world of late Renaissance Italy. This magnificent prayerbook, made for a Prince of the Church by Giulio Clovio, follows, nonetheless, in its pictorial arrangement the medieval system of typological correspondence: events prefigured in the Old Testament are fulfilled in the New. On the first double-spread reproduced (pp. 162–63), Adam and Eve tasting the forbidden fruit in the Garden of Eden are seen opposite the shepherds gathered around the infant Christ and his Mother. Theologians spoke of Mary as the new Eve through whose Son the evil brought into the world by the serpent which tempted Eve would finally be overcome. The Fathers of the Church made this message clear to the simplest minds by pointing out that EVA when reversed spelt AVE – 'Hail', the first word in the prayer recalling the Archangel Gabriel's message at the Annunciation: *Ave Maria gratia plena*.

Leaving aside these theological niceties, the eye is bewitched by the artist's virtuosity in handling his pictorial and decorative themes. The two confronting miniatures are set in architectural frames packed with nude figures in Michelangelesque postures, whose white bodies contrast with the bronzed *atlantes* supporting the pedestals on which they stand. At top and bottom of the page are small pictures painted in black and white in the manner of antique cameos: the Angel's Announcement to the Shepherds and the Boy Christ in the Temple on the left-hand page, the Creation of Eve and Expulsion from Eden on the right. Subsidiary sacred themes appear on the plinths flanked and mounted by *putti*.

The shepherds who bring gifts of sheep, the humble equivalent of the rich gifts of gold, frankincense and myrrh presented by the Three Kings, form a masterly group. In contrast, the picture on the opposite page is occupied by two figures only, the totally nude Adam and Eve glimpsed in the moment before their eyes were opened and they hastily concealed their nakedness with fig leaves. Behind them rise the Trees of Life and Knowledge, but only Eve's tree, encircled by the female-headed serpent, bears the forbidden fruit: on Adam's tree sits a parrot watching the scene below. The beasts in the garden rest and browse in happy ignorance of the sufferings which will shortly overtake them and the human pair.

VASARI'S LIFE of 'Giulio Clovio, Illuminator' opens with the words: 'For many centuries, and perhaps for yet other centuries, there has been no more excellent illuminator or painter of small things than Giulio Clovio, who has far surpassed all others in this exercise.'[1] Contemporaries considered him to have raised the art of the miniature to the level of painting, and spoke of him as the equal of Raphael, Michelangelo and Titian; a point of view diametrically opposed to that current today which holds that book illumination declined as an art form when its practitioners started treating the miniature as if it were an easel or panel painting.

A glance at the Farnese Hours tells us that Clovio indeed abandoned the integration of miniature, border and text for the Renaissance concept of paintings inside frames. His pages are like architectural frontispieces, with the exiguous text serving as lapidary inscriptions. But how beautifully composed are these confronting pairs of Old and New Testament scenes, inhabited by physically appealing Michelangelesque figures with their varied tones of white for the bodies and of bronze for the statues; how harmonious the blending of delicate washes of colour with matt gold backgrounds! Looking at these crowded yet controlled illuminations one can understand why it was said that Clovio could reproduce the ceiling of the Sistine Chapel within the confines of a page.

The text is written in the *cancelleresca formata* script, a small rounded hand with reduced ascenders and descenders which consorts impeccably with Clovio's paintings. The scribe was Francesco Monterchi, secretary to Pier Luigi Farnese, Duke of Parma, the father of Clovio's patron Cardinal Alessandro. Nor is the binding, though not quite contemporary, unworthy. It dates from sometime after 1589 when Cardinal Odoardo Farnese, on inheriting the book from his great-uncle Cardinal Alessandro, commissioned from the Roman goldsmith Antonio Gentili (known as *il Faenza*) a sumptuous silver-gilt binding with *doublures* decorated with the names and arms of the two Cardinals. This binding was later attributed to Benvenuto Cellini; the temptation to link Clovio and Cellini, the two most famous artists of the time after the great painters and sculptors, must have been irresistible.

Clovio was not a native of Italy. His birthplace was the village of Grižane in Croatia at the northern end of the Adriatic Sea. When he was born there in 1498 as Juraij (George) Glovičić, the province was under Hungarian rule though disputed by Venice which had claims to control this marchland. At an early age the young Glovičić moved to Venice where he italianized his name and learnt to paint by copying coins, medals, pictures and woodcuts (including one of the Virgin by Dürer). The patronage, protection and friendship of a succession of cardinals bearing some of the proudest names in Italy – Grimani (two of them), Campeggio, Farnese – secured Clovio's entry into the most cultivated and richest circles in Italy. Yet his career almost ended prematurely when he was taken prisoner during the Sack of Rome in 1527, maltreated and nearly killed. During this ordeal he vowed to become a monk if he escaped with his life. A year later he entered the monastery of San Ruffino, a house of the Scopetine Order (flagellants) outside Mantua. His career as a monk lasted three years, much of the time being spent in the monastery of Candiana near Padua where he met and is said to have received instruction from the illuminator Girolamo da Verona. Here he broke a leg. Following a long illness, his then patron Cardinal Marino Grimani secured for Clovio Papal dispensation from his vows. The Cardinal did not wish his protégé's sparkling gifts to be submerged in the preoccupations and observations of monastic life. Though Clovio put off his monkish habit he remained always a man of the Church, never marrying and requesting in his will to be buried in the garb of his order. His superlative gifts as an artist were graced by a personality that was kindly, generous and devout, as several anecdotes confirm. In the early 1540s, if not before, he moved to Rome to join the household of the young Cardinal Alessandro Farnese, son of the dissolute Piere Luigi, who had been made a Cardinal by his grandfather Paul III in 1534 at the age of fourteen, and who wore the purple for more than half a century until his death in 1589. Of this 'supremely cultivated connoisseur and patron of the arts', James Wardrop wrote that 'he did as much to illustrate, as his sire had done to degrade, the name of Farnese'.[2] At the Palazzo Farnese, then in the course of construction, Clovio remained for the rest of his life, except for occasional visits to Florence and Parma; he died in 1578 aged eighty.[3]

The modern cult of Clovio began in the eighteenth century. For many years he was regarded, as Vasari had prophesied, as the greatest master of miniature painting who had ever lived, *il piccolo Michelangelo*. Clovio became almost a generic term, any fine example of sixteenth-century Italian illumination being attributed to him. The effusive Thomas Frognall Dibdin, librarian to Earl Spencer, devotes several pages to him in the *Bibliographical Decameron* (1817): 'What Cabinets of Popes, Monarchs, Princes, and Cardinals have not been enriched by his matchless pencil?' This admiration long persisted. In 1891 John W. Bradley wrote of the Farnese Hours: 'The multiplicity of the accessories, the elegance of the pose of the naked figures, the correctness of the perspective, the beauty of the trees, everything that drawing requires or colouring demands, serves to render this MS. a monument unique in the world.'[4]

It was inevitable that this Clovio worship should produce a reaction. Twenty years later we find the severe comment in J.A. Herbert's *Illuminated Manuscripts* (1911) that 'Giulio Clovio is a typical master of the decadence; fond of weak suave forms, cheap sentiment, and soft broken colours. His work, though often technically good, never rises above an insipid elegance ... [his] usual weaknesses peep out continually, especially in the large compositions: his mawkish sentiment, want of dignity and florid taste.'[5]

Now that decadence is no longer an emotive term, we can appreciate Clovio's art in a wider historical and psychological context. We are aware of Mannerist ambiguities in his work, of figures disturbingly confined in architectural niches too small for their size, of the refined yet unmistakable sexuality of his nudes. It is the latter, one suspects, that aroused J. A. Herbert's censure. In an historical context Clovio appears as an artist peculiarly fitted by temperament and training to give visual expression to the antiquarian, devout, artistic and pleasure-seeking ethos which characterized the clerically dominated Roman society of his time. To the medieval tradition of Books of Hours he contributed a brilliant coda by painting in the grandest manner on the smallest scale.

Sancte Andrea or.
Sancte Iacobe or.
Sancte Ioannes or.
Sancte Thoma or.
Sancte Iacobe or.
Sancte Philippe or.
Sancte Bartholomeę or.
Sancte Matthæe or.
Sancte Simon or.
Sancte Thadæe or.
Sancte Mathia or.
Sancte Barnaba or.
Sancte Luca or.
Sancte Marce or.
Omnes ſancti Apoſtoli, & Euangeliſte, orate pro nobis
Omnes ſancti diſcipuli domini, orate pro nobis
Omnes ſancti Innocentes, orate

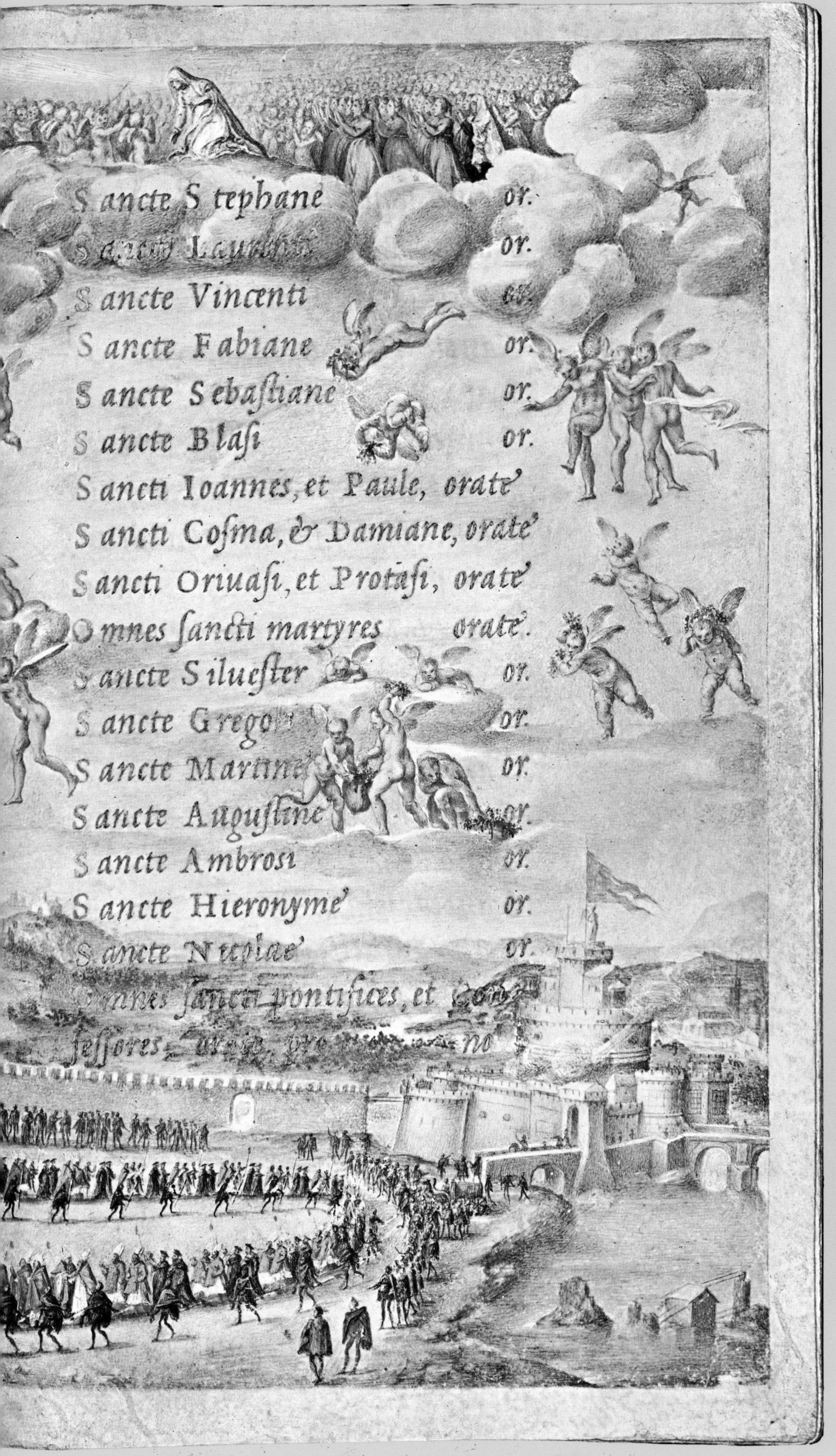
Sancte Stephane or.
or.
Sancte Vincenti
Sancte Fabiane or.
Sancte Sebastiane or.
Sancte Blasi or.
Sancti Ioannes, et Paule, orate
Sancti Cosma, & Damiane, orate
Sancti Oriuasi, et Protasi, orate
Omnes sancti martyres orate.
Sancte Siluester or.
Sancte Grego or.
Sancte Martine or.
Sancte Augustine or.
Sancte Ambrosi or.
Sancte Hieronyme or.
Sancte Nicolae or.
Omnes sancti pontifices, et Con-
fessores,

The Hours of Cardinal Alessandro Farnese

Use of Rome. Italy, Rome, completed 1546.
14.5 × 10.5 cm ($5\frac{3}{4} \times 4\frac{1}{8}$ in), 114ff. 28 miniatures with historiated borders.
Pierpont Morgan Library, New York, M. 69

166–67 **Corpus Christi Procession in border**
ff.72v–73
See also pages 162–63

THE MOST ARRESTING PAGE in the Farnese Hours, one of the most spectacular in any Book of Hours, is the double-spread at the Litany (pp. 166–67), showing the Corpus Christi procession to St Peter's in Rome. This panoramic scene may be compared with the procession of St Gregory from the *Très Riches Heures* of the Duke of Berry and the Soane Hours (pp. 66–67, 151). The Tiber and Castel Sant'Angelo with St Michael on the summit appear in all three of these procession pages; but unlike the earlier examples the scene in the Farnese Hours is painted with the accuracy of a topographical record. On the left is Old St Peter's, with wide steps leading up to the atrium and three-storied Loggia of Benediction with its supporting tower, the tallest in Rome. Linking the two pages is the fortified wall containing the *passetto* which gave direct access to Castel Sant'Angelo from the Vatican. Along this secret corridor Popes hurried to seek safety in the fortress when danger threatened: the Borgia Alexander VI in 1495 when Charles VIII and his French army invaded the Holy City, the Medici Clement VII during the Sack of Rome by Imperial troops in 1527.

Less than twenty years after this disaster Giulio Clovio painted the peaceful, resplendent Corpus Christi procession here reproduced. We seem already to be in the Baroque age. A long line of cardinals, bishops, clergy, Swiss Guards, acolytes and others accompany the Pope, who sits in his *sedia gestatoria* holding the *ostensorium* or monstrance that exhibits the Host. Clouds open above to reveal visions of the Holy Trinity and the Virgin Mary adored by saints and angels as they look down on the procession. *Putti* in the clouds are furnished with flowers to cast down on the worshippers below.

PRINTED BOOKS OF HOURS

THE IMMEDIATE descendants of manuscript Books of Hours, the printed *Horae* of the late fifteenth and early sixteenth centuries, have received detailed study in a number of specialized works.[1] Some are examples of incunabula, dating from the 'cradle' period of printing before 1500. So great was the interest of bibliophiles and connoisseurs in early printed books from the days of Dibdin in the beginning of the nineteenth century onwards that the systematic study of the printed *Horae* preceded that of the manuscript examples from which they depend.

The invention of printing from movable type in the mid fifteenth century, together with the use of engraving techniques for illustration, removed much of the drudgery from the Books of Hours industry and speeded up their production. While royalty and other wealthy patrons continued to commission superlative manuscript prayerbooks, the presses catered for a much larger public unable or unwilling to spend money on costly handwritten copies. Around 1490 several enterprising publishers in Paris captured this profitable market. During the next half-century and longer, printed Books of Hours rolled off the presses of Paris and Lyons to become one of the Northern Renaissance's best-sellers, satisfying not only an eager home demand but also the export trade to England and the Netherlands.

In purpose and format, printed Books of Hours followed the older manuscript examples. The more luxurious specimens were printed on vellum, the cheaper ones on paper: both types contained the same prayers and devotions and followed the traditional scheme of illustration established in manuscript copies. The differences were at first more in matters of technique than appearance. Woodcut illustrations replaced individually painted miniatures, and printed vignettes the familiar ivy-leaf or 'strewn-flower' borders. But the cuts were often coloured by hand and initials left blank to be filled in by a scribe in imitation of manuscripts. It was only later that the printed *Horae* became a distinct, peculiarly French genre of book production. The change occurred when the *manière criblée*, or 'dotted manner', with black backgrounds speckled with white dots or lines, appeared in illustrations printed from the engraved metal plates which gradually replaced wood blocks. The increasing secularization of the subject matter in illustrations and borders is a further characteristic of the printed *Horae*.

The first printed Book of Hours was a nondescript little volume published in 1486 by Antoine Vérard, the royal bookseller, and intended to be coloured by hand. A second edition appeared the following year. A professional calligrapher and miniature-painter, Vérard was one of the first to realize the commercial possibilities of printing for the production of Books of Hours. His pioneer efforts were quickly followed by numerous and finer examples published by himself, Simon Vostre, Jean du Pré, Philippe Pigouchet and their followers and rivals. Vostre, like Vérard, was a publisher rather than a printer, who used Pigouchet's press until at least 1502. Each of his books is specifically stated to be *imprimé pour Simon Vostre*, not *imprimé par*. Pigouchet was both a publisher and printer whose first known *Horae* dates from 1491; thenceforth he became pre-eminent in this field.

As the number of printed Books of Hours increased new pictorial subjects began to appear – finely designed printers' marks; the Astrological Man; the Chalice (sometimes inaccurately called the Holy Grail) containing Christ's wound (*plaie*) in his side shown in its supposed dimensions; the Tree of Jesse, signifying the Church Militant and Triumphant; David and Goliath in combat;

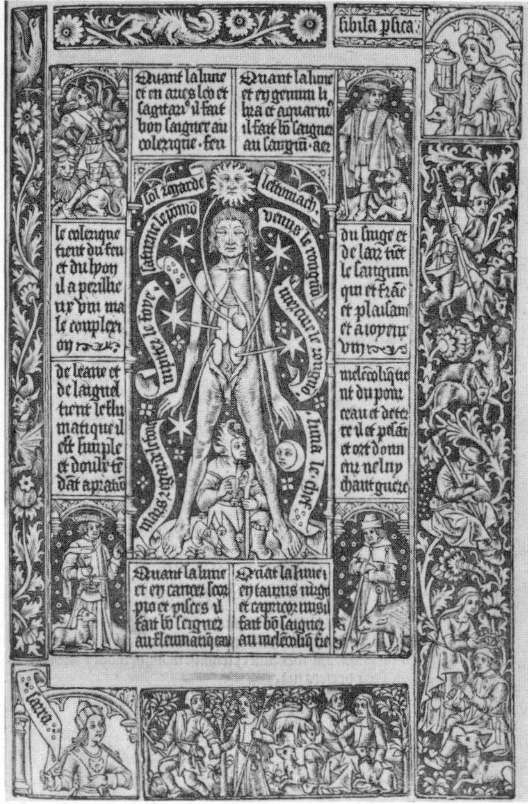

Ces presentes heures à lusaige de Rome ont esté faictes pour S. Vostre . . ., Paris, P. Pigouchet, 1500–01. Zodiacal Man. In borders: prophetesses, pastoral scenes.

Ces presentes heures . . . (*see above*). Chalice containing Christ's Wound. In borders: prophetesses, hunting scenes.

David watching Bathsheba in her bath, with the death in battle of her husband Uriah the Hittite (the old association of love and war) shown often on the facing page.

Some of these subjects had appeared occasionally in manuscript Books of Hours – the Astrological or Zodiac Man, once only, in the *Très Riches Heures*, the Holy Chalice in the Playfair Hours in the Victoria and Albert Museum, David and Bathsheba more frequently in French Books of Hours of the later fifteenth century but without the complementary scene of Uriah's death. In the printed *Horae* the Astrological Man precedes the Calendar. He is often shown as a skeleton or an eviscerated corpse, with a jester in cap and bells crouching between his feet, to symbolize the human brain and its vagaries under the influence of the moon.[2] The jester looks at the moon and points to his fool's-cap in allusion to lunar madness.[3] In the corners of the text are small pictures representing the four temperaments or 'humours'. The whole design summarizes in pictorial form current medical belief concerning the influence of the planets and signs of the zodiac upon different parts of the human body.

These large single subjects are accompanied by borders in which the decorative repertoire is greatly increased by new religious and profane imagery. In addition to foliage ornament there appear series of vignettes illustrating scenes from the Life of Christ and Mary, the Prodigal Son, Joseph, the Seven Sacraments, the Theological Virtues, the Apocalypse, the Dance of Death and many more.

In the borders of the printed *Horae* secular and religious themes mingle in incongruous but not altogether inappropriate juxtaposition. The Triumphs of Caesar occasionally occur, but a more frequent classical intrusion is the Twelve Sibyls. These prophetesses were regarded by the Church as foretelling the coming of Christ. Wearing turbans and fantastical late Gothic dress, they appear as half-length figures holding their individual attributes: the Tiburtine Sibyl a severed hand, the Erythraean Sibyl the lily of the Annunciation, the Cumaean Sibyl a bowl, the Cimmerian Sibyl a horn, the Delphic Sibyl a crown of thorns, and so on.

More immediately appealing than this recondite symbolism are the contemporary scenes of hunting, peasants dancing, gathering fruit or picnicking, children playing games and other country activities – delightful vignettes in which the gentler aspects of life are depicted with gaiety

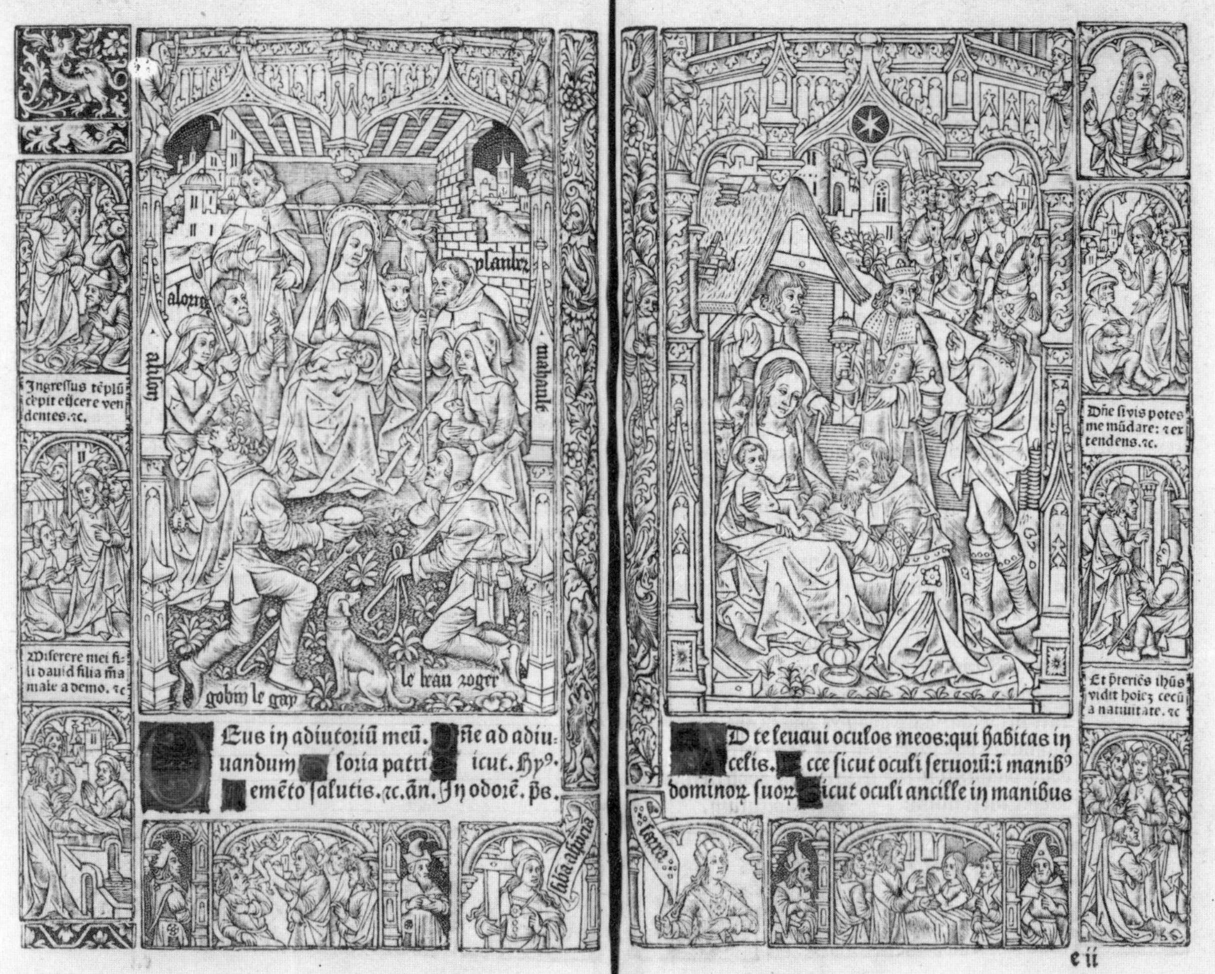

Ces presentes heures . . . (*see opposite*). Adoration of the Shepherds and of the Magi. In borders: prophetesses, healing miracles of Christ.

and freshness. An increasingly secular mood appears in the larger illustrations as well. The Angel's Announcement of Christ's Nativity is treated as a pastorale in which shepherds dance, play music and disport themselves with their wives. In Thielman Kerver's *Horae* they appear round the crib labelled with the names given to them in French Mystery Plays: 'Alison' and 'Mahault' for the women, 'Gobin le Gai', 'Aloris', 'Ysanber' and 'le beau Roger' for the men. They carry humble gifts as do the shepherds in the Farnese Hours (p. 162). The cuts and vignettes in printed Books of Hours are important sources for the study not only of early engraving, but of costume, social customs, agriculture and also the vernacular language, since the captions are often in French.

Of the most important printer-publishers already mentioned (there were many more), Antoine Vérard, the first in the field, kept close to his manuscript exemplars, both in format and terminology. His editions of a *Grandes Heures* (*c.* 1488, known also as the *Heures royales* because commissioned by Charles VIII) and a *Petites Heures* (1490) had wide circulation. Simon Vostre and Philippe Pigouchet worked together in producing the greatest number of Books of Hours under one imprint. They were celebrated for their borders, in which the Dance of Death sequence constantly appears. In the Calendars short verse quatrains in Latin or French were sometimes added comparing the different ages of man with the months of the year.

Thielman Kerver's full-page illustrations are harmoniously integrated with the text on the double-spreads, but his borders are considered to be inferior to those of Vostre and Pigouchet, from whom he often copied motifs. The brothers Germain and Gilles Hardouin produced almost as many examples as Vostre and Pigouchet; they are characterized by the frequent use of hand-colouring in the woodcuts in imitation of manuscript Books of Hours.

In the 1520s Geofroy Tory, calligrapher, printer, publisher and designer, transformed the traditional French Book of Hours from a Gothic survival into a modern, Renaissance book.[4] He had, indeed, already accomplished this feat in the

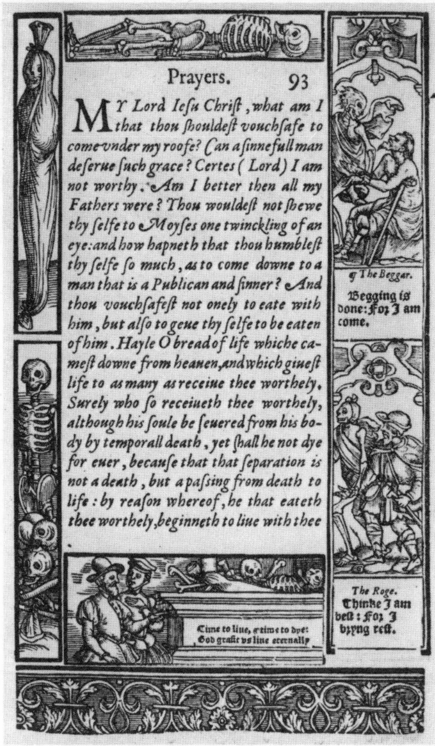

Prayers. 93

MY Lord Ieſu Chriſt, what am I that thou ſhouldeſt vouchſafe to come vnder my roofe? Can a ſinnefull man deſerue ſuch grace? Certes (Lord) I am not worthy. Am I better then all my Fathers were? Thou wouldeſt not ſhewe thy ſelfe to Moyſes one twinckling of an eye: and how hapneth that thou humbleſt thy ſelfe ſo much, as to come downe to a man that is a Publican and ſinner? And thou vouchſafeſt not onely to eate with him, but alſo to geue thy ſelfe to be eaten of him. Hayle O bread of life whiche cameſt downe from heauen, and which giueſt life to as many as receiue thee worthely. Surely who ſo receiueth thee worthely, although his ſoule be ſeuered from his body by temporall death, yet ſhall he not dye for euer, becauſe that that ſeparation is not a death, but a paſsing from death to life: by reaſon whereof, he that eateth thee worthely, beginneth to liue with thee

Booke of Christian Prayers. London, Richard Day, 1569. In borders: Dance of Death.

exquisite manuscript Book of Hours written in Roman script for Queen Claude of France which has been mentioned on p. 137. Though Tory had been anticipated in the use of Roman type by Kerver in 1504, his stylish miniatures and borders in the Italian manner have an up-to-date look which makes the so-called *Heures gothiques* seem suddenly old-fashioned. In his two Books of Hours, published in 1525 and 1527, the use of black for the African king in the Adoration of the Magi pictures is a particularly effective touch.

A last lingering look at the Middle Ages is found in the famous Prayerbook of the Emperor Maximilian (once the husband of Mary of Burgundy), which combines the new art of printing with the medieval tradition of manuscript embellishment in the margins. In the unique copy (now in the Staatsbibliothek, Munich) of the very small edition of this Prayerbook printed in Gothic type at Augsburg in 1513 by Johann Schönsperger, Albrecht Dürer provided coloured pen drawings of finely observed figures and animals in the margins.[5]

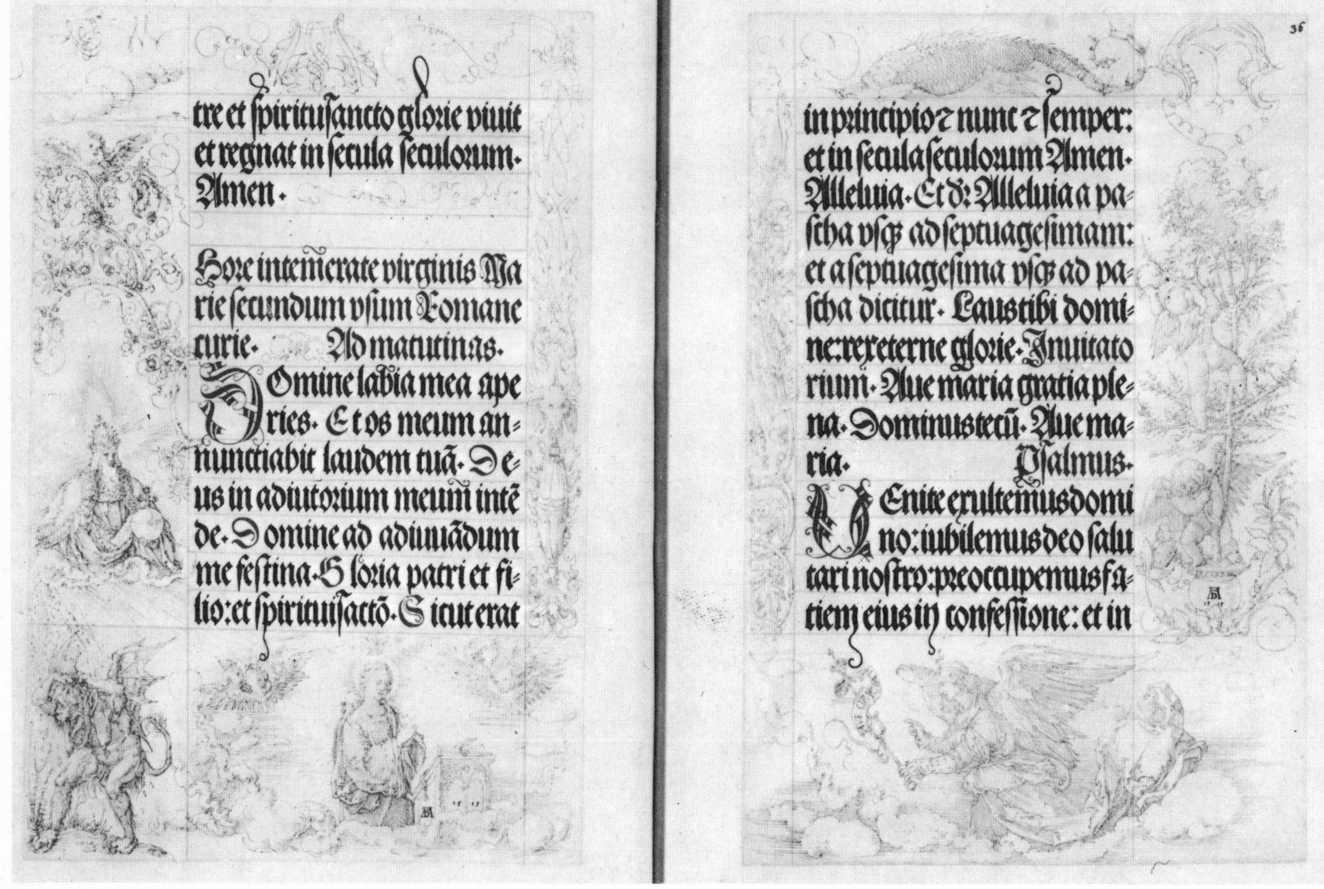

tre et ſpirituiſancto glorie viuit et regnat in ſecula ſeculorum. Amen.

Hore intemerate virginis Marie ſecundum vſum Romane curie. Ad matutinas.

Domine labia mea aperies. Et os meum annunciabit laudem tuã. Deus in adiutorium meum intẽde. Domine ad adiuuãdum me feſtina. Gloria patri et filio: et ſpirituiſactõ. Sicut erat

36

in principio et nunc et ſemper: et in ſecula ſeculorum Amen. Alleluia. Et dicitur: Alleluia a paſcha vſq; ad ſeptuageſimam: et a ſeptuageſima vſq; ad paſcha dicitur. Laus tibi domine rex eterne glorie. Inuitatorium. Aue maria gratia plena. Dominus tecũ. Aue maria. Pſalmus.

Venite exultemus domino: iubilemus deo ſalutari noſtro: preoccupemus faciem eius in confeſſione: et in

Prayerbook of the Emperor Maximilian (*Hore intemerate Virginis secundum usum Romane curie*), Augsburg, J. Schönsperger, 1513. In borders, drawings by Albrecht Dürer: God and Devil, Annunciation.

Officium Beate Marie Virginis. Venice, F. Marcolini, 1545. *Flight into Egypt at Vespers.*

Eus in adiutorium meum intende.
D omine ad adiuuan dum me feſtina.
G loria patri,& filio, & ſpiritui ſancto.
S icut erat in principio. Alleluia.
añ. Aſſumpta eſt. Pſalmus.
D Ominus regnauit, decorem indutus eſt : indutus eſt dominus fortitudinem,& præcinxit ſe.
E tenim firmauit orbem terræ,qui non commouebitur.
P arata ſedes tua deus ex tunc: à ſeculo tu es.
E leuauerunt flumina domine,eleuauerunt flumina vocem ſuam.
E leuauerunt flumina fluctus ſuos,à vocibus aquarum multarum.
M irabiles elationes maris: mirabilis in altis dominus.
T eſtimonia tua credibilia facta ſunt

Horae in laudem Beatissime Virginis Marie ad usum Romanum. Lyons, G. Rouillé, 1553. The Visitation at Lauds.

Maximilian's prayerbook is a survival from a vanishing world, as is the *Booke of Christian Prayers*, printed (1569 and later editions) for Elizabeth I of England, the champion of Protestantism. In format and in choice of such familiar subjects for the borders as the Dance of Death, the book might at first glance, text apart, be taken for a Parisian product of seventy or eighty years before. In contrast with such Gothic recalls, the *Horae* printed in France and Italy during the mid sixteenth century reflect in their embellishment the currently fashionable Mannerist styles, as seen in the striking Visitation picture at Lauds in the Book of Hours published in 1553 by Guillaume Rouillé of Lyons and the beautiful Flight into Egypt in Francesco Marcolini's 1545 Venetian Book of Hours.

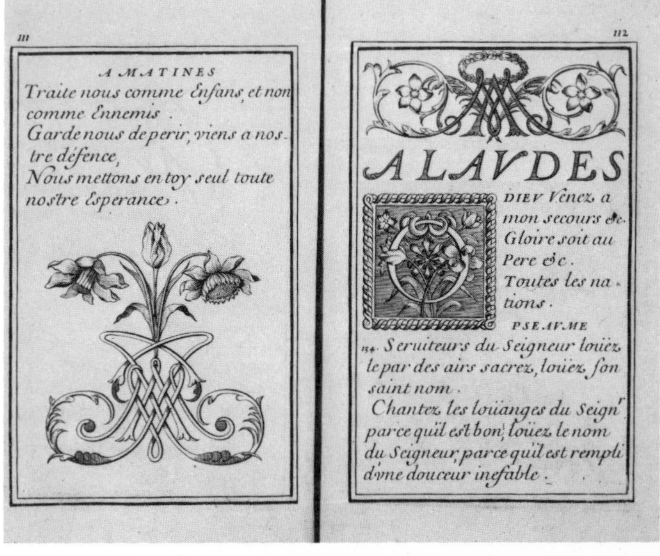

111

A MATINES
Traite nous comme Enfans, et non comme Ennemis.
Gardenous de perir, viens a nostre défence,
Nous mettons en toy seul toute nostre Esperance.

112

A LAVDES
DIEV Venez a mon secours &c. Gloire soit au Pere &c. Toutes les nations.
PSEAVME
Seruiteurs du Seigneur loüez le par des airs sacrez, louez son saint nom.
Chantez les loüanges du Seign[r] parce quil est bon; loüez le nom du Seigneur, parce quil est rempli d'vne douceur inefable.

Heures nouvelles dédiées à Madame la Dauphine, Paris, Louis Senault, *c.* 1680.
Text pages, beginning of Lauds.

For another two or three centuries Books of Hours lingered on as accessories of fashionable piety. At the court of Louis XIV in the second half of the seventeenth century there was a vogue for minute prayerbooks (*Petites Heures*) exquisitely written and embellished by Nicolas Jarry, the most accomplished calligrapher of the time, and his followers. Books of Hours with text and decorations engraved throughout were another luxury reserved for royalty. The *Heures nouvelles*

Livre d'heures d'après les manuscrits de la Bibliothèque royale. Paris, Engelmann and Graf, 1846.
Title page, showing Duke of Berry's emblems.

Livre de prières tissé d'après les enlumineurs des manuscrits du XIVe au XVIe siècle.
Lyons, A. Roux, 1886–87. Nativity.

dediées à Madame la Dauphine (Marie-Christine of Bavaria, the short-lived and unhappy wife of the Grand Dauphin) was written and engraved by Louis Senault about 1680. It was reissued for subsequent Dauphines of France until well into the eighteenth century. These stylish, sophisticated books, with their *mélange* of prayers, ornamental initials and finely engraved script, are minor examples of the opulence of the court and chapel at Versailles.

In 1846 the firm of Engelmann and Graf published a chromo-lithographed *Livre d'heures d'après les manuscrits de la Bibliothèque royale*. This book marks a revival of interest in medieval illumination. Shown a few years later in the Paris Exhibition of 1855, the volume is a technical *tour de force* in which pages from Books of Hours owned by the Duke of Berry, Anne of Brittany and others are reproduced without reference to source or date. The *Paroissien de la Renaissance*, printed in black and white, published by Engelmann and Graf in 1874 in an immaculate replica of an early sixteenth-century Tory binding, is another of these elegant *objets de piété* of the late nineteenth century, as is the *Heures romaines* of Mame of Tours.

Their ultimate refinement is represented by the *Livre de prières tissé*, woven in silk, made in 1886 in the factory of J. A. Henry of Lyons, a firm which specialized in the production of silken Books of Hours and Missals. These stylish virtuosities appeared under the imprint of the Maison A. Roux, a famous publishing house of Lyons which was succeeded by the Librairie Lardonchet. One of the designers employed by the Maison Henry was a R[everendus]. P[ater]. J. Hervier. Apart from his name, which appears in some examples, nothing is known about him.[6] The *de luxe* prayerbook he designed is a final exhalation of the medieval Book of Hours.

NOTES ON THE TEXT

THE BOOK OF HOURS pp. 11–39

1 The principal authorities used in this section have been: James, M.R., *A Descriptive Catalogue of the Manuscripts in the Fitzwilliam Museum, Cambridge*, Cambridge, 1895; Bishop, E., *On the Origin of the Prymer*, 1897, reprinted in *Liturgica Historica*, Oxford, 1918, pp. 211–37; Hoskins, E., *Horae beatae Mariae virginis, or Sarum and York Primers*, London, 1901; Dewick, E.S., *Facsimiles of Horae de Beata Maria Virgine from English MSS. of the Eleventh Century*, Henry Bradshaw Society, XXI, London, 1902; Wordsworth, C., and Littlehales, H., *The Early Service-Books of the Church*, London, 1904, ch. IX; Leroquais, V., *Le Livres d'heures manuscrits de la Bibliothèque Nationale*, 3 vols., Paris, 1927 (and *Supplément* ... Mâcon, 1943); Leclercq, H., 'Livres d'heures', in Cabrol, F., *Dictionnaire d'archéologie chrétienne et de liturgie*, vol. IX, Paris, 1930, col. 1836–82; Labarre, A., 'Livres d'heures', in *Dictionnaire de spiritualité ascétique et mystique*, vol. VII, Beauchesne, 1968, pp. 410–31. Special acknowledgment is also made to the late Dr L.M.J. Delaissé, whose notes and papers, now deposited in the Bodleian Library, Oxford, have been the source for much of the information in this section, especially the lecture 'The Production of Books of Hours in France in the Fifteenth Century', published in modified form under the title 'The Importance of Books of Hours for the History of the Medieval Book', in *Gatherings in Honor of Dorothy Miner*, Baltimore, Md, 1974, pp. 203–25.

For the text of Books of Hours *see* Littlehales, H., ed., *The Prymer or Prayer Book of the Lay People in the Middle Ages, in English, dating from about 1400 A.D. Edited from the Manuscript in St. John's College, Cambridge, by H.L.*, London, 1891; and for the Latin text of the Uses of Sarum and York, Littlehales, H., ed., *The Prymer or Lay Folk's Prayer Book*, Early English Text Society, Original Series 109, London, 1897.

2 Herolt, J., *Miracles of the Blessed Virgin Mary*, Introduction by Eileen Power, London, 1928, p. xiii. For the cult of the Virgin Mary in the later Middle Ages the following have been specially useful: Hirn, Y., *The Sacred Spring: a Study of the Poetry and Art of the Catholic Church* (first published in Swedish, 1909), London, 1958; Ahsmann, H.J.P., *Le Culte de la sainte Vierge et la littérature française profane du moyen âge*, Utrecht, 1930.

3 *See* Poole, R.L., *Medieval Reckonings of Time*, London, 1921; and for a detailed Calendar study Perdrizet, P., *Le Calendrier Parisisien à la fin du moyen âge d'après le Bréviaire et les Livres d'Heures*, Paris, 1937.

4 For the liturgical Uses and tables of localization tests for Books of Hours *see* James, op. cit. (note 1), pp. xxvi–ix; and Madan, F., 'Hours of the Virgin Mary (tests for localization)', in *Bodleian Quarterly Record*, III, 1920, pp. 41–44.

5 Lehmann-Haupt, H., *The Göttingen Model Book. A Facsimile Edition and Translation of a Fifteenth-Century Illuminator's Manual*, New York, 1972.

6 Van Buren, A.H., and Edmunds, S., 'Playing Cards and Manuscripts', in *The Art Bulletin*, LVI, 1974, pp. 12–30.

7 For the evolution of the Occupations from classical times to the thirteenth century *see* Webster, J.C., *The Labours of the Months*, Princeton, N.S., 1938; and for the later period, Le Senecal, J., 'Les occupations des mois dans l'iconographie du moyen âge', in *Bulletin de la*

Société des Antiquaires de Normandie, XXXV, 1921–23, Caen, 1924; and Willard, J., 'The Occupations of the Months in Mediaeval Calendars', in *Bodleian Quarterly Record*, VII, 1932, pp. 33–39.

8 The shepherd's *houlette* derives from *houler*, to throw, an allusion to the use of the shovel end for throwing loose earth. The hook at the other end, or below the shovel, was for catching and holding sheep while inspecting them for mange and disease and bleeding or applying other remedies. For a detailed description see the extract from Jehan de Brie, *Le Bon Berger, ou le vray regime des bergers et bergères*, quoted in Delamarre, M.J.B., *Bergers de France* (exhibition catalogue), Musée des arts et traditions, Paris, 1962, published in Paris: Société d'Ethnographie française, *Arts et traditions populaires*, X, 1962. Jehan de Brie's treatise, written in 1379, appeared in several Paris editions during the sixteenth century and was reprinted in 1879 with introduction by Paul Lacroix. I am indebted to Mr Eustace. A. Alliott for this reference and for practical information concerning *houlettes. See also* Jacobeit, W., *Schafhaltung und Schäfer in Zentraleuropa bis zum Beginn des 20. Jahrhunderts*, Berlin, 1961, especially ch. viii, 'Das Arbeitsgerät des Schäfers'; and Spriggs, G.M., 'Shepherds Abiding', in *Country Life*, 5 December 1974, pp. 1710–14.

9 For the illustrations at the Office of the Dead *see* Meiss, M., 'La Mort et l'Office des Morts à l'époque du Maître de Boucicaut et des Limbourg', in *Revue de l'art*, No. 1–2, 1968, pp. 17–25.

10 Evans, J., *Art in Medieval France*, London, 1948, p. 201.

11 Delaissé, ms. Notes, Bodleian Library, Oxford.

12 Payment from the royal accounts for a *petite paellet d'yvoire pour attacher la chandelle quant la Royne dist ses heures* is quoted in Meiss, M., *The De Levis Hours and the Bedford Workshop*, New Haven, Conn., 1972, p. 8, note 5; *see also* Tovell, R.M., *Flemish Artists of the Valois Court*, Toronto, 1950, p. 5.

13 Waterton, P., *Pietas Mariana Britannica*, London 1879, p. 125; and Hoskins, E., *Horae beatae Mariae Virginis*, London, 1901, p. xvii.

14 The will of Queen Blanche of Navarre is printed in *Mém. Soc. de l'Hist. de Paris,* XII, 1885, pp. 1–64.

15 The inventory of Marguerite of Brittany is printed in *Bibliothèque de l'Ecole des chartes*, XXIII, 1862, pp. 45–6.

16 These references are taken from Wordsworth and Littlehales, op. cit. (note 1), pp. 248–50; and Waterton, op. cit. (note 13), pp. 123ff.

17 This translation comes from Panofsky, E., *Early Netherlandish Painting*, Cambridge, Mass., 1953, vol. I, p. 68.

18 For the rosary *see* Wilkins, E., *The Rose-Garden Game. The Symbolic Background to the European Prayer-Beads*, London, 1969, especially ch. 2, pp. 44–63; and Ward, M., *The Splendour of the Rosary*, London, 1946. For the miniature from the Hours of Catherine of Cleves *see* pl. 116 in the facsimile edited by J. Plummer, London, 1966; and Gorissen, F., *Das Stundenbuch von Katharina von Kleve*, Berlin, 1973.

19 Delaissé, ms. Notes, Bodleian Library. For the St Apollonia miniature from the Chevalier Hours *see* Sterling, C., and Schaefer, C., *The Hours of Etienne Chevalier* (facsimile), London and New York, 1972, pl. 45.

20 Steele, R., 'Dies Aegyptiaci', in *Proceedings of the Royal Society of Medicine* (History of Medicine Section), vol. XII, 1919, pp. 108–21.

21 La Trémoille, F. de, ed., *Livre de comptes 1395–1406. Guy de la Trémoille et Marie de Sully. Publié d'après l'original*, Nantes, 1887, p. 73.

22 MacGibbon, D., *Jean Bourdichon*, Glasgow, 1933, p. 13.

23 Baldass, L., *Jan van Eyck*, London and New York, 1952, colour plate facing p. 10.

24 Harris, E., 'Mary in the Burning Bush; Nicolas Froment's Triptych at Aix-en-Provence', in *Journal of the Warburg Institute*, I, 1938, pp. 281–86.

25 For the Llangattock Hours *see* Kraus, H.P., *Monumenta Codicum Manu Scriptorum* (exhibition catalogue), New York, 1974, no. 36, pp. 86–89; and Schilling, R., 'Das Llangattock Stundenbuch', in *Wallraf-Richartz Jahrbuch*, XXIII, 1961, pp. 211–56. For the Flemish Book of Hours, *c.* 1510,

from the workshop of Gerard Horenbaut, *see* Sotheby Parke Bernet & Co., *Catalogue of Western Manuscripts and Miniatures*, 5 July 1976, lot 68.

26 For the Bedford Hours *see* Spencer, E. P., 'The Master of the Duke of Bedford: the Bedford Hours', in *Burlington Magazine*, CVII, 1965, pp. 495–502. The manuscript contains the armorials of the Duke of Bedford and of his wife Anne, sister of Philip the Good of Burgundy. Anne gave the book to the young King Henry VI shortly before his coronation as King of France in Paris in 1430.

27 These quotations come from Dearden, J. S., 'John Ruskin, Collector', in *The Library*, XXI, 1966, pp. 125, 139.

28 For what follows *see* Labarre's article 'Livres d'heures', op. cit. (note 1).

The Hours of Jeanne d'Evreux, Queen of France pp. 40-44

1 The rediscovery of Jean Pucelle was pioneered by Leopold Delisle in *Les Heures dites de Pucelle*, Paris, 1910. Modern authorities from which many of the details in this section are taken include Rorimer, J. J., *The Hours of Jeanne d'Evreux at the Cloisters, the Metropolitan Museum of Art* (facsimile), New York, 1957; Morand, K., *Jean Pucelle*, Oxford, 1962; and the special issue, 'Jean Pucelle – Facts and Fictions', of the *Bulletin of the Metropolitan Museum of Art*, February 1971.

2 Baron, F., 'Enlumineurs, peintres et sculpteurs Parisiens des XIVe et XVe siècles, d'après les archives de l'Hôpital Saint-Jacques-aux-Pélerins', in *Paris: Comité des Travaux historiques et scientifiques, Bulletin archéol.*, N.S. 6, 1970, pp. 87–88, 112. Dr Françoise Baron's important discovery of the date of Pucelle's death has upset the chronology of his work hitherto accepted.

3 For Jeanne d'Evreux, *see* Dreux du Radier, H. L., *Mémoires des reines de France*, Amsterdam, 1776; Martin, H., *Histoire de France*, 4th edn, IV, 1860, p. 562; Guilhermy, M. F. de, *Inscriptions de l'histoire de la France (Collection des Documents inédits)*, II, 1875, pp. 135–37 (for the effigy and heraldry in Saint-Denis Abbey); and *Musées et Monuments de France*, II, 1907, pp. 17–18 (for the statues of herself and her husband commissioned for their tomb from Hennequin de Liège).

4 The codicil to Jeanne d'Evreux's will and the entry in the Berry inventories are reproduced in full in Morand, op. cit. (note 1), p. 31.

The Grey-FitzPayn Hours p. 43

1 The Grey-FitzPayn Hours is fully described in Egbert, D. D., *The Tickhill Psalter and Related Manuscripts*, New York, 1940, ch. 3 and Appendix III. *See also* Wormald, F., and Giles, P. M., *Illuminated Manuscripts in the Fitzwilliam Museum* (exhibition catalogue), Cambridge, 1966, no. 53; and Verdier, P., and others, *England and France from 1259 to 1328* (exhibition catalogue, National Gallery of Canada), Ottawa, 1972, no. 35, p. 105. For a list of the birds in the Grey-FitzPayn Hours *see* Hutchinson, G. E., 'Attitudes towards Nature in Medieval England. The Alphonso and Birds Psalters', in *Isis*, 65, no. 226, 1974.

2 Cox, J. C., *Memorials of Old Derbyshire*, London, 1907, p. 12.

The Taymouth Hours pp. 48–49

1 The Taymouth Hours is fully described in James, M. R., *A Descriptive Catalogue of the Second Series of Fifty Manuscripts (Nos. 51–100) in the Collection of Henry Yates Thompson*, Cambridge, 1902, no. 57, pp. 50–74. Use has also been made in this section of the description of the Taymouth Hours in Klingender, F., *Animals in Art and Thought to the End of the Middle Ages*, London, 1971, pp. 415–27. The account of the rituals of the stag hunt is taken direct from this source.

2 Pächt, O., 'A Giottoesque Episode in English Illumination', in *Journal of the Warburg Institute*, VI, 1943, p. 53, note 3.

3 Little, A. G., *Franciscan History and Legend in English Medieval Art*, Manchester, 1937, pp. 75–76.

The Saint-Omer Hours p. 52

1 Quoted in Evans, J., *English Art 1307–1461*, Oxford, 1949, p. 38.

2 Pierpont Morgan Library, *Exhibition of Illuminated Manuscripts held at the New York Public Library* (exhibition catalogue), New York, 1934, no. 74, pp. 38–39.

John, Duke of Berry p. 53

1 For the political career of the Duke of Berry, *see* Lehoux, F., *Jean de France, duc de Berri, sa vie, son action politique*, 4 vols., Paris, 1966–68.

2 For patronage and manuscripts, *see* Meiss, M., *French Painting in the time of Jean de Berry*, especially the first and third parts, *The Late Fourteenth Century and the Patronage of the Duke*, London and New York, 1967, and *The Limbourgs and their Contemporaries*, London and New York, 1974.

The Très Belles Heures de Notre Dame of John, Duke of Berry p. 56

1 For the *Très Belles Heures de Notre Dame*, *see* Durrieu, P., *Les Heures de Turin*, Paris, 1902 (revised edn. by Chatelet, A., 1967); Hulin de Loo, G., *Les Heures de Milan*, Brussels, 1911; Durrieu, P., *Les Très Belles Heures de Nostre Dame du Duc de Berry*, Paris, 1922; and Meiss, *The Late Fourteenth Century*, London and New York, 1967, ch. VI, XI.

The Petites Heures of John, Duke of Berry p. 57

1 For the *Petites Heures*, *see* Panofsky, E., *Early Netherlandish Painting*, Cambridge, Mass., 1953, pp. 43–49; and Meiss, *The Late Fourteenth Century*, London and New York, 1967, ch. VIII.

The Brussels Hours of John, Duke of Berry p. 60

1 For the Brussels Hours, *see* Fierens-Gevaert, H., *Les Très Belles Heures de Jean de France, duc de Berry*, Brussels, 1924; Gaspar, C., and Lyna, F., *Les principaux manuscrits à peintures de la Bibliothèque Royale de Belgique*, Paris, 1937, vol. I, pp. 399–409; Meiss, *The Late Fourteenth Century*, London and New York, 1967, ch. IX-X; and Calkins, R.G., 'The Brussels Hours reevaluated', in *Scriptorium*, XXIV, 1970, pp. 3–26.

The Grandes Heures of John, Duke of Berry p. 61

1 For the *Grandes Heures*, *see* Thomas, M., *Les Grandes Heures de Jean, duc de Berry* (facsimile), London and New York, 1971; and Meiss, *The Late Fourteenth Century*, London and New York, 1967, ch. XII.

2 Meiss, op. cit. (note 1), p. 69.

The Belles Heures of John, Duke of Berry p. 64

1 For the *Belles Heures*, *see* Porcher, J., *Les Belles Heures de Jean de France*, Paris, 1953; Freeman, M., 'A Book of Hours made for the Duke of Berry', in *Bulletin of the Metropolitan Museum of Art*, New York, XV, 1956, pp. 93–104; Rorimer, J.J., *The Belles Heures of John, Duke of Berry*, New York, 1958; Meiss, M., and Beatson, E.H., *Les Belles Heures de Jean, duc de Berry* (facsimile), London, 1974; and Meiss, *The Limbourgs and their Contemporaries*, London and New York, 1974, ch. V.

The Très Riches Heures of John, Duke of Berry pp. 65–69

1 For the *Très Riches Heures*, *see* Longnon, J., and Cazelles, R., *Les Très Riches Heures du Duc de Berry* (facsimile), London and New York, 1969; Baldass, L., *Jan Van Eyck*, London, 1952, pp. 8–14; and Meiss, *The Limbourgs and their Contemporaries*, London and New York, 1974, ch. VI.

2 Meiss, op. cit. (note 1), pp. 321ff.

3 Aumale, H., duc d', *Chantilly. Le Cabinet de livres: manuscrits*, Paris, 1900, pp. 59–71.

The Hours of Marshal Jean de Boucicaut pp. 72–73

1 For the Boucicaut Hours, *see* Meiss, M., *French Painting in the Time of Jean de Berry. The Boucicaut Master*, London and New York, 1968, especially ch. I and V; and Panofsky, E., *Early Netherlandish Painting*, Cambridge, Mass., 1953, pp. 53–61.

2 Hirn, Y., *The Sacred Shrine*, London, 1957, p. 234.

2 Michaud, J. E., and Poujoulat, J.J. F., eds., *Le Livre des faicts du bon Messire Jean le Maingre, dit Boucicaut*, in *Nouvelle Collection des mémoires rélatifs à l'histoire de France*, II, Paris, 1881.

4 Meiss, op. cit. (note 1), p. 9.

5 Huizinga, J., *The Waning of the Middle Ages*, Garden City, N.Y., 1954, and London, 1955, p. 222.

6 Meiss, op. cit. (note 1), p. 69.

The Hours of Giangaleazzo Visconti, Duke of Milan pp. 76–77

1 Meiss, M., and Kirsch, E. W., *The Visconti Hours: Biblioteca Nazionale, Florence*, London, 1972. Acknowledgment is made here to the Forewords by Professor Meiss and Dr Kirsch.

2 Hobson, A. R. A., 'The Visconti Hours', letter to the *Times Literary Supplement*, 9 March 1973.

3 Pächt, O., 'Early Italian Nature Studies and the Early Calendar', in *Journal of the Warburg and Courtauld Institutes*, XIII, 1950, pp. 13–14.

The Hours of Mary of Guelders pp. 80–81

1 For the Hours of Mary of Guelders *see* Wegener, H., *Beschreibende Verzeichnisse der Miniaturen-Handschriften der preussischen Staatsbibliothek zu Berlin*, Leipzig, 1928, pp. 136–40; Keller, K., *Zwei Stundenbücher aus dem geldrischen Herzogshause. Das Stundenbuch der Herzogin Maria und das ihres Gemahls*, Geldern, 1969; Panofsky, E., 'Guelders and Utrecht; a footnote on a recent acquisition of the Nationalmuseum at Stockholm', in *Konsthistorisk Tidskrift*, XII, 1953, pp. 90–102; *Rhein und Maas Ausstellung* (exhibition catalogue), Aachen, 1972, especially Vermeeren, P. J. H., 'Kodikologische Notizen zum Gebetbuch der Herzogin Maria von Geldern (Q.10)', pp. 473–77. At some time fairly early in its history the manuscript was divided. The Berlin-Dahlem portion was in the possession of the Electors of Brandenburg by the seventeenth century, the second part held by the Hapsburgs in Vienna (Cod. 1908). Nothing is known about the date or circumstances of the splitting of the manuscript. The two parts were shown together in the 'Europe 1400' exhibition (Vienna, 1962) and are described in the catalogue (no. 208, p. 217).

2 Panofsky, E., *Early Netherlandish Painting*, Cambridge, Mass., 1953, pp. 100–101.

3 Guiffrey, J., *Inventaires de Jean, duc de Berry*, Paris, 1894, I, no. 1142, p. 304; no. 1186, p. 316.

4 Lehoux, F., *Jean de France, duc de Berri*, Paris, 1966–68, vol. 2, p. 40–41, with reference to Jarry, E., *La Vie politique de Louis de France, duc d'Orléans, 1372–1407*, Paris, 1889, pp. 320–21.

5 Delaissé, L. M. J., *A Century of Dutch Manuscript Illumination*, Berkeley, Calif., 1968, especially pp. 9–10 (for *devotio moderna*). *See also* Marrow, J., 'Dutch Illumination and the Devotio Moderna', in *Medium Aevum*, XLII, 1973, pp. 251–58, where Delaissé's conclusions are examined in a critical but appreciative manner.

The Grandes Heures de Rohan pp. 84–85

1 For the Rohan Hours *see* Heimann, A., 'Der Meister des "Grandes Heures de Rohan" und seine Werkstatt', in *Städel-Jahrbuch*, Frankfurt, VII–VIII, 1932, pp. 1–61; Porcher, J., *The Rohan Book of Hours*, London and New York, 1959, and *French Miniatures from Illuminated Manuscripts*, London and New York, 1960, p. 69; Meiss, M., and Thomas, M., *The Rohan Book of Hours*, London and New York, 1973; and Meiss, M., *The Limbourgs and their Contemporaries*, London and New York, 1974, pp. 256–77.

2 This summary of Yolanda's political role derives from Orliac, J. d', *Yolande d'Anjou: la reine des Quatre Royaumes*, Paris, 1933.

3 Meiss and Thomas, op. cit. (note 1), pp. 22–26. In *The Limbourgs and their Contemporaries*, London and New York, 1974, p. 478, note 93a, Professor Meiss expresses doubts about the hypothesis of the Rohan Master's limited participation in the *Grandes Heures*.

4 Martin, F., *Art and the Religious Experience: the 'Language' of the Sacred*, Lewisburg, Pa, 1972, p. 26.

The Paris Hours of René of Anjou pp. 88–89

1 The theological implications of the washing of the infant Christ are summarized in Hirn, Y., *The Sacred Shrine*, London, 1958, pp. 250–52.

2 For René's Paris Book of Hours, *see* Leroquais, V., *Les Livres d'heures manuscrits de la Bibliothèque Nationale*, Paris, 1927, vol. I, no. 20, p. 64.

3 Lecoy de La Marche, A., *Le roi René*, 2 vols., Paris, 1875.

4 Sources used in this section include, beside Lecoy de La Marche: Quatrebarbes, T. de, *Œuvres completes du roi René, avec un biographie et de notices*, 4 vols., Paris, 1843–46; Des Garets, M. L., *Un Artisan de la renaissance française au XVe siècle. Le roi*

René, 1409–80, Paris, 1946; Quarre, P., 'Le roi René, prisonnier du duc de Bourgogne à Dijon, et son œuvre de peintre', in *Revue du Louvre*, XIV, 1964, pp. 67–74 (with illustration of the Tour de Bar at Dijon); and Levron, J., *Le Bon Roi René*, Paris, 1972. *See also* Arnaud d'Agnel, G., *Les comptes du Roi René, publiés d'après les originaux inédits conservés aux Archives des Bouches-du-Rhône*, 3 vols., Paris, 1908–10. Nos. 506, 508 and 710 record the making of three Books of Hours (one, in August 1452, by 'Berthelmy Deick' for the King, and no. 1887 a payment in December 1478 to 'père Jehan', who recited the Hours with King René).

5 Pächt, O., 'René d'Anjou et les Van Eyck', in *Cahiers de l'Association internationale des études françaises*, 1955, pp. 41–67, and the expanded version 'René d'Anjou-Studien. I. Teil', in *Jahrbuch der kunsthistorischen Sammlungen in Wien*, Neue Folge, XXXIII, 1973, pp. 85–126. *See also* Ring, G., *A Century of French Painting 1400–1500*, London, 1949, pp. 18–21, 206–07.

6 *See* Unterkircher, F., ed., *Le Livre du cueur d'amours espris*, London, 1975, where the sixteen large paintings are reproduced in facsimile. (The US edn is published as *King René's Book of Love*, New York, 1975.)

The London Hours of René of Anjou pp. 92–93

1 For René's London Book of Hours, *see* Schilling, R., 'The Master of Egerton 1070 (Hours of René d'Anjou)', in *Scriptorium*, VIII, 1954, pp. 272–82; and Meiss, M., *French Painting in the Time of Jean de Berry. The Boucicaut Master*, London, 1968, pp. 95–96; and ibid., *The Limbourgs and Their Contemporaries*, London, 1974, pp. 328–29.

2 This and the following paragraphs are based entirely on Pächt, O. (*see* 'The Paris Hours', note 5), who reproduces all five miniatures added to René's London Hours.

The Hours of Philip the Bold, Duke of Burgundy pp. 96–97

1 Wormald, F., and Giles, P.H., 'Description of Fitzwilliam Museum ms. 3–1954. Book of Hours made for Philippe le Hardi', in *Transactions of the Cambridge Bibliographical Society*, IV, 1964, pp. 1–28, pls. I–VI.

2 The older histories of the Burgundian Dukes (Barante, 4th edn, 7 vols., Paris, 1826; and Laborde, 3 vols., Paris, 1849–50) have been consulted for this section but most of the historical material comes from Professor Richard Vaughan's four monographs on the Valois Dukes: *Philip the Bold*, London and Cambridge, Mass., 1962; *John the Fearless*, London and New York, 1966; *Philip the Good*, London and New York, 1970; *Charles the Bold*, London, 1973, and New York, 1974. Use has also been made of Cartellieri, O., *The Court of Burgundy*, London, 1929; Calmette, P., *The Golden Age of Burgundy*, London, 1962; and Tyler, W.R., *Dijon and the Valois Dukes of Burgundy*, Oklahoma City, 1971.

3 For the economic unity and uniform coinage of the Burgundian territories in the Low Countries, *see* Spufford, P., *Monetary Problems and Politics in the Burgundian Netherlands, 1433–1496*, Leyden, 1970.

4 Spencer, B.W., 'Medieval Pilgrim Badges', in *Rotterdam Papers: a Contribution to Medieval Archaeology. Symposium edited by J.C.N. Renaud*, Rotterdam, 1968, pp. 137–53. *See also* Köster, K., 'Pilgerzeichen und Wallfahrtsplakatten von St Adrian in Geraardsbergen', in *Städel-Jahrbuch*, Frankfurt, Neue Folge 4, 1973, pp. 103–20.

5 Gaspar, G., and Lyna, F., *Les Principaux manuscrits à peintures de la Bibliothèque Royale de Belgique*, Paris, 1937, vol. I, pp. 349–51, 419–23.

6 Delaissé, L.M.J., *Medieval Miniatures from the Royal Library of Belgium*, London and New York, 1965, pp. 100–103 (with coloured reproduction of the Madonna of the Crescent from ms. 11035–7, Bibliothèque Royale, Brussels).

7 Vaughan, R., *Philip the Bold*, London and Cambridge, Mass., 1962, p. 197.

The Hours of John the Fearless, Duke of Burgundy pp. 100–01

1 For John the Fearless, *see* Vaughan, R., *John the Fearless*, London and New York, 1966.

2 For John the Fearless's Book of Hours, *see* Leroquais, V., *Un livre d'heures de Jean Sans Peur, duc de Bourgogne*, Paris, 1930, and *Supplément aux Livres d'heures manuscrits de la Bibliothèque Nati-*

onale, Mâcon, 1943, no. 2, pp. 5–9; *see also Bibliothèque de l'Ecole des Chartes,* vol. 100, 1939, pp. 416–17.

3 Palliser, Mrs B., *Historical Devices, Badges and War-Cries*, London, 1870, p. 35.

4 Chestret de Hanette, J. de, *Histoire de la Maison de la Marck y compris les Clèves de la seconde race*, Liège, 1898, p. 43.

5 Baltimore, Walters Art Gallery, *Illuminated Books of the Middle Ages and Renaissance* (exhibition catalogue compiled by Dorothy Miner), Baltimore, Md, 1949, no. 125, p. 47 (W.166).

6 The portrait of John the Fearless, in the Antwerp Museum, shows him in profile with hands folded above a tapestry of the arms of France over which is suspended a shield of the Burgundian arms – a succinct heraldic expression of his political ambitions. The portrait is reproduced as frontispiece to Professor Vaughan's monograph (*see* note 1 above).

The Hours of Philip the Good, Duke of Burgundy pp. 104–05

1 For The Hague Book of Hours, *see* Byvanck, A.W., *Les Principaux Manuscrits à peintures de la Bibliothèque Royale des Pays-Bas à La Haye*, Paris, 1924, pp. 55–59; Delaissé, L.M.J., *La Miniature flamande: le mécénat de Philippe* (exhibition catalogue, Brussels, Palais des Beaux-Arts), Brussels, 1959, pp. 92–94; Lieftinck, G.I., 'Grisailles in the Book of Hours of Philip the Good and the Master of Mary of Burgundy', in *Oud Holland*, vol. LXXXV, 1970, pp. 237–41; and Leroquais, V., *Le Bréviaire de Philippe le Bon*, Brussels, 1929, pp. 146–50.

2 The payment to Le Tavernier is quoted in full and discussed by the Abbé Leroquais, who does not accept the identification of The Hague Book of Hours in its present form with the payment description (op. cit. note 1).

3 Delaissé, L.M.J., *Medieval Miniatures from the Royal Library of Belgium*, London and New York, 1965, p. 158.

4 The following paragraphs are based on Bonenfant, P., *Philippe le Bon*, 3rd edn, Brussels, 1955; and Vaughan, R., *Philip the Good*, London and New York, 1970, especially ch. 5, 'The Ruler and his Court'. For the Burgundian Library *see* Gaspar, C., and Lyna, F., *Philippe le Bon et ses beaux livres*, Brussels, 1944; and *La Librairie de Bourgogne* (Introduction by L. Gilissen), Brussels, Fondation Cultura, 1970.

5 Pasquier, E., *Les Recherches de la France*, Paris, 1643, book IV, ch. 32.

The Black Hours of Charles the Rash, Duke of Burgundy pp. 108–09

1 For Charles the Rash the following sources have been used: Bartier, J., *Charles le Téméraire*, Brussels, 1972; Vaughan, R., *Charles the Bold, Last Duke of Burgundy*, London, 1973; and Tyler, W.R., *Dijon and the Valois Dukes of Burgundy*, Oklahoma City, 1971. For the Burgundian booty *see* Deuchler, F., *Die Burgunderbeute. Inventar der Beutestücke aus den Schlachten von Grandson, Murten und Nancy, 1476–77*, Berne, 1965.

2 Deuchler, op. cit. (note 1), no. 316, p. 349.

3 The Franc or Liberty of Bruges comprised a territorial district outside the jurisdiction of the city. It was governed by a *châtelain* who was the lieutenant of the Counts of Flanders and possessed its own town hall or Palais du Franc in Bruges; *see* Letts, N., *Bruges and its Past*, London, 1924, p. 24, note 31. Art historians, except for A. van Schryver (*see* 'The Hours of Mary of Burgundy', note 1), consistently and inaccurately describe the mourning Book of Hours presented to Charles the Rash by the Franc de Bruges as a gift from the magistrates and Town Council of Bruges – the democratic rivals of the aristocratic, feudal Franc.

4 For the Black Hours *see* Trenkler, E., *Das schwarze Gebetbuch*, Vienna, 1948; and Delaissé, L.M.J., *La Miniature flamande* (exhibition catalogue), Brussels, 1959, no. 135, p. 119.

The Hours of Mary of Burgundy pp. 112–13

1 Unterkircher, F., and Schryver, A. de., eds., *Gebetbuch Karls des Kühnen vel potius Stundenbuch der Maria von Burgund, Codex Vindobonensis 1857*, 2 vols, Graz, 1969; Unterkircher, F., *European Illuminated Manuscripts in the Austrian National Library*, London, 1967, pp. 244–46. Also indispensable is Pächt, O., *The Master of Mary of*

Burgundy, London, 1948, to which acknowledgment is here made. The manuscripts by or connected with the Master of Mary of Burgundy are discussed by Lieftinck, G. I., 'Boekverluchters uit de omgeving van Maria van Bourgondië, *c.* 1475–*c.* 1485' (with English translation of the Introduction), in *Verhandelingen van de Koninklijke Vlaamse Academie voor Wetenschappen, Letteren en Schone Kunsten van België*, XXXI, no. 66, Brussels, 1969. Lieftinck (p. xxix) observes that the church choir in Mary of Burgundy's Book of Hours (*see* p. 110) is reminiscent of St John's Church in Ghent.

2 Schryver, in Unterkircher and Schryver, op. cit. (note 1), p. 44.

3 Pächt, op. cit. (note 1), p. 32.

The Hours of Isabella Stuart, Duchess of Brittany pp. 116–17

1 For the history and anecdotes in this section the following works have been consulted: Lobineau, G.A., *Histoire de Bretagne*, 2 vols., Paris, 1707 (reprinted 1973); Morice, P.H., *Histoire ecclésiastique et civile de Bretagne*, 2 vols., Paris, 1750–56; La Borderie, A. de, *Histoire de la Bretagne* (continued by B. Poquet), vol. 4, Rennes, 1906; Raison de Cleuzieu, A., *La Bretagne*, 3rd edn, Saint-Brieuc, 1925; Durtelle de Saint-Sauveur, E., *Histoire de Bretagne*, Rennes, 1935; and Rebillon, A., *Histoire de Bretagne*, Paris, 1957.

2 Heimann, A., 'Der Meister der "Grandes Heures de Rohan" und seine Werkstatt', in *Städel-Jahrbuch*, Frankfurt, VII, 1932, pp. 5–6; and Meiss, M., *The Limbourgs and their Contemporaries*, London and New York, 1974, pp. 264, 306–7.

3 James, M.R., *A Descriptive Catalogue of the Manuscripts in the Fitzwilliam Museum, Cambridge*, Cambridge, 1895, no. 62, pp. 156–74.

4 For the manuscripts belonging to Isabella Stuart, which include three Books of Hours, *see* Toynbee, M.R., 'The Portraiture of Isabella Stuart, Duchess of Brittany', in *Burlington Magazine*, LXXXVIII, 1946, pp. 300–06. Isabella's appearances in these manuscripts are among the earliest painted Stuart portraits on record.

5 Molière's version of John V of Brittany's *bon mot* occurs in *Les Femmes savantes*, act II, where Chrysale, in a long speech directed against too much learning in women, observes that:

Nos pères sur ce point étoient gens bien sensés,
Qui disoient qu'une femme en sait toujours assez
Quand la capacité de son esprit se hausse
A connoître un pourpoint d'avec un haut de chausse.
Our fathers on this point were men of sense,
Who said: a woman always knows enough
Providing that her intellect suffice
To tell a pair of breeches from a coat.

The Hours of Peter II, Duke of Brittany pp. 120–21

1 For the Hours of Peter II *see* Leroquais, V., *Les Livres d'heures manuscrits de la Bibliothèque Nationale*, vol. I, no. 24, p. 75.

The Hours of Marguerite de Foix, Duchess of Brittany pp. 124–25

1 A transcription of the prayer added to Marguerite de Foix's Hours, made by the late F.C. Eeles, is in the typescript catalogue (unpublished) of the Manuscripts in the Victoria and Albert Museum Library. *See also* Burlington Fine Arts Club, *Exhibition of Illuminated Manuscripts*, London, 1908, no. 217, pp. 106–07.

The Grandes Heures of Anne of Brittany, Queen of France pp. 128–29, 132–33

1 In addition to the sources for Breton history given above ('The Hours of Isabella Stuart', note 1), A.J. Leroux de Lincey's basic work, *Vie de la reine Anne de Bretagne*, 4 vols., Paris, 1857, has been consulted for this section. The catalogue of the exhibition *Anne de Bretagne et son temps*, held at the Musée Dobrée, Nantes, 1961, contains much information concerning her iconography, heart reliquary and other aspects of her life.

2 The Curmer facsimile, *Le Livre d'heures de la reine Anne de Bretagne*, Paris, 1861, 2 vols., contains a French translation of the Latin text by the Abbé Delaunay, and a catalogue of the plants found in the border by J. Decaisne. *See also* Delisle, L.V., *Les Grandes Heures de la reine Anne de Bretagne et l'atelier de Jean Bourdichon*, Paris, 1913; Emile Mâle's commentary to the pages reproduced in *Verve*, IV, 1946; and Leroquais, V., *Les Livres d'heures manuscrits de la Bibliothèque Nationale*, pp. 298–305.

3 For Jean Bourdichon *see* Ritter, G., *Manuscrits à peintures de l'école de Rouen*, Paris, 1913; MacGibbon, D., *Jean Bourdichon*, Glasgow, 1933 (with excellent documentation); and Limousin, R., *Jean Bourdichon, peintre et enlumineur*, Lyons, 1954.

The Primer of Claude de France pp. 136–37

1 For the Primer of Claude de France, *see* James, M. R., *A Descriptive Catalogue of the Manuscripts in the Fitzwilliam Museum*, Cambridge, 1895, no. 159, pp. 356–59.

2 For Books of Hours owned by Francis I *see* Backhouse, J., 'Two Books of Hours of Francis I', in *The British Museum Quarterly*, XXXI, 1967, pp. 90–96.

3 Dibdin, T. F., *Bibliographical Decameron*, London, 1817, I, p. clxxxi. For the Hours of Claude de France *see* Sterling, C., *The Master of Claude de France, a Newly Defined Miniaturist*, New York, 1975; and Kraus, H. P., *Monumenta Codicum Manu Scriptorum* (exhibition catalogue), New York, 1974, pp. 110–11, whence some of the details in this section are taken.

The Hours of Lorenzo dei Medici, the Magnificent pp. 140–41

1 For the Hours of Lorenzo dei Medici, *see* Levi d'Ancona, M., *Miniatura e miniatori a Firenze dal XIV al XVI secolo*, Florence, 1962, pp. 108–11, where previous literature is cited; and Barfucci, E., *Lorenzo de' Medici e la società del suo tempo*, 2nd edn, Florence, 1964, pp. 256–58. For other pages from the manuscript, *see* Biagi, G., *Reproductions from Illuminated Manuscripts, Fifty Plates from Mss. in the R. Medicean Library*, Florence, 1914, p. 12, and pls. XXIV–XXVIII. *See also* D'Ancona, P., *La miniatura fiorentina*, Florence, 1914, vol. 2, pp. 397–99.

2 Gombrich, E. H., 'Renaissance and Golden Age', in *Journal of the Warburg Institute*, vol. XXIV, 1961, pp. 306–09.

3 Spengler, O., *The Decline of the West* (English translation by C. F. Atkinson), London and New York, 1926, vol. 2, p. 291.

4 For the Laurentian Library *see* Hobson, A., *Great Libraries*, London and New York, 1970, pp. 85–91.

The Hours of Yolande de Lalaing pp. 144–45

1 For the Hours of Yolande de Lalaing, *see* Byvanck, A. W., *La Miniature dans les Pays-Bas septentrionaux*, Paris, 1937, pp. 88, 152, pl. LXXIV–LXXV; and Pächt, O., and Alexander, J. G., *Illuminated Manuscripts in the Bodleian Library*, vol. I, no. 218, p. 17.

2 Delaissé, L. M. J., *A Century of Dutch Manuscript Illumination*, Berkeley, Calif., 1968, p. 40, note 73.

3 For the psychology of chivalry, *see* Painter, S., *French Chivalry: Chivalric Ideas and Practices in Mediaeval France*, Baltimore, Md, 1940, especially ch. III, 'Religious Chivalry'; Harvey, R., *Moriz von Craun and the Chivalric World*, Oxford, 1941; and Barber, R., *The Knight and Chivalry*, London and New York, 1970.

4 Langland, W., *Piers the Ploughman*, translated into Modern English with an Introduction by J. F. Goodridge, London, 1966, pp. 217–18; Gaffney, W., 'The Allegory of the Christ-Knight in Piers Plowman', in *Publications of the Modern Language Association of America*, vol. XLVI, 1931, pp. 155–68; and Montaiglon, A. de, ed., *Le Livre du chevalier de la Tour Landry*, Paris, 1854, pp. 206–08. I am greatly indebted to Dr Ruth Harvey for these references and for other information used in this section.

5 For details of the Lalaing family, *see* Brassart, F., *Le Blason de Lalaing*, pt I, Douai, 1879, pp. 88–94.

6 Rudnitzki, P., *Der Turnierroman 'livre des faits du bon chevalier Messire Jacques de Lalaing'*, Münster, 1915; and the earlier editions by Chifflet, Brussels, 1634, and Buchon, Paris, 1825.

The Simon Marmion Hours pp. 148–49

1 Marmion's most celebrated Book of Hours is the one known as 'La Flora', decorated for Charles VIII of France and now in the Biblioteca Nazionale, Naples (ms. I B 51).

2 The most detailed account of the Victoria and Albert Museum's Simon Marmion Hours is in the unpublished doctoral thesis by Edith W. Hoffman, 'Simon Marmion', 1958 (deposited in the Courtauld Institute, London), to which grateful acknowledgment is made here, as also to Dr

Hoffman's article 'Simon Marmion Re-Considered', in *Scriptorium*, vol. XXIII, 1969, pp. 243–71. *See also* Delaissé, L.M.J., *La Miniature flamande à l'époque bourguignonne* (exhibition catalogue, Palais des Beaux-Arts), Brussels, 1959, no. 263, pp. 188–89; and *Burlington Fine Arts Club. Exhibition of Illuminated Manuscripts*, 1908, no. 235, p. 114.

The Soane Hours pp. 152–53

1 For the Soane Hours, *see* Millar, E., 'Les Manuscrits à peintures des bibliothèques de Londres', *Bulletin de la Société française de reproductions de manuscrits à peintures*, Année 4, no. 1, 1920, pp. 95–108.

2 Ibid., where the inscriptions are quoted.

The Serristori Hours p. 156

1 Magherini-Graziani, G., *L'Uffiziolo della famiglia Serristori conservato nel Museo South Kensington*, Città di Castello, 1913.

2 Attribution of the miniatures to Boccardino and Monte di Giovanni derived verbally from Dott. Mirella Levi d'Ancona, to whom acknowledgment is here made.

3 Marquand, A., *Robbia Heraldry*, Princeton, N.J., 1919, no. 20, p. 23. A Ristoro di Serristori was captain and *commissario* of Cortona in 1482. His coat of arms, including a human-faced griffin crest, appears in the passage leading to the courtyard of the Palazzo Casale, Cortona.

4 Vasari, G., *Lives*, London and New York, 1963, vol. 4, p. 34.

The Hours of Alfonso of Aragon, Duke of Calabria p. 157

1 De Marinis, T., *La Biblioteca dei re d'Aragona*, 4 vols., Milan, 1947–52 (and *Supplemento*, 2 vols., Verona, 1969). For the Hours of Alfonso of Aragon, Duke of Calabria, *see* vol. 1 (Introduction), p. 158, and vol. 2 (Catalogue), pp. 113, 324.

The Hours of Reynalt von Homoet pp. 160–61

1 This section derives mainly from Dr Paul Pieper's two studies of the Homoet Hours published in the *Wallraf-Richartz Jahrbuch*: 'Miniaturen des Bartholomäus-Meisters', vol. XV, 1953, pp. 135–56; and 'Das Stundenbuch des Bartholomäus-Meisters', vol. XXI, 1959, pp. 97–158; *see also* Delaissé, L.M.J., *A Century of Dutch Manuscript Illumination*, Berkeley, Calif., 1968, pp. 51–53.

2 For the Mystery Plays *see* Davidson, C., 'The Realism of the York Realist and the York Passion', in *Speculum*, L, 1975, pp. 270–83.

3 Holroyd, C., *Michael Angelo Buonarroti*, London, 1903, p. 279; and for the Italian text, A.L. Cerchiari's edition of D'Ollanda, F., *Parla Michelangelo*, Milan, 1946, p. 27.

The Hours of Cardinal Alessandro Farnese pp. 164–65, 168

1 Vasari, G., *The Lives of the Painters, Sculptors and Architects*, London and New York, 1963, vol. IV, pp. 244–49.

2 Wardrop, J., 'Civis Romanus sum: Giovanbattista Palatino and his Circle', in *Signature*, N.S., XIV, 1952, p. 8.

3 There is an extensive modern literature on Clovio starting with Bradley, J.W., *The Life and Works of Giorgio Giulio Clovio, Miniaturist*, London, 1891. Sources used in this section include Bye, A.S., 'Two Clovio Manuscripts in New York', in *Art Bulletin*, vol. V, 1917, pp. 88–99; Bonnard, F., *Un hôte du Palais Farnèse: Don Giulio Clovio, miniaturiste*, Paris, 1929; *Exhibition of Illuminated Manuscripts held at the New York Public Library* (exhibition catalogue), New York, 1933; *Italian Manuscripts in the Pierpont Morgan Library* (exhibition catalogue), New York, 1953, no. 102, pp. 57–58; La Coste-Messelière, M.C. de, 'Don Giulio', in *L'Œil*, no. 52, April 1959, pp. 4–9; Levi d'Ancona, M., 'Illuminations by Clovio Lost and Found', in *Gazette des Beaux-Arts*, ser. VI, 37a, 1959, pp. 55–76; and Smith, W., 'Giulio Clovio and the "Maniera di figure piccole"', in *Art Bulletin*, vol. XLVI, 1964, p. 395.

4 Bradley, op. cit. (note 3), p. 274.

5 Herbert, J.A., *Illuminated Manuscripts*, London, 1911, p. 304–5.

PRINTED BOOKS OF HOURS pp. 169–74

1 The copious literature on printed Books of Hours consulted for this section has included: Soleil, F., *Les heures gothiques*, Rouen, 1882;

Claudin, A., *Histoire de l'imprimerie en France au XVe et XVIe siècle*, Paris, 1901, vol. II, ch. xxi; Lacombe, P., *Livres d'heures imprimés, XVe–XVIe siècle*, Paris, 1907; *Pierpont Morgan Library. Catalogue of Manuscripts and Early Printed Books*, London, 1907, vol. III, pp. 1–43; Fairfax Murray, C., *Catalogue of a Collection of Early French Books ... compiled by H. W. Davies*, London, 1910, pt. I, pp. 265–335; Pollard, A.W., *Early Illustrated Books*, 2nd edn, London, 1917, ch. 8, and 'The Illustrations in French Books of Hours, 1486–1500', in *Bibliographica*, III, 1897, pp. 430–70; Hind, A.M., *An Introduction to the History of Woodcut*, London, 1935, vol. II, pp. 676–98; Mortimer, R., *Harvard College Library. Catalogue of Books and Manuscripts. Part I. French 16th century Books*, Cambridge, Mass., 1964, pp. 363–408.

2 Bober, H., 'The Zodiacal Miniature of the *Très-Riches Heures* of the Duke of Berry – its Sources and Meaning', in *Journal of the Warburg Institute*, XI, 1948, pp. 1–34.

3 Alès, A., *Description des livres liturgiques imprimés aux XVe et XVI siècles ... de la bibliothèque de Charles-Louis de Bourbon (Comte de Villafranca)*, Paris, 1878, p. 287.

4 Pollard, A.W., 'The Books of Hours of Geofroy Tory', in *Bibliographica*, I, 1894, pp. 114–22.

5 *Kaiser Maximilians I. Gebetbuch mit Zeichnungen von Albrecht Dürer und anderen Künstlern* (facsimile, edited by K. Giehlow), Vienna, 1907; and the more recent facsimile, *The Book of Hours of the Emperor Maximilian I, decorated by Albrecht Dürer ... Edited with a detailed commentary by W.L. Strauss*. New York, 1974.

6 Information from the Musée Historique des Tissus, Lyons; *see also* Marais, P., 'Livre de prières tissé', in *Bulletin du Bibliophile*, 1889, pp. 163–66.

SELECT READING LIST

The literature on individual Books of Hours is cited in the Notes. Titles listed below include only the more important general works dealing with the subject.

ACHTEN, G., and KNAUS, H., *Die Handschriften der Hessischen Landes- und Hochschulbibliothek*: I. *Deutsche and niederländische Gebetbuchhandschriften*, Darmstadt, 1959, and 3. *Lateinische Gebetbuchhandschiften*, Wiesbaden, 1972. (A detailed catalogue of the Books of Hours in the Hessian Landesbibliothek at Darmstadt: a German equivalent of Leroquais.)

BACKHOUSE, J. M., *The Madresfield Hours. A Fourteenth Century Manuscript in the Library of Earl Beauchamp* (Roxburghe Club), Oxford, 1976. (Contains an Appendix of twenty-four Books of Hours made for English owners between *c.* 1240 and *c.* 1350).

BUTTERWORTH, C. C., *The English Primers, 1529–45: their Publication and Connection with the Bible and the Reformation in England*, Philadelphia, 1953.

DELAISSÉ, L. M. J., 'The Importance of Books of Hours for the History of the Medieval Book', in *Gatherings in Honor of Dorothy Miner*, Baltimore, Md, 1974, pp. 203–25.

HOSKINS, E., *Horae Beatae Mariae Virginis, or Sarum and York Primers*, London, 1901.

JAMES, M. R., *A Descriptive Catalogue of the Manuscripts in the Fitzwilliam Museum, Cambridge*, Cambridge, 1895, pp. xxii–xxxvii.

LABARRE, A., 'Livres d'Heures', in *Dictionnaire de spiritualité ascétique et mystique*, vol. VII, Beauchesne, 1968, pp. 410–31.

LECLERCQ, H., Livres d'Heures', in Cabrol, F., *Dictionnaire d'archéologie chrétienne et de liturgie*, Paris, 1930, col. 1836–82.

LEROQUAIS, V., *Les Livres d'heures manuscrits de la Bibliothèque Nationale*, 3 vols., Paris, 1927 (and *Supplément . . . Acquisitions récentes et donations Smith-Lesouef*, Mâcon, 1943).

LITTLEHALES, H., *The Prymer or Prayer Book of the Lay People in the Middle Ages*, London, 1891.

MEISS, M., *French Painting in the Time of Jean de Berry*, 3 pts (in 5 volumes), London and New York, 1967–74. (Indispensable for the study of the Books of Hours of the Duke of Berry.)

RITTER, G., *Manuscrits à peintures de l'Ecole de Rouen. Livres d'Heures normands*, Rouen and Paris, 1913.

SEARLE, W. G., *The Illuminated Manuscripts in the Library in the Fitzwilliam Museum, Cambridge*, Cambridge, 1876, pp. xiii–lxiv.

WORDSWORTH, C., ed., 'Horae Eboracenses ... With other devotions used by the lay-folk in the XVth and XVIth Centuries', in *Proceedings of the Surtees Society*, 132, Durham and London, 1920.

WORDSWORTH, C., and LITTLEHALES, H., *The Early Service-Books of the Church*, London, 1904, ch. IX.

GENEALOGIES

The following genealogies have been taken largely from Isenburg, Prince W.K., *Stammtafeln zur Geschichte der europäischen Staaten*, Marburg, 1953, supplemented by Jougla de Morénas, H., *Grand Armorial de France*, vol. 1, Paris, 1934. **Names shown thus** are those of persons whose Books of Hours are described or mentioned in the text.

The House of Capet

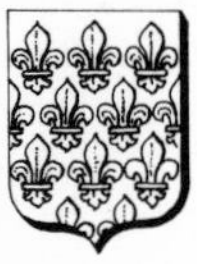

France-Ancient

Louis IX (St Louis, 1215–70)
King of France 1226–70
m. Marguerite of Provence (1221–95)

- Philip III (1245–85)
  King of France 1270–85
  m.
  (1) Isabella of Aragon (1243–71) (2) Marie of Brabant (1260–1322)
  - [by (1)] Philip IV, *le Bel* (1268–1314)
    King of France 1285–1314
    m. Jeanne of Navarre (1271–1304)
    - Louis X, *le Hutin* (1289–1316)
      King of France 1314–16
      m. Clemence of Hungary (1293–1328)
      - John I (15–19 November 1316)
        King of France 1316
        (a posthumous infant)
    - Philip V, *le Long* (1291–1322)
      King of France 1316–22
      m. Jeanne of Burgundy (1294–1329)
    - Isabella (1292–1357)
      m. Edward II (1284–1327)
      King of England 1307–27
      - Edward III (1312–77)
        King of England 1327–77
      - **Joan of the Tower** (1321–62)
        m. David II (1323–70)
        King of Scotland 1329–70
    - Charles IV *le Bel* (1295–1328)
      King of France 1322–28
      m. **Jeanne d'Evreux** (1304–70)
      - Blanche (1328–92)
        m. Philip (1336–75)
        Duke of Orleans
  - [by (1)] Charles (1270–1325)
    Count of Valois
    m. Marguerite of Anjou (d. 1298)
    Valois
    - Philip VI
      Count of Valois (1293–1350)
      King of France 1328–50
      m. **Blanche of Navarre** (d. 1398)
  - [by (2)] Louis (1276–1319)
    Count of Evreux
    m. Marguerite of Artois (d. 1311)
    Evreux
    - **Jeanne d'Evreux** (1304–70)

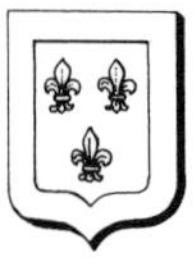

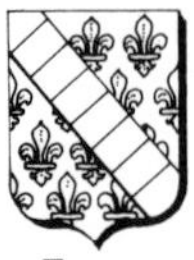

The Houses of Valois – Orleans – Angoulême

France-Ancient

Valois

Philip VI, Count of Valois
(1293–1350)
King of France 1328–50
m. (1) Jeanne of Burgundy (1294–1348) (2) **Blanche of Navarre** (1328–98)

John II, le Bon
(1319–64)
King of France
1350–64
m. Bonne of Luxembourg
(1315–49)

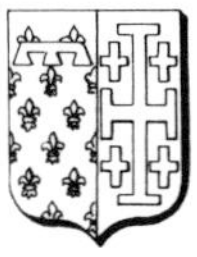
Anjou-Sicily

Berry

Burgundy

Visconti

France-Modern adopted in the reign of Charles V

Charles V, *le Sage*
(1338–80)
King of France
1364–80
m. Jeanne de Bourbon
(1338–77) (*see below*)

Louis (1339–84)
Duke of Anjou

John (1340–1416)
Duke of Berry

Philip (1342–1404)
Duke of Burgundy

Isabella (1348–72)
m. **Giangaleazzo Visconti**
(1351–1402)
Duke of Milan

Orleans

Charles VI (1368–1422)
King of France
1380–1422
m. **Isabeau of Bavaria**
(1369–1435)

Louis (1372–1407)
Duke of Orleans
m. Valentina Visconti
(1366–1408)

Angoulême

Charles VII (1403–61)
King of France
1422–61
m. Marie of Anjou
(1404–63)

Catherine
(1401–37)
m. Henry V
(1387–1422)
King of England
1413–22

Charles
(1391–1465)
Duke of Orleans
m. Marie of Cleves
(1426–86)

Marguerite
(1406–66)
m. Richard,
Count of Etampes
(1395–1438)

John (1404–1467)
Count of
Angoulême
m. Marguerite de
Rohan (d. after 1496)

Louis XI (1423–83)
King of France
1461–83
m. Charlotte of Savoy
(1443–83)

Henry VI (1422–71)
King of England
1422–61

Francis II (1435–88)
Duke of Brittany
m. **Marguerite de Foix**
(d. 1486)

Charles (1460–96)
Count
of Angoulême
m. Louise of Savoy
(1476–1531)

Charles VIII
(1470–98)
King of France
1483–98
m. **Anne** (1477–1514)
Duchess
of Brittany

Louis XII (1462–1515)
Duke of Orleans
King of France
1498–1515
m. **Anne** (1477–1514)
Duchess of
Brittany

Claude de France (1499–1524) m. **Francis I** (1494–1547)
King of France
1515–47

Bourbon

Peter I (1311–56)
Duke of Bourbon
m. Isabelle of Valois
(d. 1383)

Louis II
(1337–1410)
Duke of Bourbon
m. Anne of Auvergne
(1358–1417)

Jeanne (1338–77) (*see above*)
m. Charles V, *le Sage*
(1338–80)
King of France
1364–80

Catherine (d. 1427)
m. John (1342–88)
Count of Harcourt

Reinald IV (d. 1423) Duke of Guelders m. Marie d'Harcourt **(Mary of Guelders)** (d. 1425)

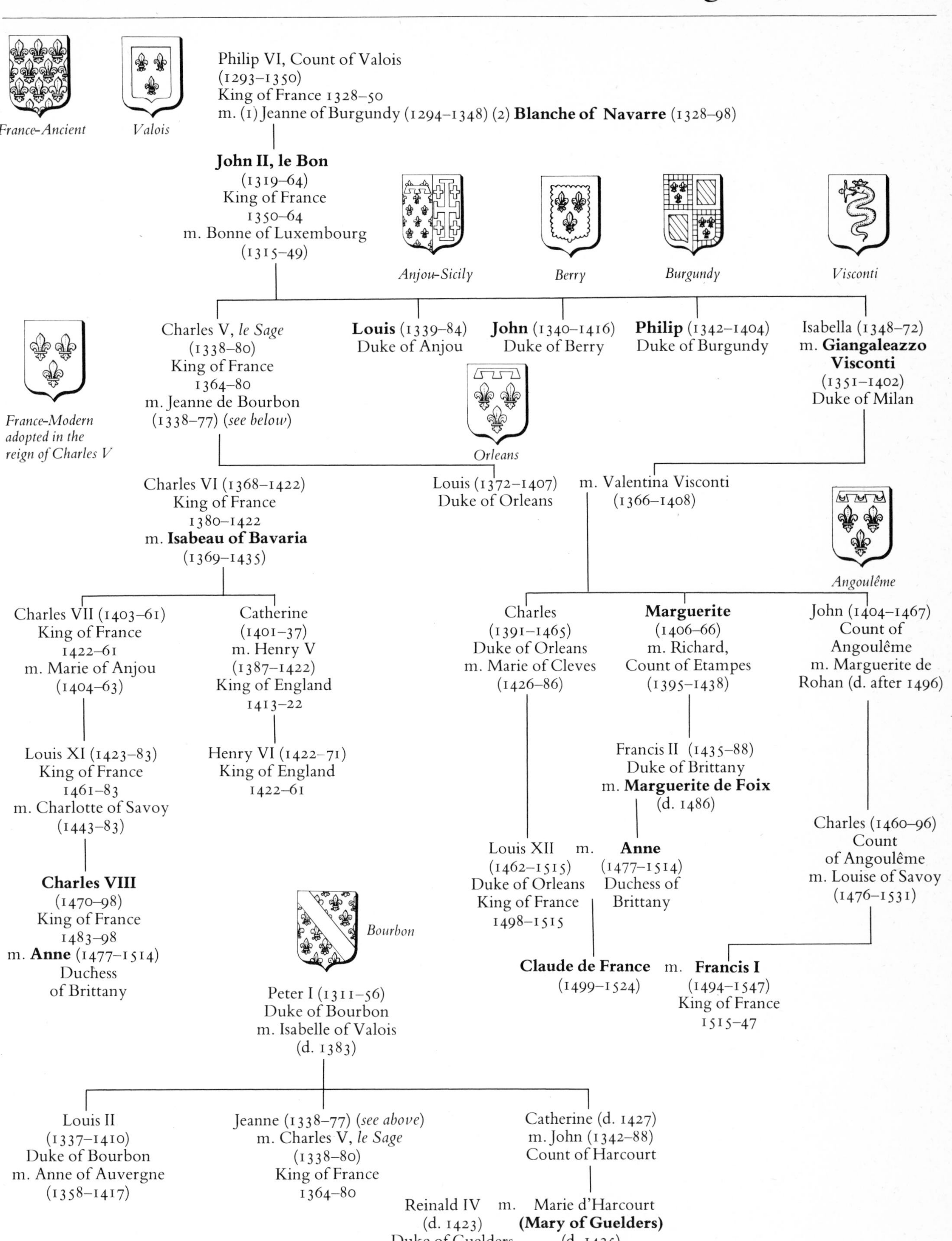

The House of Anjou

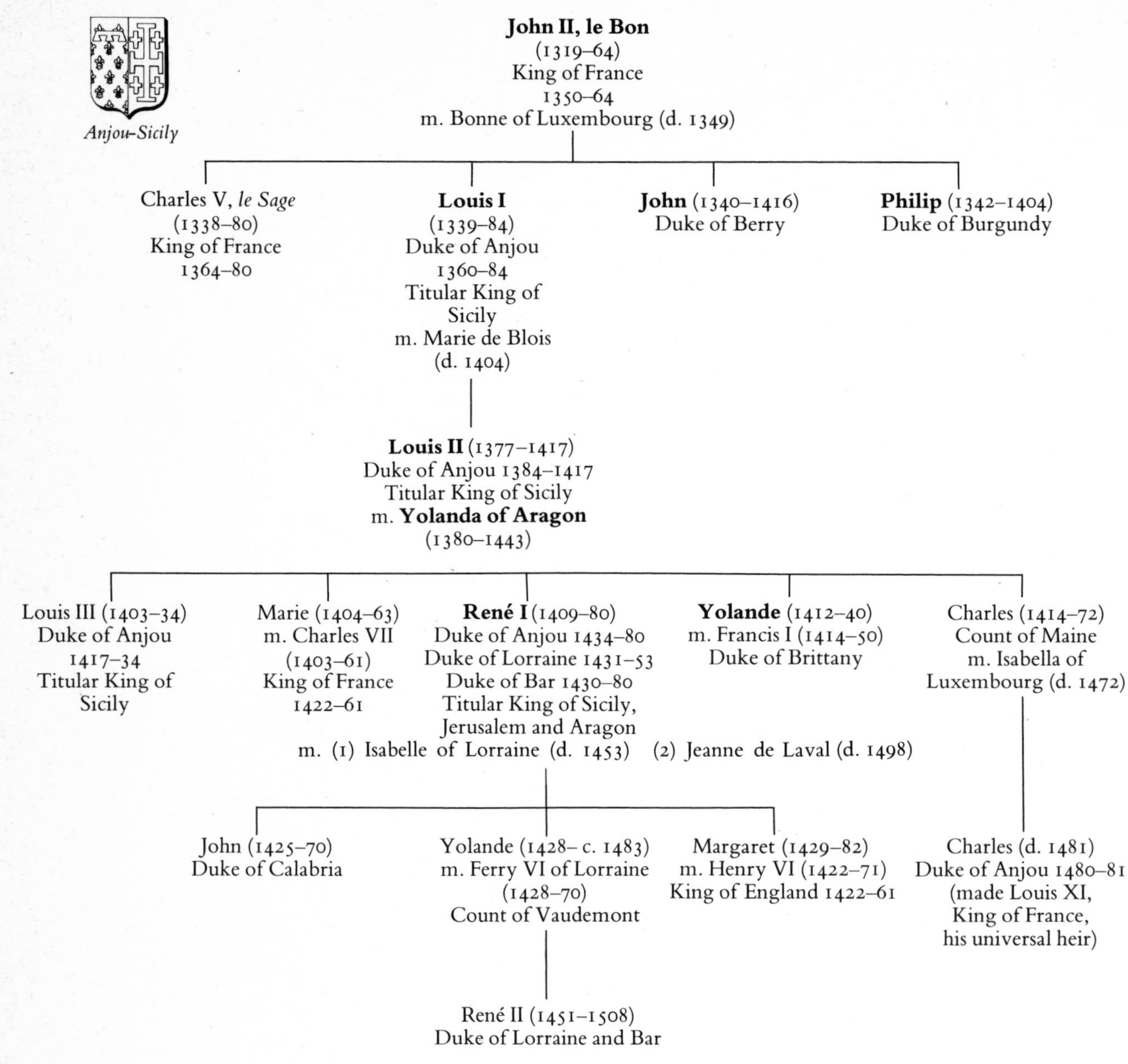
Anjou-Sicily
John II, le Bon
(1319–64)
King of France
1350–64
m. Bonne of Luxembourg (d. 1349)
Charles V, *le Sage*
(1338–80)
King of France
1364–80
Louis I
(1339–84)
Duke of Anjou
1360–84
Titular King of
Sicily
m. Marie de Blois
(d. 1404)
John (1340–1416)
Duke of Berry
Philip (1342–1404)
Duke of Burgundy
Louis II (1377–1417)
Duke of Anjou 1384–1417
Titular King of Sicily
m. **Yolanda of Aragon**
(1380–1443)
Louis III (1403–34)
Duke of Anjou
1417–34
Titular King of
Sicily
Marie (1404–63)
m. Charles VII
(1403–61)
King of France
1422–61
René I (1409–80)
Duke of Anjou 1434–80
Duke of Lorraine 1431–53
Duke of Bar 1430–80
Titular King of Sicily,
Jerusalem and Aragon
m. (1) Isabelle of Lorraine (d. 1453) (2) Jeanne de Laval (d. 1498)
Yolande (1412–40)
m. Francis I (1414–50)
Duke of Brittany
Charles (1414–72)
Count of Maine
m. Isabella of
Luxembourg (d. 1472)
John (1425–70)
Duke of Calabria
Yolande (1428– c. 1483)
m. Ferry VI of Lorraine
(1428–70)
Count of Vaudemont
Margaret (1429–82)
m. Henry VI (1422–71)
King of England 1422–61
Charles (d. 1481)
Duke of Anjou 1480–81
(made Louis XI,
King of France,
his universal heir)
René II (1451–1508)
Duke of Lorraine and Bar

The House of Burgundy

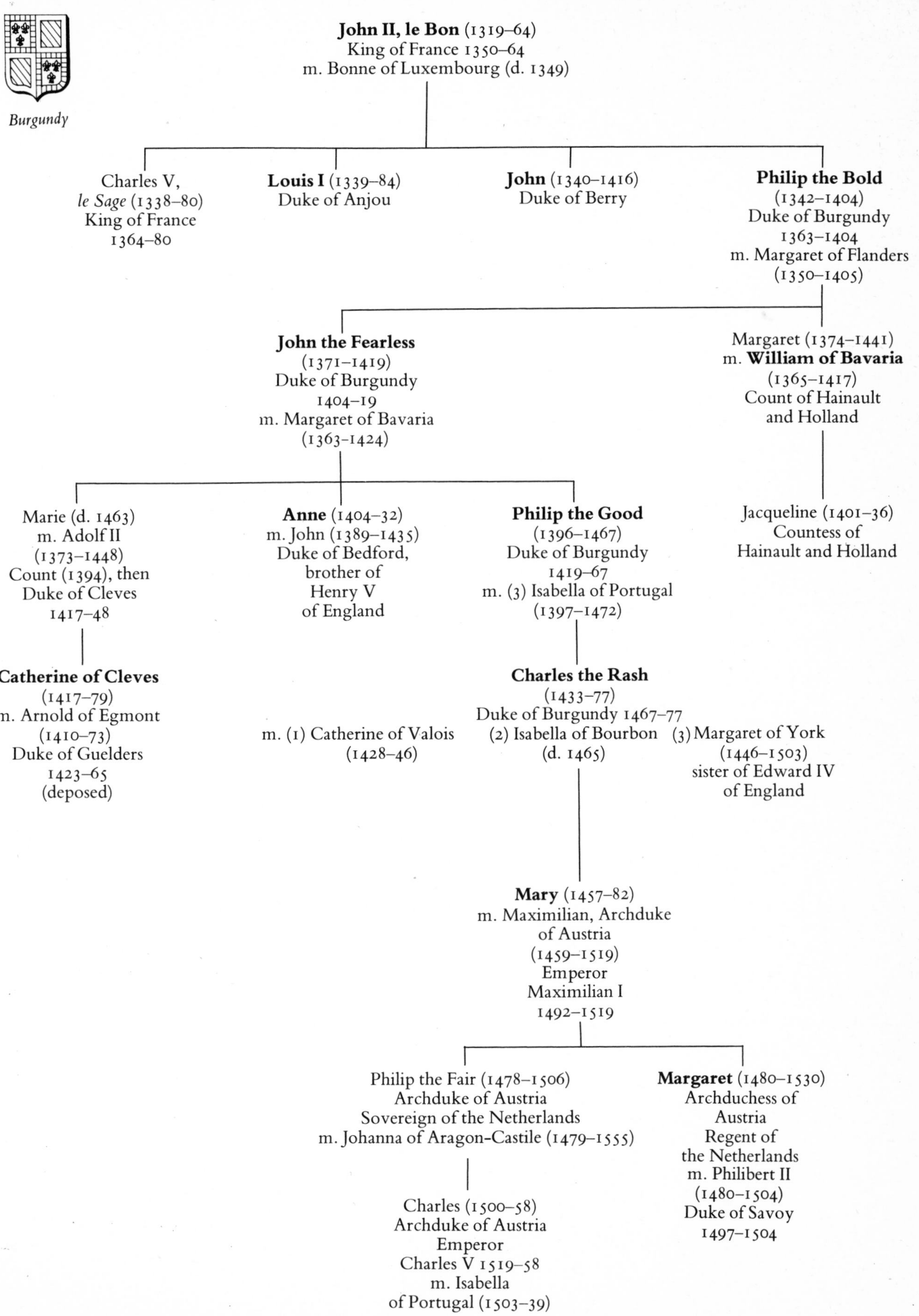
Burgundy
John II, le Bon (1319–64)
King of France 1350–64
m. Bonne of Luxembourg (d. 1349)
Charles V, *le Sage* (1338–80) King of France 1364–80
Louis I (1339–84) Duke of Anjou
John (1340–1416) Duke of Berry
Philip the Bold (1342–1404) Duke of Burgundy 1363–1404 m. Margaret of Flanders (1350–1405)
John the Fearless (1371–1419) Duke of Burgundy 1404–19 m. Margaret of Bavaria (1363–1424)
Margaret (1374–1441) m. **William of Bavaria** (1365–1417) Count of Hainault and Holland
Marie (d. 1463) m. Adolf II (1373–1448) Count (1394), then Duke of Cleves 1417–48
Anne (1404–32) m. John (1389–1435) Duke of Bedford, brother of Henry V of England
Philip the Good (1396–1467) Duke of Burgundy 1419–67 m. (3) Isabella of Portugal (1397–1472)
Jacqueline (1401–36) Countess of Hainault and Holland
Catherine of Cleves (1417–79) m. Arnold of Egmont (1410–73) Duke of Guelders 1423–65 (deposed)
Charles the Rash (1433–77) Duke of Burgundy 1467–77
m. (1) Catherine of Valois (1428–46)
(2) Isabella of Bourbon (d. 1465)
(3) Margaret of York (1446–1503) sister of Edward IV of England
Mary (1457–82) m. Maximilian, Archduke of Austria (1459–1519) Emperor Maximilian I 1492–1519
Philip the Fair (1478–1506) Archduke of Austria Sovereign of the Netherlands m. Johanna of Aragon-Castile (1479–1555)
Margaret (1480–1530) Archduchess of Austria Regent of the Netherlands m. Philibert II (1480–1504) Duke of Savoy 1497–1504
Charles (1500–58) Archduke of Austria Emperor Charles V 1519–58 m. Isabella of Portugal (1503–39)

The House of Brittany

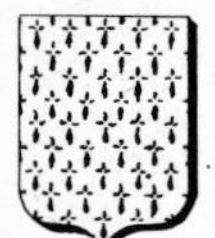

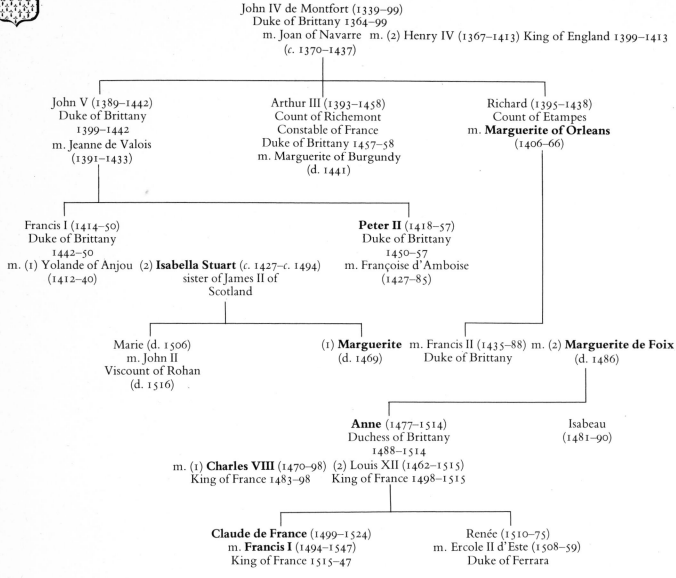

John IV de Montfort (1339–99)
Duke of Brittany 1364–99
m. Joan of Navarre (*c.* 1370–1437) m. (2) Henry IV (1367–1413) King of England 1399–1413

- John V (1389–1442)
  Duke of Brittany 1399–1442
  m. Jeanne de Valois (1391–1433)
  - Francis I (1414–50)
    Duke of Brittany 1442–50
    m. (1) Yolande of Anjou (1412–40) (2) **Isabella Stuart** (*c.* 1427–*c.* 1494) sister of James II of Scotland
    - Marie (d. 1506)
      m. John II Viscount of Rohan (d. 1516)
    - (1) **Marguerite** (d. 1469) m. Francis II (1435–88) Duke of Brittany m. (2) **Marguerite de Foix** (d. 1486)
  - **Peter II** (1418–57)
    Duke of Brittany 1450–57
    m. Françoise d'Amboise (1427–85)
- Arthur III (1393–1458)
  Count of Richemont
  Constable of France
  Duke of Brittany 1457–58
  m. Marguerite of Burgundy (d. 1441)
- Richard (1395–1438)
  Count of Etampes
  m. **Marguerite of Orleans** (1406–66)
  - Francis II (1435–88) Duke of Brittany, m. (1) **Marguerite** (d. 1469), m. (2) **Marguerite de Foix** (d. 1486)
    - **Anne** (1477–1514)
      Duchess of Brittany 1488–1514
      m. (1) **Charles VIII** (1470–98) King of France 1483–98 (2) Louis XII (1462–1515) King of France 1498–1515
      - **Claude de France** (1499–1524)
        m. **Francis I** (1494–1547)
        King of France 1515–47
      - Renée (1510–75)
        m. Ercole II d'Este (1508–59)
        Duke of Ferrara
    - Isabeau (1481–90)

INDEX

Page numbers in italic refer to illustrations